Educating Democratic
Citizens in Troubled Times

Educating Democratic Citizens in Troubled Times

Qualitative Studies of Current Efforts

Edited by
Janet S. Bixby
and
Judith L. Pace

Published by
State University of New York Press, Albany

© 2008 State University of New York

All rights reserved

Published in the United States of America

No part of this book may be used or reproduced in any manner whatsoever without written permission. No part of this book may be stored in a retrieval system or transmitted in any form or by any means including electronic, electrostatic, magnetic tape, mechanical, photocopying, recording, or otherwise without the prior permission in writing of the publisher.

For information, contact State University of New York Press, Albany, NY
www. sunypress. edu

Production by Kelli LeRoux
Marketing by Michael Campochiaro

Library of Congress Cataloging-in-Publication Data
Educating democratic citizens in troubled times : qualitative studies of current
efforts / edited by Judith L. Pace and Janet S. Bixby ; foreword by Walter C. Parker.
   p.   cm.
  Includes bibliographical references and index.
  ISBN 978-0-7914-7639-0 (hardcover : alk. paper) — ISBN 978-0-7914-7640-6
(pbk. : alk. paper)
   1. Citizenship—Study and teaching—United States. 2. Democracy—United States.
I. Pace, Judith L. II. Bixby, Janet S.
  LC1091.E3835 2009
  370.11'5—dc22   2008003125

10 9 8 7 6 5 4 3 2 1

Contents

In the Community

Foreword

Walter C. Parker

This is an excellent and needed collection. When its editors, Janet S. Bixby and Judith L. Pace, invited me to write the foreword, I accepted knowing only that it would contain new and well-selected qualitative studies of democratic education. Now that I've read them, I want to recommend a close and comparative reading of each. Much is to be learned here about civic education in the United States today—both broadly (thanks to reading these studies as a set) and particularly (thanks to reading each one as a context-specific inquiry). Six themes appear to be central to the collection: knowing about democracy and engaging in democracy, social context and identity formation, and curriculum and instruction for democracy. In each pair there is tension; each "and" can be replaced, for a different effect, with "versus." Now, permit me to set the stage with a bit of personal and social history.

My working-class parents were members of the United Methodist Church in Englewood, Colorado; therefore, so were my sister and I. Such is the thrownness of life. None of us chooses the social contexts of our birth or the primary discourses that come with them because we have already been "thrown" into them by the time we become aware of them. But my parents worried about provincialism. Caught up in the Roosevelt-era social-democratic liberalism that was still alive in postwar America (before its death at the hands of Thatcher and Reagan), they set about assembling a group of families who attended other Christian churches which, at least to my sister and me, were strangely different—Mormon, Baptist, and Catholic.

But they reached farther than ecumenism, for there were nonchristians too: other monotheists (a Jewish couple) plus polytheists (a Hindu couple) and nontheists (a Buddhist couple). As the initial exoticism of this experiment in grassroots multiculturalism subsided, the group became ordinary friends. The women were the primary glue: they gathered monthly at one another's homes to talk and sew (they referred to themselves as the "sewing group'). But the couples gathered now and then, too, and always celebrated New Year's Eve together. The children became friends, attending one another's birthday parties and gathering at the annual sewing-group picnic on Labor Day.

It was a thoroughly modern thing my parents did, for it assumed that their faith was but one of many. "Modern faith becomes reflexive," Jürgen Habermas writes (2006, p. 152), "for it can only stabilize itself through self-critical awareness of the status it assumes within a universe of discourse restricted by secular knowledge and shared with other religions." Modern society is characteristically self aware in this way, thus affording the possibility of pluralism, or the acknowledgement and acceptance of diversity.

This modern reflexivity has important political consequences, not the least of which is the idea of the neutral, secular state. There was no more quick or effective solution to perpetual religious warfare among European states, recall, than the disestablishment of religion. But there is another political consequence: the spread of constitutional democracies. These are not merely electoral democracies in which citizens, via more-or-less free and fair elections, empower elected officials to administer society; they are also liberal democracies in which pluralism is accepted and civil liberties (the rights of women and minorities, for example) are protected by law—at least that's the ideal and the basis for civil rights movements that struggle to realize it. Voting, then, is not the only form of popular political participation in a society that is trying to be a liberal democracy and certainly not the most demanding. There are other citizens with other viewpoints—ideological and cultural—and relating to them is part and parcel to creating, maintaining, and deepening the democratic project.

We arrive at a decentralized and discursive image of democratic life. On this model, democracy's location is not mainly in the political system or what is colloquially (in the United States) called "the government" or "politicians," but is distributed throughout society. Here is John Dewey's conception of democracy as a "mode of associated living, of conjoint communicated experience" (1985, p. 93). Here also is Danielle Allen's (2004) argument that any utopian and anti-democratic notion of "oneness" must be given up as both false and illiberal—false because gross inequalities within U.S. society belie it (e.g., we have the most highly paid CEOs amid the highest rate of childhood poverty in the rich nations of the world) and illiberal because the idealization of oneness requires too much repression of difference and forces an assimilation model on the education system. Freed of the "oneness" ideal, popular sovereignty can be diversified and decentralized through political parties, cultural groups, unions, faculty meetings, faith communities, schools, social movements, the Internet, book clubs, ball fields, and my parents' sewing club. Citizens' rights are secured not only by "the government" but also by the efforts of fellow citizens. Citizens, therefore, have not only rights but obligations: to relate democratically to fellow citizens—to recognize, accept, and communicate with them—and to take some responsibility for nurturing this mode of associated living.

Powerful social forces compete with this communicative model of democracy, draining the associational highways and byways of the public sphere of their potential for democratic education and mobilization. These include religious fundamentalism and other forms of aggressive monism, certainly, but also free-market fundamentalism (neoliberalism), which not only prevents serious attention to eliminating poverty but is in hock to a culture industry that manufactures mass somnolence. Each of these undercuts a citizen's political maturation, or what I've described as growth from "idiocy" to "puberty" (Parker, 2003). But there's another force: Even as liberal democracies increase in number and extend the franchise and civil rights to people previously denied them, this says nothing about what people *do* with them. Indeed, "inclusion" is entirely mute about the active deployment of citizen powers by anyone.

The important and timely collection of studies in this volume speaks creatively to this problem space. Across an intriguing array of concerns and locations, it asks: How are citizens of the world's oldest liberal democracy, a nation now possessing unparalleled power, helped to understand and exercise citizen powers? What meanings of equality, politics, justice, democracy, difference, and now terrorism are they afforded, and how? To whom are they encouraged to speak and listen? What rationales are they given for engaging in political life? And in what range of settings does this education take place?

Thankfully, these are empirical studies. An educational endeavor filled with so many "musts" and "shoulds" and given to so many earnest exhortations begs for description, analysis, and explanation. Moreover, they are qualitative studies that offer thick, on-the-ground accounts of contemporary

Walter C. Parker

democratic education as it is practiced in particular—unique and contingent—circumstances. They deploy in one variation or another the scientific method of knowledge construction, of course, which has three anchors: evidence, plausible rival explanations, and public inspection. Perhaps readers will keep these three in mind as a way of interacting with the chapters. What kinds of data were gathered and why? What interpretations do the authors offer and with which plausible alternatives are they (or might they be) compared? As for the third, their claims and methods await your scrutiny.

Political scientists subsume political education within the concept "political socialization" and therein are concerned mainly with what Amy Gutmann (1999) calls unconscious social reproduction. Educators by contrast are concerned to intervene in history and to intentionally shape society's future, not only to diagnose but also to remediate and transform; that is, they are concerned with conscious social reform. Accordingly, in these chapters we see the researchers' questions, methods, and findings along with their hope for a more vibrant democratic education. I share that hope.

References

Allen, D. (2004). *Talking to strangers: Anxieties of citizenship since Brown v. Board of Education.* Chicago: University of Chicago Press.

Dewey, J. (1985). *Democracy and education. The middle works of John Dewey, 1899–1924* (Vol. 9). Carbondale: Southern Illinois University Press.

Gutmann, A. (1999). *Democratic education* (2nd ed.). Princeton, N. J.: Princeton University Press.

Habermas, J. (2006). *Time of transitions.* Cambridge, England: Polity.

Parker, W. (2003). *Teaching Democracy: Unity and diversity in public life.* New York: Teachers College Press.

Educating Democratic Citizens in Troubled Times

CHAPTER 1

Introduction: Studying Citizenship Education in Troubled Times

Judith L. Pace and Janet S. Bixby

The education of democratic citizens has always been of paramount concern in the United States. But since the early 1990s, the literature on democratic citizenship education has virtually exploded (Johanek & Puckett, 2005). One could reasonably inquire, "Why publish yet another book on this topic?"

The preparation of informed and concerned citizens is especially urgent due to the troubling political, educational, and sociological problems that confront us every time we read the news. (In this book, the word "citizens" is inclusive of U. S. residents; we do not mean to exclude those who do not have legal status as citizens.) In this post 9/11 era, the United States is still at war in Iraq and Afghanistan and embroiled in domestic conflict over topics such as immigration and religion. Heated debates continue about what constitutes good citizenship and what democracy means. Critical questions proliferate about free speech, privacy, and other civil liberties; trust in the government; the role of the United States in foreign affairs; environmental protection; and criminalization of youth. These questions generate yet another: How are today's young citizens, upon whom the future of our democracy depends, being educated to understand these issues, make informed decisions, and contribute to building a more just society?

In addition to politics, the current educational scene begs the question of how we are educating citizens for democracy. The federal government is attempting to exercise unprecedented control over schools through systems of accountability, specifically No Child Left Behind. This new increase in federal control over schools both reflects and generates huge controversy over public schooling. At the same time, education for democratic citizenship is absent from these systems of accountability that focus on reading and math (Johanek & Puckett, 2005).

Another critical factor is the prominent view that young people are inadequately prepared for democratic citizenship. Findings about youth civic knowledge are mixed. Niemi and Junn (1998) examined the 1988 National Assessment of Educational Progress (NAEP) data and concluded that in the United States, high school seniors possess important civic knowledge. Specifically:

> As students leave high school, they are well informed about citizens' rights in general . . . They are well-informed about the division of powers among the various levels of government and about state and local governments. They are also able to make rudimentary comparisons of the government of the United States and that of other countries. In all of these instances, although students are somewhat hazy on details, they nonetheless perform relatively well on these aspects of the test. (p. 50)

However, according to the Civic Mission of Schools Report, 75 percent of students scored at "basic" or "below basic" levels on the 1998 NAEP civic assessment (Gibson & Levine, 2003). In the International Association for the Evaluation of Educational Achievement (IEA) study of civic education, U.S. ninth graders performed well on assessments of civic knowledge compared to youth in other countries (Baldi, Petri, Skidmore, & Greenberg, 2001). But Gibson and Levine (2003), drawing on data from this same study, conclude that "the range between the best- and the worst-prepared students . . . is exceptionally large in the United States, and this gap may foreshadow continued or worsening political inequality in decades to come" (p. 19). Hahn (2002) argues:

> The results from Phase 2 of the IEA study and from the 1998 NAEP Civics point to the need to learn more about the quality of civic education for particular subgroups of students. In both those assessments, achievement was related to socioeconomic factors, as measured by eligibility for free and reduced lunch program, parental education level,

and number of books in the home. . . . In both there were significant differences by race and ethnicity. . . . In a country that prides itself on valuing equality and justice for all, it is especially important that researchers, policy makers, and educators direct their attention to these glaring inequalities in the outcomes of civic education. (pp. 88–89)

In addition to concerns about civic knowledge, multiple indicators, in recent years, have shown disturbingly low levels of political and civic interest and engagement among youth as compared to both contemporary adults and youth in previous generations (Galston, 2001; Putnam, 2000). Another cause for concern is that while demographic diversity in the U.S. continues to increase, the rights and entitlements of citizenship continue to be denied to various groups. Today the place of millions of U.S. residents is threatened by their illegal status. Ongoing inequalities and discrimination in and outside of schools create significant impediments to the development of civic identity and engagement among low-income and minority youth (Hart & Atkins, 2002).

Within these four troubling conditions—the war on terror; the federal press for school accountability; concerns about civic knowledge, interest, and engagement among youth; and disenfranchisement of marginalized groups—the need to focus on education for democratic citizenship is urgent.

The study of the education of youth for democratic citizenship is multifaceted. Numerous books and articles discuss the connection in the United States between schooling and democracy writ large (see Fuhrman & Lazerson, 2005). The IEA research provides case studies and comparative findings on citizenship education in over twenty countries (see Torney-Purta, Schwille, & Amadeo, 1999; Torney-Purta, Lehmann, Oswald, & Schultz, 2001). Other scholarship proscribes particular approaches to citizenship education (for example see Parker, 2003). Still others report empirical findings on citizenship education outcomes, such as students' civic knowledge and attitudes based on standardized tests and surveys (Niemi & Junn, 1998).

Despite the plethora of writing on the topic, we know little about enactments of citizenship education in the United States. There are studies of classes that teach for citizenship (Baldi et al., 2001; Dilworth, 1994; Hahn, 2002; Hess, 2002; Kahne, Rodriguez, & Smith, 2000), special curricula (Patrick, Vontz, & Nixon, 2002), and programs such as community service (Walker, 2002). Parker's (2002) collection of essays and studies presents specific ideas and cases that speak to a vision of education for liberal democracy. But to better understand how young people are being prepared to play their role as citizen, we need far greater knowledge about what constitutes specific programs, how youth participants and adult educators make meaning of their experiences with citizenship education, and how these experiences are shaped by local and larger contexts, such as ever-increasing demographic diversity along with continued socioeconomic and racial inequality in schools and society. We need to know much more about the relationship between theory about how citizenship education should proceed and what actually happens in various educational settings.

This book is a collection of qualitative studies on formal programs that provide citizenship education for contemporary youth, either school or community-based, and located within the United States. These programs include social studies classes and curricula, school governance, and community-based education efforts. Because schools operate under many constraints that inhibit certain kinds of educational experiences, it is vital to explore programs in alternative settings that have taken up the aims of citizenship education. In fact, by juxtaposing studies of efforts in mainstream high schools, alternative high schools, and community-based organizations, much can be learned about the contextual factors that shape these efforts and the challenges and possibilities that exist across a range of educational sites.

As a collection, the studies in this book investigate the diversity of purposes of citizenship education, meanings of citizenship held by participants, and approaches to teaching and learning. The studies present the voices of educators and youth involved in these civic education efforts and analyze key elements of their practices. The authors utilize a wide variety of theoretical lenses and qualitative methodologies, including ethnography, focus group interviews, and content analysis of textbooks. All of the chapters offer findings that bear valuable and specific implications for strengthening citizenship education. The authors' analyses deepen the often tenuous connections between research and practice.

Research Questions

The studies in this volume address three research questions:

1. What are the purposes of education for democratic citizenship enacted in a particular setting?

2. What understandings of citizenship are held/exhibited by the curriculum, the educators, and/or the youth in a particular program?

3. What is the nature of teaching and learning evident in these programs and how do these educational enactments limit and enable various kinds of education for democratic citizenship?

The purposes of citizenship education have changed over time according to the historical context and political/social needs of the nation (Reuben, 2005). The fundamental aim is to prepare young people with knowledge, skills, and dispositions to be the good citizens upon whom democracy depends. But debates over the aims of citizenship education in public schools have intensified along with battles over the social studies curriculum in part due to tension between the ideals of pluralism and unity. Questions of purpose also center on what kind of democracy is desirable, and how much/what kind of knowledge and engagement is required of citizens (Galston, 2001). Ross (2001) argues that while there is widespread agreement that "citizenship education" is "the proper aim of social studies" in the public schools, "there is no consensus on what "citizenship" means nor on the implications of "citizenship" for curriculum and instruction" (p. 23). This is equally true outside of public schools.

Conservative thinkers promote coherent coverage of content and transmission of particular values such as unity, patriotism, and consent to the status quo. This approach aims at providing students with knowledge about the U.S. system of government and "developing understandings of and pride in the contributions that American democracy has made to U.S. citizens and to the world" (Simon, 2005, p. 108). The central aim here is to prepare citizens who vote and support the nation.

Progressive education scholars who dominate the recent literature on citizenship education reform advocate "deliberative pedagogies" (Simon, 2005, p. 107), and more specifically an "issues centered curriculum" (Evans and Saxe, 1996; Ochoa-Becker, 2007) in which students research, analyze, and discuss controversial public issues, and engage in simulations, debates, and decision-making. Democratic deliberation is meant to develop critical thinking and "help students gain the skills they need to address the complex problems facing society" (Simon, 2005, p. 107). The ultimate purpose is to prepare citizens who will actively and thoughtfully participate in the social and political arena. (See chapter 2 for more discussion of conservative vs. progressive orientations.)

Parker (1996) explicitly critiques both the conservative and progressive models. Although he favors the progressive aim of developing intellectually able citizens who participate more directly rather than the conservative aim of transmitting knowledge and values to future voters, he points out that both camps disregard matters of social and cultural diversity and inequality. He argues that rather than teaching students that democracy is a finished product, citizenship education should prepare young people to become involved in democracy as an ongoing work in progress (Parker, 2003). To be successful, citizenship education must promote both democratic enlightenment and political engagement. Political engagement means participation in the form of voting, deliberating public problems, campaigning, civil disobedience, and so on. Democratic enlightenment refers to understanding the ideals of democratic living and the commitment to freedom and justice (pp. 33–34). Similarly, according to Banks (1997), students should develop the knowledge, attitudes, and skills to transform society, to close the gap between the ideals and realities of democracy in the United States.

Two quotes from a recent issue of *Phi Delta Kappan* on patriotism and civic education articulate purposes pertinent to our contemporary situation:

> Even as we strive for balance and fairness, we should provide our students with the analytical skills to critique and evaluate information they are exposed to so that they can develop a logical and historically grounded framework for comprehending present conflicts and foreign engagements (Noguera & Cohen, 2006, p. 576).

> Rather than "teaching" students to love their country, teachers need to help students build an explicit connection between their "love of country" and democratic ideals—ideals that include the role of informed analysis and, at times, critique; the importance of action; and the danger of blind loyalty to the state (Kahne & Middaugh, 2006, p. 606).

Given the vast amount of writing on what should be the aims of citizenship education, what purposes are actually enacted in particular settings? How do these purposes vary, depending on contextual factors, such as location within mainstream classrooms, alternative schools, or the community? And how are these purposes influenced by the educators and the youth who bring these educational efforts to life?

Secondly, what meanings of citizenship are manifested by the curriculum, the educators, and the youth in these programs? Findings from the IEA Civic Education Study conducted with adolescents in twenty-eight countries provide general information about the views of youth: "The large majority of young people surveyed in 1999 believed that citizens should obey the law and should vote. Between 80% and 90% in the United States . . . thought these activities important or very important. In contrast, only 58% of these students believed it important or very important for the citizen to participate in political discussions, and the figure was 48% for affiliating with a political party" (Torney-Purta, 2002, p. 208). Baldi et al. (2001) found that in the United States "more than 80% of students thought it important or very important for adult citizens to participate in activities helping the community, promoting human rights, and protecting the environment" (Torney-Purta, 2002, p. 208).

Research points to the separation young people make between involvement in community service and politics: "Many students actively involved in community service say that they have chosen service as an antidote to politics" (Battistoni, 2000), which they hold in disdain (Walker, 2002). Chiodo and Martin (2005) also find that students do not relate to politics, but rather to the social side of citizenship, such as community service and being respectful, helpful, and obedient. These findings indicate the need for more explicit and broader conceptions of citizenship in curricula.

How do meanings of citizenship and democracy vary for youth from different racial, ethnic, and socio-economic backgrounds? Sherrod, Flanagan, and Youniss (2002) ask how the definition of citizenship changes for people who are not offered full rights as U.S. citizens, for example immigrants and sexual minorities. The activism of these groups is vital to the expansion of democracy: "In this regard, we are reminded that it was the collective resistance of Black citizens and their civil disobedience of laws on the books that denied them full inclusion as citizens that eventually resulted in the passage of a Civil Rights Act in this country" (Sherrod, Flanagan, & Youniss, 2002, p. 265).

Sanchez-Jankowski (2002) and Junn (2004) find that young people from marginalized minority groups develop civic understandings and skills that may not manifest themselves in standardized measures but are adaptive to the real life situations of their communities. Do educational efforts acknowledge and adapt to these differences, or further marginalize youth from low income and underrepresented backgrounds?

Westheimer and Kahne (2004) investigate different visions of citizenship exhibited by ten school programs: the *personally responsible citizen,* the *participatory citizen,* or the *justice-oriented citizen.* How do these models pertain to curricula, educators, and youth in different kinds of settings? Content analysis of the National Standards for Civics and Government (Gonzales, Riedel, Avery, & Sullivan, 2001) shows a heavy focus on the rights and freedoms of citizens versus responsibilities to the public good and civic virtue. Also, the role of political engagement is de-emphasized, as are the contributions of women and minorities to society. Programs that enjoy freedom from the structural and curricular constraints imposed on classrooms may be much more inclusive in the views of citizenship they embrace.

Finally, what is the nature of teaching and learning evident in these programs, and how do these educational enactments both enable and limit various kinds of education for democratic citizenship? Numerous scholars, including Gutmann (1999), Newmann (1989), and Parker (1996), agree that "the most important component of effective democratic citizenship preparation involves teaching young people how to deliberate about the nature of the public good" (Hess, 2002, p. 12). Indeed, research indicates that social studies classes with discussion of controversial issues in an open climate foster citizenship learning and involvement (Hahn, 1998; Hess & Posselt, 2002; Patrick & Hoge, 1991). And twelfth grade civics classes that include a variety of topics and frequent discussion of current events increase political knowledge according to the National Assessment of Educational Progress (NAEP) Civics Assessment (Niemi & Junn, 1998). However, studies show that discussion of controversial public issues and other "deliberative pedagogies" (Simon, 2001) are rarely employed (Hahn, Dilworth, Hughes, & Sen, 2001; Kahne et al., 2000). Instead, Ross (2001), taking an historical look at research on the social studies curriculum in schools, states that within social studies classes "citizenship transmission" or "conservative cultural continuity" is the dominant approach practiced in the schools" (p. 24). This is true even though in one national survey of social studies teachers "respondents identified more strongly with social studies as "reflective inquiry" and "informed social criticism" than with approaches to social studies as "citizenship transmission'" (Vinson, 1998 as quoted in Ross, 2001, p. 24).

One highly publicized nontraditional approach to education for democratic citizenship within the schools is service-learning, although there are multiple interpretations of exactly what service-learning means. According to the Center for Information and Research on Civic Learning and Engagement

(CIRCLE), service learning "consists of sustained community service projects that are closely connected to formal instruction and curriculum . . . [and] often involves close partnerships between schools or colleges and communities" (http://www.civicyouth.org/research/areas/serv_learn.htm). A recent study of high school students who participated in service-learning found that in regards to increasing students' civic knowledge, behaviors, and dispositions, "service-learning is effective when it is implemented well, but it is no more effective than conventional social studies classes when the conditions are not optimal" (Billig, Root, & Jesse, 2005, p. 1).

What approaches are employed in classrooms, given the well documented constraints of schooling? How do educators break out of the traditional mold of textbook and lecture centered classes that typify high school social studies? How does civic development differ in school governance projects or community based youth organizations that provide opportunities for authentic and experiential education? How do authority relationships between educators and youth, which greatly bear on the quality of teaching and learning (Pace & Hemmings, 2007), shape citizenship education experiences? And, considering the gap between recommendations for practice and actual practices in schools (Gibson & Levine, 2003), how do specific approaches in these diverse locations relate to scholarship on citizenship education?

This volume provides answers to these key questions. In doing so, it both builds upon and challenges prior scholarship in the field. We aim to encourage greater support for citizenship education efforts, both within schools and in the community, that foster enlightenment and engagement, to use Parker's terms. The book also generates critical questions, for example how citizenship education is being affected by the accountability movement and other reforms, and how educators can be better prepared to employ recommendations for practice. Future research and policy must attend to these fundamental concerns.

Contents of the Book

Section 1: Inside Classrooms

Chapter 2, "Teaching for Citizenship in 12th Grade Government Classes," addresses a serious gap in research on classroom practices in citizenship education. Judith L. Pace describes different versions of Government classes taught by four teachers in two racially/ethnically diverse metropolitan high schools during fall 2004 and the Presidential election. Using data from classroom observations and interviews with teachers and students, she analyzes the teachers' approaches and students' responses to the enacted curricula. The Government classes were all knowledge-based, and according to recommendations from the Civic Mission for Schools (Gibson & Levine, 2003) and others (see Hahn, 1998; Parker, 2003), classes did not adequately prepare most students to be politically engaged citizens. But the classes varied significantly in levels of student participation, critical thinking, attention to social justice and contemporary political issues, and promotion of active citizenship. Variation was influenced by a set of inter-related factors—track level, views of students, and school demographics and culture. At both schools, students in the Advanced Placement classes had greater opportunities for learning than did students in college preparatory classes. Also, the smaller high school with a higher percentage of White and Asian American students was more progressive; teachers encouraged more student participation in class, and contemporary events, including the war on terror and fights over civil liberties, were more openly discussed. The larger high school, with a higher percentage of African American and Latino students, was a more controlled environment and classes were teacher-centered. Contemporary political and social issues were not as central to the curriculum. However, students at this school organized political activity outside of class, and fought the administration for the right to hold an anti-war rally at school. Pace's chapter both reveals and contradicts the view that adolescents are politically apathetic and paves the way for more, sorely needed, research on how Government classes do and do not teach for political engagement and are shaped by institutional factors.

Chapter 3, "Connecting Diversity, Justice, and Democratic Citizenship: Lessons from an Alternative U.S. History Class," showcases one teacher's efforts to enact multicultural democratic education (Marri, 2005) with marginalized, academically struggling youth. Anand Marri outlines the classroom practices of Mr. Sinclair, a well-educated and committed social studies teacher at a public alternative high school, by focusing on a month-long unit on the Civil Rights Movement. Mr. Sinclair enacts ideas and approaches advocated by citizenship education experts, such as Walter Parker (2003). For example, he engages students in applying Kohlberg's theory of moral development to civil rights activists' law breaking. He gets his class to grapple with political action that is illegal yet morally justified. The teacher also involves students in inquiry-based lessons that draw connections between segregation in the South and contemporary housing and school segregation patterns in their own city. And he conducts a seminar on Dr. Martin Luther King, Jr.'s *Letter from Birmingham Jail*. Marri's analysis points to elements of teaching that aims to empower marginalized students and educate them for multicultural democratic citizenship. These elements are inclusive pedagogy, a diverse learning community, critical thinking, discussion, and transformational knowledge. The author identifies a missing element from Mr. Sinclair's curriculum—mainstream academic knowledge and skills—which raises the question of how to provide struggling students with the range of educational experiences needed to become empowered citizens.

In chapter 4, "Urban Youth and the Construction of Racialized and Classed Political Identities," Kysa Nygreen uses participatory action research to explore the emerging political identities of three urban youth (age 16–19) as they worked together to design and teach a social justice class. The class was located at an urban continuation high school serving a predominantly African American and low-income student body, where the research participants were/had been students. Working from a sociocultural perspective, Nygreen conceptualizes political identity as a way of acting and interacting as a certain "kind" of political subject. Political identity is fluid, dynamic, and shaped by local and larger factors, including shared counter-narratives about the government and its relationship to marginalized communities (i.e., poor people, people of color). Political identity grew out of (to differing degrees) the youth's lived experiences of social marginalization, and the "disjuncture" (Rubin, 2007) they experienced or witnessed between the ideals and realities of U.S. democracy. While the youth developed and taught their weekly class, as social justice educators they enacted, confirmed, and strengthened their political identities. Nygreen's study shows the processes through which this occurred, and makes a unique and important contribution to sociocultural theories of identity formation and youth political agency. Her work implies that efforts to educate for democratic citizenship begin by seeking to understand youths' existing and emerging political perspectives, and recognizing the critical political insights and potential agency youth possess even if they score poorly on civics tests or surveys.

Chapter 5, "Service-Learning as a Promising Approach to High School Civic Engagement," presents findings from a national study of service-learning and high school students' civic engagement. Susan Root and Shelly Billig discuss service-learning as a teaching strategy wherein students learn important curricular objectives by providing service that meets authentic community needs, and they review the possibilities and challenges of service-learning. Their chapter first outlines a national study that involves quantitative and qualitative measures, and then focuses on qualitative data from three sites. It argues that service-learning can be used to revitalize citizenship education within high schools when particular design components are in place, even at a time when the curriculum is undergoing increased constriction under accountability pressures. Successful programs in this study featured components that required students to learn about political institutions and processes and practice skills for political participation. These components included:

1. **Preparation** for service that included research, advocacy, and student voice;
2. **Action/Implementation** of service activities that were of sufficient duration and offered cognitive challenges, opportunities to empathize with the community, and skillful teacher facilitation of student work; and
3. **Reflection** activities that were continuous and in-depth;
4. **Public demonstration** of results in which students engaged in a public demonstration of learning with previously unfamiliar adults.

Importantly, the teachers at these sites had extensive experience implementing service-learning and were comfortable in allowing students voice and choice in the activities they conducted.

Chapter 6, "Democracy's Practice Grounds: The Role of School Governance in Citizenship Education," shows how schools can engage students in democratic citizenship by providing exercises in community governance and public problem solving. Richard Battistoni's chapter showcases Project 540, a national initiative involving 270 American high schools. It uses interviews with students, teachers, and administrators to analyze the opportunities and challenges involved in using student governance as a tool in citizenship education. This "democratic school practice" approach to civic education—as opposed to the "formal civics instruction" approach—allowed students to participate in a process of dialogue, decision making, and action. Students, teachers, and administrators spoke about key opportunities: civic communication, participation in public policy decisions, and making change in their schools and communities. In Project 540 learning was experiential, project and performance based, and authentic; it was situated in actual practices of governance and involved deliberative decision making in collaborative, heterogeneous groups. Students spoke about how they applied the civic skills they gained in Project 540 to other aspects of their life: leadership in student government, cocurricular activities, even work and family life. Project 540 also confronted challenges. Often it conflicted with the institutional culture of high schools, where adult educators were used to being in control and making most if not all of the decisions for the school. Another challenge was competing demands, such as pressures for school accountability. Findings suggest that giving students opportunities for practicing democracy, through involvement in real school governance, can enhance democratic citizenship education, especially in the area of students' civic skills and values/attitudes, as well as improve school climate and foster the educational goals of the institution.

Chapter 7, "Civic Development in Context: The Influence of Local Contexts on High School Students' Beliefs about Civic Engagement," examines the salience of social context in youth civic development and civic education. Using focus group interviews with high school seniors, Ellen Middaugh and Joseph Kahne reveal the ways students make sense of their own roles as citizens. Data collection was conducted in May and June of 2005 with focus groups of 4–6 students each from five schools including urban, suburban, and rural schools across the state of California. The schools all are engaged in a process of working to create new opportunities for civic education aligned with the six recommendations of the Civic Mission of Schools Report (Gibson & Levine, 2003). The findings point to similarities as well as important differences within and among groups of students. All the students expressed an appreciation for democracy, but varied in the extent to which they believed the current system of government truly is democratic. More affluent students believed this more strongly than did low income students. Students in very different contexts shared a relative disinterest in politics and political action. The reasons behind this differed across groups. In affluent and majority white communities, students reported few local problems. In demographically diverse and in lower-income, urban, majority Latino communities, students indicated they did not view politics as a viable means for addressing relevant problems. For students across groups, political engagement was seen as a matter of personal inclination rather than the responsibility of citizens. Students did speak positively about service-learning experiences, but often perceived them as separate from politics. Students also said they liked classroom debates and wanted to have more discussion of contemporary social issues. The chapter points to particular implications for civic education. First, exploring only the virtues of democratic institutions is problematic. Forging stronger connections between government curriculum and civic and political engagement is needed. And attending to contextual differences may help build commitments to civic engagement. The authors conclude that there is yet much we have to learn about the influence local contexts have on youth civic development.

Chapter 8, "Examining the Treatment of 9/11 and Terrorism in High School Textbooks," analyzes textbook coverage of 9/11. Diana Hess, Jeremy Stoddard, and Shannon Murto present findings based on a study of top-selling U.S. history, world history, and government textbooks that were published between 2003 and 2005 and included the events of 9/11 and the war on terrorism. The study had two primary aims. The first was to examine critically what curricula are communicating about 9/11, its aftermath, and terrorism more generally. The second aim was to investigate which topics or questions related to 9/11, its aftermath, and terrorism are presented to students as genuinely controversial and which either explicitly or implicitly present a "correct" answer that the curriculum writers expect students to believe. Their analysis focuses on the depth of information on the events, and what students were asked to do with that information. The textbooks used a neutral, compact style and events were presented as matter of fact or used to promote ideas of heroism, patriotism, and unquestioned citizenship. They did not endorse active deliberation about the roots of terrorism, the causes of 9/11, or how the United States should have responded. These texts overall identify 9/11 as an iconic and tragic event with no equal among terrorist attacks, provide examples of terrorism that emphasize attacks on the U.S. over attacks on other countries or peoples, and present inconsistent definitions of terrorism and examples as universally accepted truths.

Implications from this analysis include the importance of utilizing a range of curricular materials in social studies courses. Specifically, schools districts and funders should support materials developed by democratic education organizations with more ideological freedom than textbook publishers who operate under a system of perceived and real market constraints.

Section 3: In the Community

Chapter 9, "Engaging Urban Youth in Civic Practice: Community-Based Youth Organizations for Democratic Education," explores community-based youth organizations (CBYOs) as a meaningful alternative to urban public schools in providing a space where youth can learn democratic citizenship skills. Authors Jennifer O'Donoghue and Ben Kirshner examine the features of CBYOs that impact youth's development as citizens. They conducted qualitative studies consisting of observations and interviews in five youth organizations located in low-income urban areas between 2001 and 2003. While varying in specific mission and goals, all programs sought to engage young people in civic action. In total, these five organizations worked with over 150 youth (with program size varying from 7 to 80). O'Donoghue and Kirshner identify five shared civic education practices across the organizations: working with others, decision-making, interpreting public problems, taking action, and promoting youth public efficacy. They illustrate these practices through vignettes and present participants' perspectives on their learning experiences.

The authors find that the youth involved in these programs developed important competencies for democratic participation, including collaboration, decision-making, and knowledge about local issues and how to make an impact on them. They also document particular challenges, such as the need for adult educators who are skilled in particular ways in working with young people. Also, by focusing on local issues, youth were not engaged in national or international issues, nor did they learn traditional civic content knowledge. The chapter shows that despite the tensions, CBYOs are vital, emancipated spaces for urban youth to learn about and practice active democratic citizenship to improve their communities.

In chapter 10, "To Think, Live and Breathe Politics: Experiencing Democratic Citizenship in Chicago," Janet S. Bixby examines the experiences of alumni from citizenship education programs run by a private foundation called the Mikva Challenge for urban high school students in Chicago. The Mikva programs have impacted a large number of students, involving over forty schools and 1500 students. The programs provide multifaceted opportunities for youth to engage in authentic forms of civic activism and to experience democracy as a way of life (Dewey, 1966), for example by acting as election judges, hosting a debate for gubernatorial candidates, volunteering for campaigns, and interning with elected officials. The youth in the Mikva programs are predominantly African American, Latino, and/or immigrants, from middle- to low-income backgrounds. Bixby collected data for eighteen months through individual interviews and focus groups with alumni of the programs; interviews with teachers and staff; observations of student, alumni, and teacher events; and materials produced by the foundation. Bixby's analysis utilizes Lave and Wenger's (1991) framework for understanding learning as apprenticeship to examine how alumni of the Mikva programs interpreted the meaning of their participation in these programs and its significance in their lives. All of the twenty alumni she studied reported that their work in the Mikva programs had a dramatically positive, transformative impact on their sense of themselves as civic actors. Their experiences stood in stark contrast to reports that urban youth have little opportunity to participate constructively in the public sphere (McLaughlin, 2000). Their political interest and activity also contrasts with findings related to low levels of civic knowledge and engagement associated with poor and minority youth.

The volume ends with an epilogue by Judith L. Pace titled "Citizenship Education in Diverse Settings: Findings, Tensions, and Future Research." It identifies the major findings of these studies in relation to the three research questions that guide the book. Pace points to the influence of institutional contexts and the tensions that arise in teaching for democracy, as well as the need for further qualitative research.

Note

We are grateful to Lyndsey Schlax and Matt Magansay, former students in the Teacher Education Department at the University of San Francisco, for their helpful research assistance.

References

Baldi, S., Perie, M., Skidmore, D., & Greenberg, E. (2001). *What democracy means to ninth-graders: U.S. results from the international IEA civic education study.* Washington, DC: U.S. Department of Education National Center for Education Statistics.

Banks, J. (1997). *Educating citizens in a multicultural society.* New York: Teachers College Press.

Battistoni, R. (2000). Service learning and civic education. In S. Mann & J. Patrick (Eds.) *Education for civic engagement in democracy.* Bloomington, IN: ERIC Clearinghouse for Social Studies.

Billig, S., Root, S., & Jesse, D. (2005). The impact of participation in service learning on high school students' civic learning. *CIRCLE.* Available at www.civicyouth.org

Chiodo, J., & Martin, L. (2005). What do students have to say about citizenship? An analysis of the concept of citizenship among secondary education students. *Journal of Social Studies Research, 29*(1), 23–31.

Dewey, J. (1966). *Democracy and education.* New York: Free Press.

Dilworth, P. (2004). Multicultural citizenship education: Case studies from social studies classrooms. *Theory and Research in Social Education, 32*(2), 153–186.

Evans, R. & Saxe, D. (1996). *Handbook on teaching social issues.* Washington, DC: National Council for the Social Studies.

Fuhrman, S., & Lazerson, M. (Eds.) (2005). *The public schools.* New York: Oxford University Press.

Galston, W. (2001). Political knowledge, political engagement, and civic education. *Annual Review of Political Science (4),* 217–234.

Gibson, C., & Levine, P. (2003). *The civic mission of schools.* New York and Washington, DC: The Carnegie Corporation of New York and the Center for Information and Research on Civic Learning.

Gonzales, M., Riedel, E., Avery, P., & Sullivan, J. (2001). Rights and obligations in civic education: A content analysis of the national standards for civics and government. *Theory and Research in Social Education, 29*(1), 109–128.

Gutmann, A. (1999). *Democratic education, 2nd ed.* Princeton, NJ: Princeton University Press.

Hahn, C. (1998). *Becoming political: Comparative perspectives on citizenship education.* Albany: State University of New York Press.

Hahn, C., Dilworth, P., Hughes, J., & Sen, T. (2001). Democratic understanding: Cross-national perspectives. *Theory into Practice, 40*(1), 14–22.

Hahn, C. (2002). Education for democratic citizenship: One nation's story. In W. Parker (Ed.), *Education for democracy: Contexts, curricula, assessments* (pp. 63–92). Greenwich, CT.: Information Age Publishing.

Hart, D., & Atkins, R. (2002). Civic competence in urban youth. *Applied Developmental Science, 6*(4), 227–236.

Hess, D. (2002). Discussing controversial public issues in secondary social studies classrooms: Learning from skilled teachers. *Theory and Research in Social Education, 30* (1), 10–41.

Hess, D., & Posselt, J. (2002). How high school students experience and learn from the discussion of controversial public issues. *Journal of Curriculum and Supervision, 17*(4), 283–314.

Johanek, M., & Puckett, J. (2005). The state of civic education: Preparing citizens in an era of accountability. In S. Furhman & M. Lazerson (Eds.), *The public schools* (pp. 130–159). Oxford: Oxford University Press.

Junn, J. (2004). Diversity, immigration, and the politics of civic education. *P.S.: Political Science and Politics, 37,* 253–255.

Kahne, J., & Middaugh, E. (2006). Is patriotism good for democracy? A study of seniors patriotic commitments. *Phi Delta Kappan* 87(8), 600–607.

Kahne, J., Rodriguez, M., & Smith, B. (2000). Developing citizens for democracy? Assessing opportunities to learn in Chicago's social studies classrooms. *Theory and Research in Social Education, 28*(3), 311–338.

Lave, J. & Wenger, E. (1991). *Situated learning: Legitimate peripheral participation.* Cambridge: University of Cambridge Press.

Marri, A. (2005). Building a framework for classroom-based multicultural democratic education: Learning from three skilled teachers. *Teachers College Record, 107* (5), 1036–1059.

McLaughlin, M. (2000). *Community counts: How youth organizations matter for youth development.* Washington, DC: Public Education Network.

Newmann, F. (1989). Reflective civic participation. *Social Education, 53*(October), 357–360.

Niemi, R., & Junn, J. (1998). *Civic education: What makes students learn.* New Haven: Yale University Press.

Noguera, P., & Cohen, R. (2006). Patriotism and accountability: The role of educators in the war on terrorism. *Phi Delta Kappan* 87(8), 573–578.

Ochoa-Becker, A. (2007). *Democratic education for social studies: An issues-centered decision making curriculum.* Greenwich, CT: Information Age Publishing.

Pace, J., & Hemmings, A. (2007). Understanding classroom authority: A review of theory, ideology, and research. *Review of Educational Research, 77* (1), 4–27.

Parker, W. (1996). "Advanced" ideas about democracy: Toward a pluralistic conception of citizen education. *Teachers College Record, 98*(1), 104–125.

Parker, W. (2003). *Teaching democracy: Unity and diversity in public life.* New York: Teachers College Press.

Patrick, J., Vontz, T. & Nixon, W. (2002). Issue-centered education for democracy through project citizen. In W. Parker (Ed.), *Education for democracy; Contexts, curricula, assessments* (pp. 93–112). Greenwich, CT: Information Age Publishing.

Patrick, J., & Hoge, J. (2001). Teaching government, civics, and law. In J. Shaver (Ed.), *Handbook of research on social studies teaching and learning.* New York: Macmillan.

Parker, W. (Ed.) (2002). *Education for democracy: Contexts, curricula, assessments.* Greenwich, CT: Information Age Publishing.

Putnam, R. (2000). *Bowling alone: The collapse and revival of American community.* New York: Simon & Schuster.

Reuben, J. (2005). Patriotic purposes: Public schools and the education of citizens. In S. Fuhrman & M. Lazerson (Eds.) (2005). *The public schools* (pp. 1–24). New York: Oxford University Press.

Ross, E. (2001). The struggle for the social studies curriculum. In E. W. Ross (Ed.), *The social studies: Purposes, problems, and possibilities* (pp. 19–41). Albany: State University of New York.

Rubin, B. (2007). There's still not justice: Youth civic identity development amid distinct school and community contexts. *Teachers College Record, 109*(2), 449–481.

Sanchez-Jankowski, M. (2002). Minority Youth and Civic Engagement: The impact of group relations. *Applied Development Science, 6*(4), 237–245.

Sherrod, L., Flanagan, C., & Youniss, J. (Eds.). (2002). Dimensions of citizenship and opportunities for youth development: The what, why, when, where, and who of citizenship development. *Applied Developmental Science, 6*(4), 264–274.

Simon, K. (2001). *Moral questions in the classroom: How to get kids to think deeply about real life and their school work.* New Haven, CT: Yale University Press.

Simon, K. (2005). Classroom deliberations. In S. Fuhrman & M. Lazerson (Eds.). *The public schools* (pp. 107–129). New York: Oxford University Press.

Torney-Purta, J. (2002). What adolescents know about citizenship and democracy. *Educational Leadership, 59*(4), 42–22.

Torney-Purta, J., Lehmann, J., Oswald, R., & Schultz, W. (2001). *Citizenship and education in twenty-eight countries: Civic knowledge and engagement at age fourteen.* Amsterdam: IEA <http://www.wam.umd.edu/~iea/>

Torney-Purta, J., Schwille, J., & Amadeo, J. (1999). *Civic education across countries: Twenty-four national case studies from the IEA Civic Education Project.* Amsterdam: IEA <htp://www.wam.umd.edu/~iea/>

Vinson, K. (1998). The traditions revisited: Instructional approach and high school social studies teachers. *Theory and Research in Social Education, 26,* 50–82.

Walker, T. (2002). Service as a pathway to political participation. *Applied Developmental Science, 16*(4), 183–188.

Westheimer, J., & Kahne, J. (2004). What kind of citizen? The politics of educating for democracy. *American Educational Research Journal, 41*(2), 237–269.

Inside Classrooms

CHAPTER 2

Teaching for Citizenship in 12th Grade Government Classes

Judith L. Pace

A wealth of scholarship discusses lack of political engagement among Americans and the crucial role of schools and especially social studies courses in cultivating that engagement (see Fuhrman & Lazerson, 2005; Gibson & Levine, 2003). Yet little is known about classes that teach for citizenship in U.S. high schools. Much research indicates that classroom curriculum and instruction has a negligible impact on political involvement (Ehman, 1980; Patrick & Hoge, 1991).

However, researchers also have found that classes with discussion, debates, and decision making in a climate that is open to expression of ideas encourage students' political interest, knowledge, competence and tolerance (see Hahn, 1998; 2001; Kahne, Rodriguez, Smith, & Thiede, 2000; Niemi & Junn, 1998; Torney-Purta et al., 2001). But few[1] have documented the content and processes of particular classes, how they align with theories of citizenship education, and how they influence the development of democratic citizens. In their review of scholarship, Patrick and Hoge (1991) call for improved research that can inform classroom practice. Likewise, Kahne et al., (2000), in a quantitative study on classroom opportunities to learn about democracy, conclude: "There is an enormous need to undertake qualitative assessments of classroom practices, the motivations that drive them, and the ways they are experienced by teachers and students" (p. 332). They assert that studies must consider contextual influences that shape classroom practices, such as school structures and student demographics.

Twelfth grade civics classes play a special role in citizenship education as students approach voting age (Niemi & Junn, 1998). In addition to lack of research on classroom practices in context, virtually no studies examine how these particular classes do or do not teach for political engagement, how teachers and students think about these classes, and how local and larger factors shape them.

During the fall semester of 2004, coinciding with the U.S. presidential election, I conducted an exploratory qualitative study of 12th grade Government classes in two California high schools taught by two teachers in each school. U.S. Government[2] is a one-semester course required of California seniors for graduation. High school social studies, and government in particular, has a reputation for boring students. And in 12th grade a seemingly inevitable epidemic—senioritis—takes hold. Additionally, low commitment to learning among many high school students is a well-documented problem (National Research Council, 2005; Powell, Farrar, & Cohen, 1985; Sizer, 1984). Schools often assuage and unwittingly exacerbate students' disengagement through tracking and teaching practices that lower expectations and control knowledge (McNeil, 1981; Oakes, 1985; Pace, 2003a, 2006; Page, 1991).

To address the dual problems of political and classroom engagement, this study examines different versions of teaching for citizenship in Government classes. Variation in teaching was shaped by interrelated factors: Views of students, conceptions of the course, tracking, and school culture. In each school, opportunities for engagement in classroom learning were greater in higher-track (Advanced Placement) than in lower-track (college preparatory) classes. Opportunities were greater in the school with student centered practices that served a student body with a majority of White and Asian American students. They were fewer in the school with teacher-centered practices that served a student body with a majority of White, African American, and Latino students. Yet opportunities for learning about citizenship occurred in all classes, and despite assumptions about youth disengagement, students showed great potential for political involvement.

Research Sites and Methodology

The study was conducted in two high schools located in two small northern California cities. Each school had diverse student populations but differed in important ways. Rutherford High School in Lynvale (all names of people and places are pseudonyms) enrolled 2,000 students. Its demographics were reported as the following: Whites at 35%, Asians 27%, Latinos 10%, African Americans 5%, Filipinos 4%, and "Other" 18%. Students represented many ethnicities and different religions as well as recent immigrants to the U.S. The school prided itself on being an inclusive community.

Jefferson High School in Cedarville enrolled over 3300 students. Its demographic report was Whites at 32%, African Americans 25%, Hispanics or Latinos 20%, Asians 9%, Filipinos 8%, and "Other" 6%. Of particular note was talk among faculty, administration, and even students about the difficulty of integrating African American students with "urban attitudes" whose families were relative newcomers from a nearby city, and the lack of cohesive community at such a large school.

The original research question was the following: What is being taught and learned in discussion-based 12th grade Government classes during the fall semester of 2004? Because classes did not involve as much discussion as anticipated, I examined the teaching methods that were employed. I also explored teachers' and students' views on purposes of, approaches to, and engagement in the course, and on democracy and citizenship. During the fall semester, I visited each school one day a week, observing Government classes taught by the two participating teachers, taking field notes, and occasionally audio taping lessons.

At Rutherford the teachers were Ms. Bates, who taught college preparatory classes, and Ms. Kelly, who taught the Advanced Placement class. At Jefferson I observed Ms. Sutter who taught college prep, and Ms. Jones who taught an AP class and college prep as well.[3] Due to scheduling constraints I observed the teachers at Rutherford with the same class each time; at Jefferson I observed multiple classes taught by each teacher. I talked informally with the teachers and their students, collected pertinent documents such as class handouts, and hung out in the cafeteria, corridors, quad, library, and other spaces in the school. Toward the end of the semester I interviewed each participating teacher for at least an hour and each of ten students from the Government classes I observed at each school (total of twenty students) for at least half an hour. Students were recruited by sending around a volunteer sign-up sheet during class after briefly explaining my research. Additionally I attended a meeting of an after school politics club at Jefferson. Several months after data collection was completed, I conducted two more interviews—one with a teacher and the other with a student from Jefferson—about a surprising event that took place after I left the site.

Analysis of data involved applying concepts from both citizenship education and social foundations of education to develop an explanation of the factors that shaped unequal opportunities for student engagement across Government classes. Prior research on civics classes generally has not examined contextual factors such as teachers' views of students, tracking, and school culture. I found that these lenses provided a powerful framework for understanding inequality across these classes.

Conceptual Frameworks

Citizenship Education and Socio-cultural Foundations of Education

According to Galston (2001), debates in citizenship education have centered on what kind of democracy is desirable and what knowledge is required of citizens. Stanley (2005) compares progressive and conservative models of citizenship education. The former aims to build intellectual capacity, including the ability to think critically about social problems and make reasoned decisions about solutions (see Dewey, 1916). Progressives believe that political knowledge and engagement among youth must be increased in order to support "strong democracy" (Barber, 1984) in which citizens actively participate. The conservative model aims to transmit knowledge and values to create a unified citizenry that will vote for officials who make the decisions (Stanley, 2005).

The Civic Mission of Schools (Gibson & Levine, 2003) is aligned with the progressive orientation and asserts that effective approaches to citizenship education are characterized by elements that specifically and strongly attend to involvement in politics:

- purposeful focus on preparing youth for civic participation
- "explicit advocacy of civic and political engagement"
- "active learning opportunities" that engage students in discussion of issues and activities that relate classroom knowledge to real life (e.g., research projects and presentations, mock trials, simulations, service-learning, and so on)
- emphasis on ideas and principles central to constitutional democracy and how they influence everyday institutions and "problems, opportunities,

controversies, rights, and responsibilities that matter to them in the present." (p. 21)

Parker (1996) critiques both the conservative and progressive models. Although he advocates the progressive aim of developing intellectually able citizens who participate directly in political affairs rather than the conservative aim of transmitting knowledge and values to future voters, he points out that both camps disregard critical issues related to social and cultural diversity and inequality. He argues that citizenship education must develop two vital attributes—democratic enlightenment and political engagement. Parker defines political engagement as citizenship participation, which includes voting, contacting public officials, deliberating public problems, campaigning, and engaging in political protest. Democratic enlightenment means understanding and embracing democratic ideals, including the commitment to freedom and justice for all people (Parker, 2003, p. 33–34).

The extent to which the classes I observed represented citizenship education guidelines and ideals reveals the gap between research and practice. All the classes in my study emphasized acquisition of knowledge (Hess & Posselt, 2002). None took a systematic approach to discussion of controversial public issues, so widely recommended by scholars (Hess, 2002; Parker, 2003), yet infrequently found by researchers (Hahn, 2002). None involved students in substantial and authentic political participation or social action (Westheimer & Kahne, 2004). But within the general knowledge-based paradigm, teaching and learning for citizenship varied a great deal. Research in the social foundations of education in combination with scholarship in citizenship education helps to explain this variation.

Numerous sociocultural studies on schooling identify teachers' views of students as a major influence on teaching (see Anyon, 1983; McNeil, 1986; Metz, 1978; Oakes, 1985; Page, 1991). They find that when students are perceived as low-income, low-track, and/or hostile to school, teachers are likely to lower expectations, emphasize rote learning, control discourse, and/or mistreat them. When students are seen as high-income, high-track, and/or invested in school, teachers are likely to have higher expectations, engage students in higher-order thinking and discussion, and show them more respect. These studies also have found that students respond accordingly: "Defensive teaching" (McNeil, 1981, 1986) provokes various forms of resistance, ranging from covert to overt, while responsive teaching can engender student empowerment and consent.

School culture is an important factor in the development of students' civic attitudes and actions (Patrick & Hoge, 1991), and it also is a major influence on teaching. It may promote either rigid (Cornbleth, 2001) or nurturing (Lightfoot, 1983) classroom practices. Teachers translate a school's values and curricula in different ways (Hahn, 2002; Page, 1990); however, the dominant values, norms, and goals of the school often shape classroom relations (Metz, 1978). Student demographics influence both school culture and teaching (McLaughlin, 1993). Schools with high proportions of African American and Latino students may exercise racialized social control (Lipman, 2004) that works against education. In the IEA CivEd study[4] Hahn (2002) found that three U.S. teachers in three urban middle schools with large African American populations said it was difficult to teach students to voice their opinions when other school personnel enforced quiet and passive behavior among students in and outside of classes.

Inequalities in Teaching for Citizenship: Contrasts in School Culture

A general finding of this study was that learning opportunities among classes were unequal. Within the two schools, AP classes provided more opportunities for involvement with subject matter. Specifically, class participation, teachers' positive views of students, and academic intensity combined with a congenial atmosphere were much more evident in AP classes as compared to college preparatory classes. From an interpretive perspective, the latter were viewed similarly to the lower-track, non college-prep classes studied in earlier research on tracking (Metz, 1978; Oakes, 1985; Page, 1991) even though they were not officially designated as such.

Opportunities for classroom learning about engaged citizenship also varied across schools. Interest in classroom activity and in political issues were more apparent in classes at Rutherford as compared to Jefferson. The classes were more focused on student participation. They represented a more progressive model as they engaged students in critical thinking and exploration of political issues (Stanley, 2005), even though I did not observe systematic discussion of controversial public issues (Hess, 2002).

Classes at Jefferson were teacher-centered, discussion was limited, and the textbook and lectures played a large role in transmission of knowledge. They seemed to represent the conservative trend in citizenship education and its philosophy of democratic realism (Stanley, 2005). Stanley explains that according to this view, most citizens are not capable of understanding complex issues and making public policy decisions; instead, their key role is voting to elect officials. This philosophy suggests that "schools should help students understand how our current democracy actually works, how it might be improved, and why it is the preferred political system" (Stanley, 2005, p. 284).

Jefferson High School was a more controlled environment than was Rutherford. The sprawling facilities were newer, cleaner, and more attractive; the school was in excellent condition compared to numerous public schools in California. At the same time, student posters, artwork, and other physical signs of student life were minimal. I had a more difficult time finding out about clubs, events, and special programs because they were not so visible. During lunchtime, in the huge outdoor area in the middle of various school buildings, groups of students were spread out and relatively quiet. On the first day of class all teachers were required to review school rules; even with seniors.

In contrast, Rutherford occupied old, run down facilities, which provoked many complaints. But the walls were covered with homemade posters advertising extracurricular activities and school events, the display cases were filled with student work, and the overall appearance was a stimulating, lived-in, student-centered environment. Correspondingly, most students at Rutherford seemed more expressive, involved, and at home than did students at Jefferson. They organized lunchtime events out in the courtyard with music and voices blaring over the PA system. Students participated enthusiastically in school-wide celebrations and rituals, such as pep rallies and dress-up days.

Both high schools were middle-class. Rutherford High was mostly a mix of White and Asian American students, with a minority of Latinos and a very small percentage of African American students. The school took great pride in its cultural diversity, and espoused inclusion and celebration of ethnic differences.

Jefferson's student population was mostly constituted by fairly even numbers of Whites, African Americans, and Latinos. The school broke the stereotypical association between race and class; Ms. Jones told me that some of the more affluent families were African American. The AP Government class was racially diverse, defying pervasive findings that Advanced Placement classes have disproportionately small representations of African

American and Latino students (Lucas, 1999). But a negative attitude in the school and larger community toward the growing African American presence over recent years became apparent. My participating teachers told me that some adults in the school community complained about the "urban attitudes" brought by students coming from the city to the suburbs. They also informed me of a widespread notion that too many students did not actually reside in Cedarville but gave false addresses to attend a better school. Community members expressed resentment, as I saw in a letter to the editor published in a local newspaper, about supporting the education of outsiders with their taxes. I surmise that reactions to the large African American and Latino population at the school in addition to the school's size influenced school personnel to maintain fairly tight controls over the student body. Data suggest that subtle forms of racialized social control were evident at the school.

Although racial diversity at Jefferson was apparent, it seemed like an invisible issue in class that was never discussed (see Pollock, 2001). The absence of talk about race in Government classes implied that the curriculum was divorced from the realities of political life in the U.S., which may have had major consequences for students' engagement, especially students of color, in these classes (see Epstein, 2000).

Contrasting Classroom Discourses and Expectations for Engagement

To illustrate the impact that views of students, tracking, and school culture can have on teaching for citizenship, I present two examples of classroom discourse during Government lessons. The first was audio taped on November 8, 2004, just a few days after the presidential election, in Ms. Sutter's college prep class of 39 students at Jefferson High School. It illustrates the routine review of a five-question, multiple-choice quiz on the textbook that occurred each time the class met (three days a week on a block schedule). The quiz and review generally took about half an hour, a significant part of the period. For every review the teacher would ask the class to articulate the process of elimination strategy for every question. She told me she used this strategy to help students be better multiple choice test takers and to reinforce information they were supposed to have read in the book.

The transcription of discourse reveals the teacher's attempts to focus students on content, as well as her frustration with their lack of involvement. Ironically, her rote methods exacerbated students' apathy. The quiz was meant to hold them accountable for reading the textbook, but the review indicated they had not read it; at least, they had not absorbed the information. The teacher continued trying to persuade students to read by chastising them during the review. Absorption of textbook knowledge was a primary purpose of the course.

TS: Pass them up quickly. Don't dilly-dally. Don't be looking at other people's papers please. . . . Okay, let's review. You're going to eliminate one . . . Rick?

Rick: A.

TS: (affirms his response) Chief Justice of the Supreme Court has nothing to do with the legislative branch pretty much. Derek?

Derek: B?

TS: No, B is the correct answer.

Derek: [Unintelligible].

TS: Read it in the book, man. I'm not lying. . . . That is the correct answer, guys. The President of the Senate is the Vice President of the United States. The Vice President has two duties: 1. [?] presidential disability. 2. Preside over the Senate.

Student: [Unintelligible].

TS: No, read it in your book, man. Yes, the President of the Senate is the Vice President. Remember, Vice President is the one that breaks ties. You can have ties in the senate because there's how many people in the senate? One-hundred people in the senate, so you could theoretically have a 50/50 tie, right? The Vice President is the tie-breaker. He presides over the senate. Okay. Number two—a blank committee is set up for some specific purpose and usually exists [unintelligible] tie . . . Joe?

Joe: B.

TS: So permanent committee. It acts on major bills, yes. You're right to eliminate B . . . What's another? Derek?

Derek: D?

TS: What's a subcommittee?

Derek: Um, is there one?

TS: Yes.

Derek: Oh, I didn't know.

TS: There's such a thing as subcommittees. Ben, what's a subcommittee?

Ben: [Unintelligible].

TS: And what does a subcommittee do? You guys need to read more effectively. What's a subcommittee do? Let's say the agriculture committee is taking a look at something to do with farming, right, and there's a bill for them that needs further investigation. Let's say maybe there are 20 people on the committee. The committee chairperson can designate five, six or seven people within that committee to further investigate this bill, to conduct some interviews or do some research and report back to the committee. That's what a subcommittee does. I'm sure that's in the reading. Okay, so we've eliminated D and E. Now we're down to A, B and C. Get rid of another one please. Dan?

Dan: B?

TS: What's a conference committee? . . . It's created to iron out differences in a bill, and it is a joint body between two different groups; one group for the senate, one for the house—the conference committee, okay? So now we're down to A and C. I took the definition right out of the book, people. Which one would you like to eliminate? How many think that C needs to be eliminated, raise your hand? Okay, how many think that A needs to be eliminated? Good, A is the answer. I made up C. It doesn't exist. A select committee would be something that exists for a specific purpose. Let me give you an example. A committee that was enacted in both houses to investigate 9/11, that would be a select committee. It exists for a specific purpose, it only exists for a limited time; the answer is select committee. . . . Okay, and the committee is sometimes known as the traffic cop—House of Representatives. If you're going to eliminate one, you have to tell me what their job is. If you don't know, then open your book and look around to find the answer. I want you to eliminate one for me, Ben?

Ben: C.

TS: No, that is in the House, but it's not—the Ways and Means Committee. What is the Ways and Means Committee in the House deal with? Anybody? It's in your book. . . . Those of you who don't have your books open, shame on you, man. Come on, get going. Bottom of page 291.

Andrew: [Unintelligible].

TS: Very good, thank you, Andrew. Bottom of page 291, bottom of the first column—the speaker sends all tax measures to the House of

Ways and Means Committee. Ways and Means deals primarily with tax issues. Are we going to increase taxes, are we going to decrease taxes, what are we going to look at in terms of taxes, appropriate taxes? Because remember, Congress does have the power to tax. That's one of the express powers. So Ways and Means primarily deals with taxes, okay? (Finishes up) Okay, any questions? No? Okay. Leave the lights off because we're going right on into Chapter 11 notes. So new section in your notebook please. We're doing the first two sections today.

The above excerpt shows a low level of student involvement and a struggle over authority (see Pace & Hemmings, 2007); students appear to resist the teacher's agenda. The first indication is the teacher's attempts to prevent cheating, which she had confronted earlier in the semester. Most striking are her frequent admonitions to "read it in the book, man," which underline dependency on students' reading the textbook in order to learn the course content, and students' apparent unwillingness to do so. Class participation in the review is minimal. Ms. Sutter picks up the slack and re-lays the dry and de-contextualized information from the book. At one point the teacher references a contemporary and vital issue—investigation of 9/11—but passes over it. With this 4th period class, males were a more vocal presence, and here it seems the teacher unconsciously excludes female students. She calls only on males, and colloquially refers to students as "man," perhaps attempting with egalitarian language to make the impo-sition of the quiz, the review, and the tedious material more palatable (see Pace, 2006; Page, 1991). The transmission of knowledge continues as she launches into the daily lecture.

The emphasis on absorbing factual knowledge about the structures and processes of government from the textbook, lower order thinking, and dominance of teacher talk all contradict recommendations for citizen-ship education (Hahn, 2001). In fact the Civic Mission of Schools (Gibson & Levine, 2003) states that "it is important to underscore that teaching only rote facts about dry procedures is unlikely to benefit students and may actually alienate them from political participation, including voting" (p. 20). But Ms. Sutter's teaching was not atypical and illustrates a com-mon finding: The gap between social studies scholars' ideals and teachers' practices is very wide (Thornton, 1991). Large class size may exacerbate the problem.

The second edited transcript of discourse was audio taped on December 10, 2004 in Ms. Kelly's AP Government class of 24 students at Rutherford High School. The teacher coaches students in preparation for an upcoming competition. I regularly observed practice sessions during classroom lessons. At this point in the semester, in four person units students have prepared essays in response to particular questions that require research and critical thinking. Now they rehearse these responses verbally, in front of an audience (the class) in a small auditorium. The four students who make up the first unit sit at a table down in the front, hands folded. They openly express nervousness about their performance. After delivering their essay, they respond to impromptu questions, as they will do during the competition. Then the unit is critiqued on the content and form of their presentation. This example shows the serious involvement expected of students.

> FK: Okay, quiet please. We've got a lot to do. . . . You know, you guys did a good job yesterday, but we have to be on top of things . . . Are you all memorized? Okay.
> Rajiv: If I get nervous, [unintelligible].
> FK: If you get nervous—you're not nervous. We're going to slam dunk it, right?
> . . . In the United States, what rights does a citizen have that a resident alien does not have? Do these rights mean that citizens have responsibilities that resident aliens do not have? If so, what are they? To what extent are these responsibilities moral, and to what extent are they legal? . . .

(Students attempt to present their memorized essay but have trouble being fluid. The teacher tells them to start over.)

> Rajiv: Citizens and resident aliens are entitled to civil rights. Only citizens are entitled to political rights which include voting, jury service and running for political office. Citizens have a moral and legal responsibility to maintain and carry on democracy for participation.
> Laura: No it is not a legal responsibility to take on an active role in government. By doing such things as voting or providing public service, it is the moral duty of the citizenship to [unintelligible] and those of other [unintelligible].

Dan: Citizens have a greater responsibility than resident aliens do in maintaining their own self-interests as well as those of others. The French philosopher, Alexis de Tocqueville, believed that the ability Americans had to come together for the common good is what made Americans great. He believed that citizens were also encouraged [unintelligible] of the general welfare by pursuing their own self-interests.

Audrey: Voting, demonstrating and contacting your representatives may exhibit this enlightened self-interest. Citizens also hold legal obligations such as jury service, which is essential to the judicial system. Resident aliens, however, do not hold legal obligations such as jury service because they have not yet learned the workings of the political system.

Rajiv: In the early 19th century, [counties] established five years as a minimum amount of time for immigrants to learn the ideals of our government [unintelligible]. By immigrating to this country, aliens are giving their [unintelligible] consent to be governed by the American government. They are joining a society in which customs have already been established, and therefore, before they can become a part of society, they must understand them.

Laura: On the contrary, American citizens have given the American government their [unintelligible] consent to be governed by them. They have lived here since birth. By remaining here, they have accepted the laws and services which are provided by the government.

Dan: Aliens, however, do have the moral obligations to participate in their communities. Because they're a part of the system, they should also manifest [unintelligible] community service demonstrating and lobbying, they are able to participate in democracy and promote their own [interests] as well as those of others and their communities. Many immigrant community organizations [unintelligible] members of the American society and also help bridge the gap between cultures.

(Students continue to present the essay they have composed. The teacher then poses impromptu questions.)

FK: Given the diversity of American society, what provides the common bond that makes us Americans?

(Laura attempts a response, but gets confused. The teacher re-directs the response.)

Dan: I believe it's the chasing—[unintelligible] the pursuit of being happy, a better life is what ties Americans together. They want what's best for themselves and for their communities.

Rajiv: Many people immigrate to America to enjoy what is called the American Dream, which is the pursuit of happiness and having a good life in America, which can be acquired through pursuing your own ambitions as well as ambitions of your community.

(The teacher asks students if they memorized their essays and they say yes.)

FK: . . . you don't want to sound memorized. So you've got to go beyond memorized. You're doing this alone. We need you to perform this together, perform it with your family members . . . This is your homework. Now how many of you have put this on tape?

(Ms. Kelly continues for another couple of minutes, giving directives about how to use tape recording and how to answer the impromptu questions more effectively. She asks when the unit will be meeting to practice.)

This transcript shows that the class is focused on active learning and student performance, which requires presentation of student written essays and application of democratic principles and policies to probing questions. In these ways, it reflects recommendations from the Civic Mission of Schools (Gibson & Levine, 2003). The common goal shared by teacher and students invokes high expectations on everyone's part, indicated by the teacher's directives throughout the episode and students' nervousness and efforts to perform well. It is not a quiz grade, but a national competition that is at stake. Although students demonstrate intellectual understanding, commitment, and skill, the teacher has no qualms in pressing them to do more to improve their presentation; overt authority and assistance are accepted because everyone wants to win. Coaching also involves encouragement: She uses a sports metaphor ("slam dunk") and conveys her confidence and high standards simultaneously.

But from a social justice perspective (Westheimer & Kahne, 2004), the focus on performance constrains the opportunity to delve into the issues underlying students' statements about "resident aliens" versus "citizens." The critical importance and relevance of debates over immigration and citizenship were not addressed. While this session continued with a question and answer period in which students had to apply their knowledge, genuine exploration of controversial issues did not occur. High motivation, demonstration of knowledge, and limited examination of highly contested current issues were characteristic of the other lessons I observed in this class.

Conceptions of Teaching and Learning for Citizenship

Although all four teachers emphasized acquisition of knowledge about government and shared common state content standards, each of them exemplified a different approach (Thornton, 1991). In turn, each approach was influenced by views of students, conceptions of the course, and tracking.

Teaching by the Book

Ms. Sutter's practice in her college prep classes at Jefferson High School could be described as *teaching by the book*. Her lessons were lecture and textbook based, with little discussion and little variation in her routine. The teacher offset a controlled classroom climate with humorous colloquialisms about political figures and an informal manner. A few students would ask questions during lectures, which created short exchanges between them and the teacher. Except for these instances and review of quizzes, which involved recitation, students were mostly quiet. Every Monday, the teacher distributed copies of the newspaper and students spent the last 30–45 minutes of class reading and writing summaries of articles related to government, but there was no discussion of them. Ms. Sutter's class seemed representative of Hahn's (2002) finding from focus groups with a nationwide sample of ninth grade students about their social studies classes. Lessons were characterized by "frequent teacher talk and student recitation related to the textbook and, periodically, a simulation, written project, or discussion of a current issue" (p. 87).

Ironically, the teacher's perspective on teaching the *American Government* course seemed strongly influenced by the view that adolescents are apathetic and even antagonistic to politics. During our interview, she explained the course's purpose in conservative terms that suggested a protective stance, rather than the purpose of preparing young people for political engagement: "People overall need to know more about the government and the types of things that the government can and cannot do." She said that many people today feel disconnected from the government and it was important to teach about it because "whether students like it or not, government affects them. . . . Government affects everybody, whether they choose to participate in it or not." Ms. Sutter's articulation of purpose went from assertive to tentative: "Maybe the goal for the class is they do start to think a little differently about what government means and what their place can be. If they decide not to be involved in government then that's fine too. It's their choice."

In addition to covering the state standards, the teacher voiced concern about alienating students: "I try to put the material out there in a relevant enough way that it won't seem like an awful thing for the kids that are, "Government, blah. Do I have to vote?" "No, you don't have to vote, but here are some reasons why you should." She said she was most focused on those students who were most negative about the subject matter: "'I don't want to be here, this makes no sense to me, it doesn't pertain to me.' How do I reach that student? What can I say that will make it relevant for them? The other kids are already halfway there." Ms. Sutter also seemed influenced by teaching seniors: "So many of them want out of school so bad they can taste it." I asked Ms. Sutter how many students were negative about government. She said it was hard to tell, due to many students' silence in class, but she imagined they felt, "'Okay, I need to get out of here with a D–, so I don't believe anything this woman is saying, but that's okay, because I will do what I have to do in order to pass the class.'" The teacher continued, "I'm not offended at all by that attitude. I mean I realize that there's only so much I can do. Kids have to meet me part of the way, to be able to be receptive of ideas."

These statements contradict the press for political engagement that fills the literature on citizenship education. Instead the teacher's views reflect common perspectives and research findings that U.S. youth are both politically and educationally disengaged. In addition, they resonate with findings that teachers in lower track and/or heterogeneous classes regard students as oppositional, and teach defensively to avoid conflict (McNeil, 1986; Page, 1991). Although her classes were designated as college prep rather than lower-track, Ms. Sutter seemed to deal with the anticipation of student withdrawal by framing it as a given, over which teachers have no control. Her comments reflect the stance that students must be accommodated through a classroom treaty that makes learning an individual choice (Powell, Farrar, & Cohen, 1985). The teacher conveyed that participating in citizenship is also a choice. This understanding points to cultural trends that celebrate individual freedom over collective responsibility. It emphasizes citizens' rights over their obligations.

The teacher's conception of the course also appeared to contradict the importance of understanding democratic principles, a central feature advocated by the Civic Mission of Schools. During our interview she said she did not see the first unit of the semester as relevant to students and therefore did not pursue discussion of it. "We're just talking about concepts of democracy, the history of government . . . nothing that's going to be relevant; it's not going to be something that they're going to hang on to. I don't want to spend too much time on anything that won't have meaning for them." Ms. Sutter said the issue in which students—especially males—expressed the most interest was the possibility of reinstituting the military draft. The teacher's comments and actions appeared to reflect and re-create anti-intellectualism in American culture (Hofstadter, 1963; Pace, 2003a) and politics.

Interestingly, the five students who volunteered to be interviewed all made appreciative remarks about the teacher. They all had responses to my questions about the purposes of the class and what they had learned, although some of these were uncertain and most were brief. Three students found the course valuable in gaining knowledge about government, one found it boring because she hated to read, and one found it confusing.

Students' descriptions of what happened in the class centered on Ms. Smith's lectures. They said she was helpful in explaining the information and making it easier to understand, answering questions, and using humor. Students also referred to the daily routine. Victor said, "I know the schedule every day—you come in, you sit down, get your homework out, she comes by and stamps it . . . then we take our quiz for which we had to read the night before, then we review it, then we take lecture notes. She gives us all these notes and talks and goes on for about an hour." However, he expressed enthusiasm: "It's great because it's something I never thought I'd learn because my mom and dad dropped out of high school. . . . I get to learn more about what's going on in the world. . . . Now I'm a lot more interested in watching the news." Andrew said the class "lets you gain your own perspective on government." Molly described the class as "really fast-paced," but more informational than other classes: "I think it gives a really good overview." Students' responses spoke to the value of acquiring knowledge.

I asked Andrew why more students didn't ask questions in class. He responded, "They just believe everything is the way it should be . . . it's been this way for so long so I'm not going to ask any questions about it now, because it probably won't change anyway. Some people probably just don't care." When asked to explain, he continued, ". . . a lot of people just sit in class, just go through the class, do the work because they have to, to graduate, and that's all it is. And some people are actually into class and want to learn more about the government and all that stuff. So I guess it depends on your personality and what you prefer." His response mirrored the teacher's view that political engagement is a personal choice, and that schooling has little influence on students' civic attitudes and actions.

Presenting Expert Knowledge

Ms. Sutter worked closely with her colleague at Jefferson, Ms. Jones, but their approaches differed significantly. Ms. Jones, who taught both college prep classes and AP, could be viewed as *presenting expert knowledge.* She regularly assigned reading from the textbook but told me she tried not to lean on it because that would put students to sleep. Most classes followed a pattern, but it was varied and the content was often stimulating. Usually a class period began with one or two students presenting a news article, and Ms. Jones would illuminate the issues at play. The daily quiz on assigned textbook reading took about ten minutes, including the review. Usually a lecture followed based upon overheads that Ms. Jones created or took from various sources. These often included diagrams in addition to an outline of notes. The teacher often distributed a short reading, and posed questions for students to think or write about, and sometimes discuss. Readings came from classroom magazines such as *The New York Times Upfront, Teen Newsweek,* and adult news sources such as The *Washington Post* and other newspapers. Occasionally Ms. Jones showed a film. The atmosphere was relaxed yet focused on subject matter; the teacher was so knowledgeable that she allowed students to ask all kinds of questions to which she almost always had an informed response. Although she posed higher-order questions for students to ponder, discussions were limited, but her lectures were more interactive and students initiated more questions than in Ms. Sutter's class.

Ms. Jones expressed passion for government and a great deal of expertise drawn from years of political activity and work as a legislative aide and reporter. But she told me she was disappointed by the apathy she perceived: "I think seniors just want to get in, do what they have to do, and get out." In particular, she said this semester's students were not as interested in the presidential election as they were in 2000: "I tried to emphasize that this was an every-four-year event and 'it happens to fall right in the semester you have Government. What an opportunity!' . . . They didn't get that." She indicated that in general her own commitment to the class was not matched by students' interest in it. She also indicated that opportunities for involvement were more plentiful in the AP class, and students were more responsive.

Ms. Jones and Ms. Sutter told me the AP Government class at Jefferson lasted the entire school year instead of one semester to increase students' chances of passing the AP exam. Like high-track classes in studies of authority, the atmosphere was more relaxed and more competitive, and the dynamics between teacher and students revealed an accommodation of what Ms. Jones and I perceived as students' sense of entitlement (see Metz, 1978; Pace, 2003b). The AP class went into more depth than the college prep classes did and studied interesting special topics such as the culture wars. A fun assignment for the AP students was to write a political parody set to the tune of a holiday song; these were performed in an assembly just before winter vacation. As at Rutherford, the existence of the AP Government class and its special opportunities conferred an inferior lower-track status onto college prep classes, even though they were a higher level than the non-college preparatory class.

In contrast to Ms. Jones's disappointment regarding students' lack of interest, the five students whom I interviewed expressed enthusiasm for her teaching style. They used words such as "well-organized," "really patient," "really nice," "very friendly," "fun," "entertaining," "exciting," and "open-minded." But Kent, a student in one of Ms. Jones's college prep classes, picked up on her frustration: "She definitely wishes to cater to a more engaging class . . . But, she really tries." Although he had always been interested in government (his parents worked in government), Kent said, "I would describe it as a mandatory class . . . and that's why people take it. Most people don't find it very interesting." When I asked why, he replied, "Because most people don't care." In reference to his peers he said, "Many of them are sleeping during class. They don't take it seriously." He also said, "Many people in my class are probably going to be arrested."

Kent's comments may point to the lack of connection between the Government curriculum and many students' concerns and interests, due to its mainstream (versus multicultural or critical) content and the teacher's focus on transmission of knowledge. They may also be understood as expressing negativity that echoed adult community members' concerns about students from the inner city, with "urban attitudes," encroaching upon the school and surrounding suburbs.

It was evident from students I interviewed that Ms. Jones stood out as one of their best teachers because of her passion for the subject, good rapport with students, and efforts to make the class interesting. However, I did observe withdrawal in the form of off-topic side conversations and low levels of participation, especially in the college prep classes. Most of Ms. Jones's lessons consisted largely of lecture, reading, and recitation. Students sometimes worked together on class assignments, but not on major projects or performances. In the AP class, students seemed motivated to show off their knowledge and compete for grades, and there was more interaction among class participants. But in the heterogeneous college prep classes, many students remained passive. I wondered whether Ms. Jones's students would have been significantly more engaged in a class that emphasized participatory citizenship or social justice issues (Westheimer & Kahne, 2004).

Coaching for Competition

At Rutherford, Ms. Kelly taught her AP class as if she were *coaching an elite sports team.* The class had a dual goal—to win a competition and to empower students. Ms. Kelly brought tremendous knowledge and a long history of civic involvement to her teaching. However, different from the other classes I observed, her course was set up so that students would become experts as well. Their performance was of utmost importance; therefore, most of the class time I observed was spent preparing to skillfully exhibit their knowledge in a professional manner through rehearsal and feedback sessions. According to the teacher and students, the class spent an enormous amount of time outside of class in preparation. Commitment of time and energy was an absolute requirement. In turn, Ms. Kelly gave her students special treatment.

Ms. Kelly's AP U.S. Government class was unlike any other high school class I had seen in its intensity of academic involvement, structure as a team competition, and closeness of relationships among peers and between students and teacher. Students auditioned for the class; twenty-four were selected based on their academic record, demonstration of commitment and ability to work well with others, and passion for the subject matter. The course had a special reputation at the school, and students—many of whom had been in Ms. Kelly's AP U.S. History class—had a great deal of preliminary work to complete over the summer to prepare for the fall semester. Ms. Kelly had numerous political connections from her own scholarship and civic involvement. She tapped these resources to provide amazing educational opportunities, including internships and a trip to Washington, DC (where they met with governmen officials), for her students.

Ms. Kelly told me she wanted students to learn that "democracy works." One of the main purposes of the course was "to get them to understand why participation is important." The teacher said that academics and application of knowledge were equally important. She wanted students to understand that "you can't be passive and have democracy survive." Citizenship in a democracy was interactive, and could take many forms.

A critical influence on Ms. Kelly's teaching is that she believed her students were "amazing." She said this group was particularly special in the way they befriended one another and developed community. She found that students were excited about the presidential election and it was a perfect situation for the course: "Oh, you know, it is so much, so much fun to teach a government class during an election because everything is right there. Kids are more enthusiastic because they see it all the time on TV." The teacher did not need to assign watching the presidential candidates' debates; she could assume everyone would see them. She also spoke to the importance of connecting students with professional experts: "You know, we have a lot of government officials who will talk to the kids, a lot of kids who intern." Ms. Kelly seemed to thrive on intense involvement with her students. She was an unusually dedicated teacher and also knew about students' personal and social lives.[5] With its special curriculum, structure, and goals, the class exemplified sociocultural learning theory in that learning occurred through guided participation (Rogoff, 1990) as teachers and students collaborated on a project that was valued by all.

On the other hand, if the class had focused less on competitive performance and more on civic involvement or discussion of controversial topics, students may have gained more experience in participation and insight into social justice (see Hess, 2002; Westheimer & Kahne, 2004). Even in this impressive class, the emphasis on winning the competition compromised certain kinds of engagement. And it contributed to unequal distribution of educational opportunities to students at Rutherford High School.

However, student interviews suggested that they had learned the importance of participation. Kahlil told me, "The obvious purpose is to teach us about government and civic responsibility, but I think also importantly it's to teach us how to be active citizens, important in our community, and how to present our information. To be members of our society that have the power to change things and have the ability to make the proper adjustments in our society."

During interviews students expressed great enthusiasm that corresponded with my observations. Jim told me, "I think it's a great class. I personally love it a lot. It's my favorite class ever, in high school . . ." When I asked why, he said, "It's engaging. It's not so much read the book, take the test, write an essay, get a lecture on it. It's actually you own the information." Also he happened to like politics. Students said they were motivated by the competition and their own curiosity. Kahlil described the atmosphere of the class: "Friendly, cooperative, camaraderie. It's like a team, any sports team. We all congratulate each other, we're helping each other." Cindy said, ". . . even with the stress, some people just thrive on it. . . . There's a purpose for what you are doing and it's so much more satisfying, gratifying, in the end when you do achieve that goal. And even if you don't, you still feel that sense of satisfaction because you know that the process you went through made you a better person in the end, that all your efforts weren't in vain." She also said, "And because there's competition, we feel as though we should keep updated on issues and that's how we become better citizens because we know what's going on in the government." Romi said, "It's never boring in there. . . . someone's always finding out things and, even though there's factions within us—people don't always agree—people feel comfortable to share, and I think that's always a good idea." Students' comments reflected an internalization of high expectations for engagement and empowerment as well as understanding of democratic principles.

Facilitating Hands-on Learning and Consciousness

Ms. Bates, Ms. Kelly's colleague at Rutherford High, focused on *facilitating hands-on learning and political consciousness*. Although primarily knowledge-based, Ms. Bates's college prep Government class made forays into other approaches to citizenship education, such as exploration of issues and development of skills and values (Hess & Posselt, 2002). The class had a social justice orientation, and included a unit on the civil rights movement.

She encouraged a critical perspective on the government by raising current issues related to the Presidential campaigns, such as the war in Iraq, campaign strategies, and media coverage. She involved students in activities such as making historical timelines, posters of Constitution articles, and campaign ads, as well as projects that included research and presentations on policy debates such as abortion, gay rights, and censorship. The teacher used videos, including *The Daily Show, Outfoxed,* and *Farenheit 9/11,* and led more open discussions than in any of the other classes I observed. But students were not taught deliberation skills, and participation was scattered; a few students tended to talk a lot while others said very little or nothing at all. Those who spoke were often inaudible at the back of the room. Students said this was a relatively easy and relaxed class; Ms. Bates did not assign a lot of written work or give tough exams.

Ms. Bates characterized the course as a preparation for democratic citizenship. In our interview she invoked all three orientations towards citizenship education presented by Westheimer and Kahne (2004): personal responsibility, participation, and social justice. She characterized her goals for the course: "Being aware of current events. . . . To make it relevant so that they will play their part in democracy. They will vote." She wanted students to learn "to play their part in democracy that they have to be critical and speak out. Be involved." Her aim was to get students to celebrate and be critical of U.S. democracy, as well as to be part of shaping it. Ms. Bates said that every year her approach to the course was different, and influenced by what was happening in the world. She noted that this semester a big part of the course was the presidential election. She assigned watching the presidential debates for homework, unlike the other teachers in the study. She said the next unit would be on the Middle East because of the war in Iraq. The teacher was especially pleased about an expert panels project in which students did research and presentations on a particular issue that was important to them and relevant to contemporary partisan politics.

Ms. Bates remarked upon students' dislike of the subject matter: "A lot of kids will tell you it's boring. Okay? 'Oh, government. I don't want to learn about that. Oh, it's like history.' There's a negativity that walks into the classroom that first day." However, she said their interest in the class evolved: "But I think we do stuff that they're enthusiastic about . . . You know, kind of flaky and it's not always there, but more or less they're engaged. . . . they do the work, and they get enthusiastic about the projects that they're doing. And a lot of them . . . do, you know, really wrestle with things and expand their minds. I see that."

My observations revealed a class in which students participated, to varying extents, in interesting activities and discussions, but that did not seem challenging, consistently focused, or deeply involved in the subject matter. Of greatest concern to the teacher was a group of "Asian boys" who appeared withdrawn and even somewhat hostile. Ms. Bates told me that while she had been recognized for her ability to encourage female participation, she had trouble with Asian male students, and believed that their culture taught them to not respect female authority. Interestingly, two of these Asian-American boys voluntarily signed up for interviews with me. Jon expressed great appreciation for the class. The other boy, Ronald, voiced concern with the liberal politics supported by the teacher and most students. I wondered if a few of his peers felt similarly.

In general, students during interviews spoke enthusiastically about how they felt more relaxed than in other classes yet still learned a lot. The teacher made the class active and relevant by having discussions in which she encouraged participation, showing movies about issues they were studying, and doing projects. Students perceived that Ms. Bates was passionate about political issues and wanted them to see the Democrats' side, but was open to the expression of different opinions. She was described as a very helpful and personable teacher. Jon, whose parents were not citizens, told me his view of the purpose of the class: "Hopefully, for people like me who have never known anything much about the government to let me into the knowledge of how the government works and everything. Because, we're living in the country and it's a good thing to know how your government works, and how it helps other people." He also told me, "So whatever I learn in the class, it forms what I think about the government. So I think it's really a big impact on how I would vote in the future." Jon spoke specifically about the opportunity to discuss controversial topics, such as gay rights: "I think it's the first time where I actually talked about it with a group of people. I don't think gay marriage is a topic you'd talk just out of nowhere with your family. So Government is the class where issues are actually brought up and forced to talk about, so you actually can feel about how and what you think about the subject."

Jon's comments reveal the vital significance of Government classes to students from immigrant families, especially when important contemporary topics are explored. In fact, even though the classes I studied did not match many of the recommendations of citizenship education scholars, all four teachers included controversial topics in the curriculum. Although discussion of these topics tended to be constrained rather than in-depth, this is an important finding.

Taboo Topics and Evidence for Enlightenment

The persistence of traditional approaches to teaching social studies can be partially explained by the impact of cultural restraints on subjects deemed appropriate for classroom discussion (Evans, Avery, & Pederson, 1999). Teachers consider certain topics taboo, and this belief is influenced by fear of sanctions within the school system, the teacher's experience and gender, and the wider contemporary political culture (p. 219). Taboo topics historically have included abortion, pornography, religion, sexual orientation, and criticism of school administration (p. 220).

The Government classes I studied all addressed issues that constituted Democratic and Republican party platforms, as well as media headlines especially in the months leading up to the presidential election: gay marriage, abortion, the Bush administration, and war in Iraq. Ms. Jones and Ms. Sutter held presidential debates in which students were responsible for presenting the candidates' points of view on a range of issues. Although time allotments were limited and the quality of presentations was uneven, these topics were legitimized. Additionally, Ms. Jones and Ms. Sutter assigned essays for which students did research on proposed amendments and the First Amendment. Controversial topics came up in Ms. Kelly's class as students presented knowledge in preparation for the competition and in the context of informal discussions, for example on the anniversary of 9/11 and after seeing the presidential debates on TV. In Ms. Bates's class the topics were more explicitly and fully addressed as controversial issues, through teacher-led discussions and in the "expert panels" project related to party platforms. In this project, small groups of students researched topics including gay marriage, abortion, discrimination in the workplace, the Iraq war, the military draft, teenage pregnancy, and censorship. Each group presented their findings and a proposal related to the issue that was briefly discussed and voted on by the class. For teacher and students, the project was a highlight of the semester.

The attention to these topics is noteworthy, because it indicates a new openness in public school classrooms to topics that were considered taboo in the past. This phenomenon may be traced to the presidential election and the culture war controversies highlighted by the media, as well as to greater openness in mainstream society, due in part to lack of censorship in popular culture. And it may be a feature of classrooms in liberal regions such as northern California. Many of the students I interviewed commented that they appreciated addressing these topics, and learned to respect different points of view from listening to their classmates. In general, openness to diverse opinions appeared to encourage tolerance (see Avery, 2002) as well as engagement in learning. At the same time, a few students who identified as Republican or conservative expressed the feeling, either in class or during interviews with me, that they did not have an equal voice.

Students and School Politics

Although traditionally taboo topics were addressed, teachers and students did not discuss governance issues or politics at their own school in class (for contrast see Battistoni's chapter). However, school politics became a live issue at one site. Ironically, the controlled atmosphere at Jefferson yielded two surprising and related examples of student political activism that were unmatched by anything I saw at Rutherford. The first was the establishment of an after school club called Students for Social Justice and Peace by two seniors in Ms. Jones's AP Government class. Peter, a European American (White) student, was one of my interviewees and Omar, a Middle Eastern American student, was his friend. Upon request, Ms. Jones allowed the club to meet weekly in her classroom to discuss the news and hold discussions, watch films, and plan activities (such as attending a regional demonstration). She told me that each week about fifty students filled her room. Topics discussed included the Iraq war, the Presidential elections, and the Palestinian-Israeli conflict. She said she was genuinely impressed with the group's commitment, focus, and process. Her role was faculty advisor but she actually did very little except be present during meetings. Out of this group a specific incident developed that vividly demonstrated youth's political engagement and the school administration's repression of it. It occurred a few months after I left the site and I learned about it after Peter contacted me. Subsequently I interviewed both Peter and Ms. Jones to find out what had happened. The following narrative is based on their stories, which were consistent with one another.

Students from the Social Justice and Peace club planned a lunchtime rally for March 2005 to mark the second anniversary of the Iraq invasion. Peter and Omar submitted what Ms. Jones considered a thoughtful and in-depth plan, including copies of speeches, to request permission from Ms. Coombs, acting principal at Jefferson. She denied permission, saying the speeches were too anti-Republican and would cause a riot. Ms. Jones toned down their speeches and resubmitted their request, but it was denied. The students met with the principal, who said she would confer with the super-intendent of schools when she saw him next. Three days before the rally date, Peter and Omar asked again, and she said they had freedom of speech, but no amplification would be allowed. They were upset, wonder-ing how the rally could be effective with such a large student body and not-ing that other groups had used amplification for special events. Ms. Jones convinced them to comply and suggested they hand out copies of the speeches. The students went back to the principal and agreed to her rules. That afternoon, during their AP Government class with Ms. Jones, the two young men were called down to the main office, each to meet separately with associate principals.

At that point they were informed that each of them was receiving a two-day on-campus suspension (OCS) for harassing a military recruiter on campus. The students vehemently denied the charges, but to no avail, even after bringing their parents—who completely supported them—to meet with the administrators and the military recruiter the following day. Peter said he would refuse OCS and the associate principal threatened that he would not graduate. Terribly distressed, Peter and Omar went to OCS. The principal had already e-mailed Ms. Jones that the rally would not be hap-pening. After school, a student protest against the school administrations' actions was held across the street.

Peter and Omar with their parents appealed to the Cedarville School Board. Ms. Jones said they were "brilliantly eloquent in stating their case." The School Board said they were very interested and would look into the issue, but nothing happened. In the meantime, on Ms. Jones's advice, the students had contacted a political group in the area that took up their cause. A lawyer from this group worked with them intensively over the course of a few months to develop a case against the district and wrote a se-ries of letters to the School Board arguing for students' First Amendment rights. That summer, the lawyer set up a meeting with the school district's attorney, the principal, the superintendent, and the two students and their parents. She said the students wanted an on-campus lunchtime rally with amplification, no censoring of speeches, the right to leaflet at any time, and the removal of the suspension. If these were not granted, she would file a lawsuit. After a short private caucus with their attorney, and without a rebuttal, the administrators suddenly backed down and agreed to everything.

I asked Peter if he had learned anything in his classes that helped him with this process. He referred to electives such as Philosophy and Forensics, which taught him about using language to make an argument and to feel confident with public speaking. He mentioned doing model United Nations and mock trial. He also referred to the AP Government class: "Government helped as well. If I was in CP (college prep) Government I don't know if I would, you know, know as much." He told me that before the year started, the AP class read a book about different Supreme Court cases, such as *Tinker vs. Des Moines,* and what the plaintiffs went through. Peter said, "So that book was really helpful just to relate with other people that were kinda doing the same thing I was, just on an even larger scale." He continued, "And you got to learn about the law in *Tinker* and I could argue the cases confidently. . . . A lot of the Government stuff, yea, did help me. I would catch Omar because he would be quoting things that we just learned in class that day . . . with Ms. Jones."

Ms. Jones told me that she was really proud that the students applied what they learned from the assignment last summer, which included reading *The Courage of Their Convictions* and writing about cases in which people fought for freedom of expression. She said the experienced humbled her; it made her realize she'd forgotten her idealism and had become cynical. It gave her more faith in students' ability to see the truth and go for what's right. She saw that students could learn the material from her course and use it. When I asked if this would influence her teaching, she said she wanted to feel less constricted by the state standards and focus on what is truly important, such as the Constitution, details of what it means, and how it applies to students' lives.

I asked Peter what he was taking away from the experience. He said it was "life changing . . . on some level." He learned how people can twist things in a bureaucratic system, but it also gave him confidence in the system: "I'm more of a radical thinker, but it gave me more confidence in the way things work and the way that justice and right will always turn out in the end. Like that sounds corny and all but when we won, I felt like all right you can't lose if you're on the right side. If you're telling the truth . . . as long as you feel that you're doing the right thing. . . . There is no way you can lose."

This episode bears powerful lessons. It shows how schools suppress political engagement even as they hold the obligation to educate democratic citizens. The student activism at Jefferson was the most authentic and focused form of political activity I witnessed during the study. And Ms. Jones's ongoing support and advice, which she had to keep quiet in order not to jeopardize her relationship with the administration, made a huge difference in the process. The conundrum of engaging in democratic conflict at school contributed to her not discussing the case in her Government classes. Criticism of school administration is still a taboo topic in classroom discussions.

The incident at Jefferson highlighted that in Government classes across schools, to a large extent complacency was the norm. Most classes did not prompt questioning the status quo. Even when the government and media were critiqued, as in Ms. Bates's class, relaxed expectations, inconsistent engagement, and the absence of tools for political action undercut any urgency about change. And, in Ms. Kelly's class, intense involvement was centered on winning, not on examining causes of injustice or making a difference. At the same time, teaching and learning did occur in all the classes I studied.

Implications for Reform and Research

What are implications of this study for citizenship education and future research? First, negative views of high school students, pervasive in the media, bear revision. This study reveals how those perceptions perpetuated low expectations and weak engagement in Government classes. In contrast, the Social Justice and Peace club at Jefferson is a stunning example of young people's political interest. Second, the gap between scholarship and actual classrooms needs to be bridged. Reform of citizenship education should accommodate teachers and the contexts in which they work. It should build on what teachers already know and do and address the conceptions they hold about students, teaching and learning, and citizenship. Reformers must acknowledge that democratic realism is a popular conception in the United States. At the same time, teachers—and administrators—need opportunities to enlarge their understandings and visions of citizenship and democracy. And the conditions of their work, such as class size, must facilitate rather than impede their efficacy. Reforms must also consider all students—their diverse needs, backgrounds, concerns, and experiences. Third, citizenship education researchers need to pursue in-depth examinations of how the structures and cultures of schooling shape unequal preparation of citizens, and how this perpetuates social and political inequality. As the "Civic Mission of Schools" states, citizenship education needs to be tied to broader school reform; the two are inextricable.

Research should focus on real classrooms in context in order to narrow the huge gap between theory and practice in citizenship education. Qualitative research is difficult because of the resources it requires, but it yields the greatest understanding (Preissle-Goetz & LeCompte, 1991). More support for qualitative studies on citizenship classes may be a crucial step in furthering democracy.

Notes

This study was supported by a University of San Francisco Jesuit Foundation Grant. I also want to thank Ann McNallen for her assistance with data analysis.

1. See Dilworth (2004) and Marri (2005) for examples.
2. In fact, the official title, according to the California History/Social Science Standards, is *Principles of American Democracy*. However, it goes by various names in different schools, including *Civics, U.S. Government,* and *American Government.*
3. At each school, a non-college preparatory class was provided for especially reluctant and/or struggling students.
4. The International Association for the Evaluation of Educational Achievement's Civic Education study began in 1993.
5. Important to note is that Ms. Kelly taught fewer and smaller classes due to their AP status and her administrative responsibilities at the school.

References

Anyon, J. (1983). Social class and the hidden curriculum of work. In H. Giroux & D. Purpel (Eds.), *The hidden curriculum and moral education* (pp. 143–167). Berkeley, CA: McCutchan Publishing.

Avery, P. (2002). Teaching tolerance: What research tells us. *Social Education, 66*(5), 270–275.

Barber, B. (1984). *Strong democracy: Participatory politics for a new age.* Berkeley, CA: University of California Press.

Cornbleth, C. (2001). Climates of constraint/restraint of teachers and teaching. In W. Stanley (Ed.), *Critical issues in social studies research for the 21st century.* Greenwich, CT: Information Age Publishing.

Dewey, J. (1916/1966). *Democracy and education.* New York: Free Press.

Dilworth, P. (2004). Multicultural citizenship education: Case studies from social studies classrooms. *Theory and Research in Social Education, 32*(2), 153-186.

Ehman, L. (1980). The American school in the political socialization process. *Review of Educational Research, 50*(1), 99-119.

Epstein, T. (2000) Adolescents' perspectives on racial diversity in U.S. history: Case studies from an urban classroom. *American Educational Research Journal, 37,* 185-214.

Evans, R., Avery, P., & Pederson, P. (1999). Taboo topics: Cultural restraint on teaching social issues. *The Social Studies,* September/October, 218-224.

Fuhrman, S., & Lazerson, M. (Eds.). (2005). *The public schools.* New York: Oxford University Press.

Galston, W. (2001). Political knowledge, political engagement, and civic education. *Annual Review of Political Science (4),* 217-234.

Gibson, C., & Levine, P. (2003). *The civic mission of schools.* New York and Washington, DC: The Carnegie Corporation of New York and the Center for Information and Research on Civic Learning.

Hahn, C. (1998). *Becoming political: Comparative perspectives on citizenship education.* Albany: State University of New York Press.

Hahn, C. (2001). Democratic understanding: Cross-national perspectives. *Theory Into Practice, 40*(1), 14-22.

Hahn, C. (2002). Education for democratic citizenship: One nation's story. In W. Parker (Ed.), *Education for democracy: Contexts, curricula, assessments* (pp. 63-92). Greenwich, CT: Information Age Publishing.

Hess, D. (2002). Discussing controversial public issues in secondary social studies classrooms: Learning from skilled teachers. *Theory and Research in Social Education, 30*(1), 10-41.

Hess, D., & Posselt, J. (2002). How high school students experience and learn from the discussion of controversial public issues. *Journal of Curriculum and Supervision, 17*(4), 283-314.

Hofstadter, R. (1963). *Anti-intellectualism in American life.* New York: Vintage Books.

Kahne, J., Rodriguez, M., Smith, B., & Thiede, K. (2000). Developing citizens for democracy? Assessing opportunities to learn in Chicago's social studies classrooms. *Theory and Research in Social Studies Education, 28*(3), 311-338.

Lightfoot, S. L. (1983). *The good high school.* New York: Basic Books.

Lipman, P. (2004). *High stakes education: Inequality, globalization, and school reform.* New York: Routledge/Falmer.

Lucas, S. R. (1999). *Tracking inequality: Stratification and mobility in American high schools.* New York: Teachers College Press.

Marri, A. R. (2005). Building a framework for classroom-based multicultural democratic education: Learning from three skilled teachers. *Teachers College Record, 107*(5), 1036-1059.

McLaughlin, M. W. (1993). What matters most in teachers' workplace context. In J. Little and M. McLaughlin (Eds.), *Teachers' work: Individuals, colleagues, and contexts* (pp. 79-103). New York: Teachers College Press.

McNeil, L. (1981). Negotiating classroom knowledge: Beyond achievement and socialization. *Journal of Curriculum Studies, 13,* 313-328.

McNeil, L. (1986). *Contradicitions of control: School structure and school knowledge.* New York: Routledge & Kegan Paul.

Metz, M. H. (1978). *Classrooms and corridors: The Crisis of authority in desegregated secondary schools.* Berkeley: University of California Press.

National Research Council. (2005). *Engaging schools: Fostering high school students' motivation to learn.* Washington, DC: The National Academies Press.

Niemi, R., & Junn, J. (1998). *Civic education: What makes students learn.* New Haven, CT: Yale University Press.

Oakes, J. (1985). *Keeping track: How teachers structure inequality.* New Haven, CT: Yale University Press.

Pace, J. (2003a). Using ambiguity and entertainment to win compliance in a lower-level U.S. history class. *Journal of Curriculum Studies, 35*(1), 83–110.

Pace, J. (2003b). Revisiting classroom authority: Theory and ideology meet practice. *Teachers College Record, 105*(8), 1559–1585.

Pace, J. (2006). Saving (and losing) face, race, and authority in a 9th grade English class. In J. Pace & A. Hemmings (Eds.), *Classroom authority: Theory, research, and practice* (pp. 87–112). Mahwah, NJ: Erlbaum Associates.

Pace, J., & Hemmings, A. (2007). *Understanding authority in classrooms: A review of theory, ideology, and research, 77* (1), 4–27.

Page, R. (1987). Teachers' perceptions of students: A link between classrooms, school cultures, and the social order. *Anthropology & Education Quarterly, 18,* 77–99.

Page, R. (1990). Cultures and curricula: Differences between and within schools. *Educational Foundations, 4*(1), 49–76.

Page, R. (1991). *Lower-track classrooms: A curricular and cultural perspective.* New York: Teachers College Press.

Parker, W. (1996). "Advanced" ideas about democracy: Toward a pluralist conception of citizen education. *Teachers College Record, 98*(1), 104–125.

Parker, W. (2003). *Teaching democracy: Unity and diversity in public life.* New York: Teachers College Press.

Patrick, J., & Hoge, J. (1991). Teaching government, civics, and law. In J.Shaver, (Ed.), *Handbook of Research on Social Studies Teaching and Learning* (pp. 427–436). New York: Macmillan.

Pollock, M. (2001). How the question we ask most about race in education is the very question we most suppress. *Educational Researcher, 30*(9), 2–12.

Powell, A., Farrar, E., & Cohen, D. (1985). *The shopping mall high school: Winners and losers in the educational marketplace.* Boston: Houghton Mifflin.

Preissle-Goetz, J., & LeCompte, M. (1991). Qualitative research in social studies education. In J. Shaver (Ed.). *Handbook of research on social studies teaching and learning* (pp. 56–66). New York: Macmillan.

Rogoff, B. (1990). *Apprenticeship in thinking: Cognitive development in social context.* New York: Oxford University Press.

Sizer, T. R. (1984). *Horace's compromise: The dilemma of the American high school.* Boston: Houghton Mifflin.

Stanley, W. (2005). Social studies and the social order. Transmission or transformation? *Social Education, 69*(5), 282–287.

Thornton, S. (1991). Teacher as curricular-instructional gatekeeper in social studies. In J. Shaver (Ed.). *Handbook of research on social studies teaching and learning* (pp. 237–248). New York: Macmillan.

Torney-Purta, J., Lehmann, J., Oswald, R., & Schultz, W. (2001). *Citizenship and Education in Twenty-eight Countries: Civic Knowledge and Engagement at Age Fourteen.* Amsterdam: IEA <http://www.wam.umd.edu/~iea/>

Westheimer, J., & Kahne, J. (2004). What kind of citizen? The politics of educating for democracy. *American Educational Research Journal, 41*(2), 237–269.

CHAPTER 3

Connecting Diversity, Justice, and Democratic Citizenship

Lessons from an Alternative U.S. History Class

Anand R. Marri

How can high school social studies teachers educate students for multi-cultural democratic citizenship in the study of U.S. history? This chapter outlines curricular and pedagogical practices of Mr. Sinclair, a social studies teacher at a public alternative high school for academically struggling students. The study is significant because although the literature on citizenship education includes a great deal of theory about the importance of multicultural democratic education and what it should look like (Banks, 2003; Gay, 1997; Marri, 2003; Parker, 2003), examples from actual classrooms are rare. This case is especially important because it shows an effort to enact multicultural democratic education with low-income and otherwise marginalized students, who represent those in greatest need and with the least opportunity for empowerment (Banks, 2003; Delpit, 1995). The chapter highlights how the teacher promoted students' understanding of justice, drawing both on individual/psychological and group/sociological conceptions of justice (see Parker, 2003). These two conceptions are often dichotomized, but Mr. Sinclair's teaching provides a noteworthy example of how they can be brought together in a unit on the Civil Rights Movement.

Methodology and Context

Data for this chapter were collected as part of a larger study I conducted on three skilled social studies teachers' enactments of an approach called Classroom-based Multicultural Democratic Education (CMDE) (see Marri, 2005) using the central question of how do secondary social studies teachers teach about and for multicultural democracy in U.S. history courses? In answering this question, I aimed to generate an initial framework of how teachers can teach about and for multicultural democracy. My sub-questions included the following:

1. In what ways do these teachers use their pedagogy in working toward multicultural democracy in their classrooms?
2. In what ways do these teachers build community in working toward multicultural democracy?
3. In what ways do these teachers use disciplinary content in working toward multicultural democracy?
4. What factors play a role in working toward classroom-based multicultural democracy?
5. What factors serve as obstacles in working toward classroom-based multicultural democracy?

Mr. Sinclair was selected based on the following four criteria: (1) he provided more equitable opportunities for all students to learn through integrating multiple sources of information, (2) he used multiple perspectives in their teaching, (3) he encouraged students to expand learning beyond the classroom, and (4) he was involved in professional development activities. I chose these four criteria because they serve as a proxy for "good" teachers (Lightfoot, 1983). "Good" teachers, in this case, are teachers whose work "might tell us about the myriad definitions of educational success and how it is achieved" (Lightfoot, 1983, p. 11). In addition to these criteria, I also relied on the recommendations of the district social studies curriculum director, other teachers, and parents in selecting Mr. Sinclair.

I analyzed the data to create codes and categories of data through line-by-line inductive coding (Miles & Huberman, 1984). Mr. Sinclair, like the other teachers in the larger study, received a transcribed copy of the interviews and observations, and a copy of my analysis notes for his class, in order to provide feedback and suggestions for changes. He used these opportunities to clarify his rationale and pedagogy, raise questions, and provide further explanations.

Observations of Mr. Sinclair's teaching took place for twenty-five 50-minute class periods during the course of a unit of study, approximately four weeks. I interviewed him three times: once at the start of the unit, the second midway though the unit, and the third after the completion of my observations. Finally, teacher-generated materials, such as handouts, quizzes, exams, and projects, were also collected and analyzed.

Mr. Sinclair taught in the Homestead School District, located in a Midwestern state and serving approximately 25,000 students. Its 54 schools included 32 elementary (K–5) schools, 13 middle (6–8) schools, four comprehensive high schools and five alternative high schools. The district also had early childhood programs and secondary (6–12) alternative programs located at its 54 schools. The district covered approximately 65 square miles, including all or part of the 11 towns, villages, and cities.

The Seventh Avenue School (SAS), one of the district's five alternative high schools, served as the last chance school for students who lived on the eastside of the Homestead. Students at SAS had previously attended at least one of the district's four comprehensive high schools and left because of academic, or personal problems, or both. The SAS provided a four-semester sequence (two years) of academic courses and related work experiences that emphasized a core academic curriculum for each semester, in social studies, English, math, or science. The school's mission was to provide a program for struggling students, who are dealing with academic, family, or personal problems, that focuses on completion of requirements for a high school diploma while learning skills needed for independent adult living, work, and citizenship.

Students must have been 16 years old and have attended at least two years of high school prior to admission. Students were referred to the program by a principal, a guidance counselor, a support staff member at their high school, or a county social worker because of their academic, family, or personal problems. In addition, the student himself could have requested admission. Some students were not admitted even though they were referred because SAS could only admit about 15–20 students per semester through a selective application process involving a written application and interviews with the school's four teachers, guidance counselor, or principal.

At SAS students were classified as juniors for semesters one and two and as seniors for semesters three and four. Academic courses were scheduled for the first half of the day at the school. Students spent the other half of each day working at different work sites away from the school building. The goal was to give students on the job training in multiple work settings, such as in offices, restaurants, day care centers, retail stores, and construction worksites. The curriculum focused on four themes (human interaction, economic/consumer survival, citizenship and the law, and identity) that were infused into the core academic curriculum for each semester, in social studies, English, math, or science. During each semester there was an emphasis on the application of basic skills to career planning and employability. Class sizes ranged from fifteen to twenty, and students were assigned an individual teacher advisor.

Will Sinclair was a White 7th year high school social studies teacher in his mid-thirties. He grew up in a rural part of the state and moved to the city of Homestead upon receiving his undergraduate degree in history from a state university. He worked at a local bookstore for several years before deciding to return to school for his teaching license.

Mr. Sinclair decided to enroll in a teaching certificate program in social studies education after being inspired by Jonathan Kozol's "Savage Inequalities." He stated:

> Kozol's *Savage Inequalities* is probably the one book that really hit me as boy this is a challenge. It would be something to try to do. Obviously there is a problem here and maybe I can do something about it by being a teacher.

This book inspired Mr. Sinclair because he wondered:

> How we could have an area where kids obviously are getting a better deal, and simply because of where they lived? I mean, they were getting better resources and they were getting, for the most part, better teaching in these schools. It really took something special to get across the importance of school to kids and how school can be a wonderful place. I thought, "Well this is one way I can affect the world, one way I can make a difference."

Mr. Sinclair's concern about inequality in public education motivated him to become a public school teacher. He entered the profession intent on becoming an activist teacher in improving the lives of marginalized students, such as those at SAS.

Mr. Sinclair started teaching at Seventh Avenue School as a student teacher and became a full-time teacher there upon graduation from his teacher education program. During the semester of my observation, Mr. Sinclair was completing an MA thesis in Curriculum & Instruction, which examined the effective use of discussions in high school social studies classrooms. As a result, he was familiar with the literature on democratic citizenship education, especially the research on discussions, critical thinking, and the relationship between the two.

During my study, Mr. Sinclair's fourth semester U.S. history class consisted of fifteen students who started as a cohort at the SAS together as 1st semester students, meaning that these students had taken the same classes for the previous year and a half and were familiar with each other. There were 10 females (six White, one African American, one Native American/African American, one Hispanic, and one Asian American) and five males (4 White and 1 Hispanic) in this class. They all arrived at SAS with zero to five credits, a very low number, after two years at a comprehensive high school. According to Mr. Sinclair, his students had a range of academic abilities and were functioning at "average or below average" levels. He said they had experiences that were atypical for high school students and mentioned that his own high school experience was quite different from that of his students. For example, four students had their own children, another student was pregnant, and several students lived on their own because of family or personal problems. According to Mr. Sinclair, such circumstances negatively affected his students' academic performance because they could not concentrate on their schoolwork outside of SAS, or missed school to attend to their problems.

Virtually all of the students were on the low end of the socioeconomic scale and were very focused on finishing their high school education because, according to Mr. Sinclair, of the significant progress they made during their time at SAS. Further, because students in this semester were working at their job sites in the afternoons as part of the required curriculum and hoped to continue employment in those sites upon graduation, dropping out meant that students would be jeopardizing their next year's employment as well. Finally, Mr. Sinclair characterized his students this way: "Willing to talk about their experiences, to put stuff out on the table and they're willing to work together for the most part."

Multicultural Citizenship Education in Action

Evidence in the literature of real examples of classroom-based multicultural citizenship education is rare. Specifically, U.S. history and government courses tend to be knowledge-based, relying on the textbook and lectures (Epstein, 2000; Grant, 2001 & 2003). In those rare classes that emphasize the development of citizenship, most often students are taught to be personally responsible citizens or participatory citizens (Westheimer & Kahne, 2004). Instead, Mr. Sinclair tried to prepare students with the tools to be justice-oriented citizens, who question, debate, and change unjust systems and structures (Westheimer & Kahne, 2004). In exploring the meaning of justice, Mr. Sinclair exposed students to a tension of democratic citizenship by showing them that the rights and responsibilities of citizenship sometimes involve breaking the law.

The 4th semester, when the students took Mr. Sinclair's class, was the culminating semester of the program at SAS and students had to show that they had competencies in school and work through the skills of listening, speaking, and writing. Students had to also show that they were able to function as democratic citizens in society through their in-class evaluations as well as through their workplace evaluations. To help students achieve this goal, Mr. Sinclair emphasized discussions and examination of current events in his U.S. history class.

Mr. Sinclair told me the curriculum of the U.S. history class integrated English, psychology, sociology, and U.S. history. There was a heavy emphasis on self-identity and answering the question "What are you going to do after you're done here and how are you going to do it?" Mr. Sinclair said he used these subject areas (English, psychology, sociology, U.S. history) to help students address this question through their end-of-year portfolio projects. All students read one book together, Louis Rodriguez's *Always Running,* an autobiography of a Los Angeles gang member. Mr. Sinclair said he used this book to discuss "the underside, so to speak, of America." He said he chose it because it was "well written, easily accessible to (his) students, and something they could relate to."

This book serves as an example of the interdisciplinary nature of the curriculum in Mr. Sinclair's class used to connect the curriculum with student lives. He did not emphasize "official knowledge" (Apple, 1993), the knowledge that is emphasized in textbooks and statewide tests. He told me that he designed the curricula to help his underachieving and marginalized students relate to what they were learning and value schooling. Thus, he designed his curriculum so that his students would be empowered to bring their lived experiences into school and to use such experiences as tools for their school education. In short, he intended the curriculum to help his students to "become better students" by connecting their daily lives to school learning (Ball, 2000; Dewey, 1916; Freire, 1990).

The Civil Rights Movement: Studying Individual and Group Conceptions of Justice

I observed Mr. Sinclair teach a one-month-long unit on the Civil Rights Movement (CRM), one of several he taught on law and citizenship. I observed this unit because it was striking in its innovative and interdisciplinary enactment of multicultural democratic education. It started with an examination of Kohlberg's stages of moral development followed by an analysis of four dilemmas involving moral and political choices. Mr. Sinclair said he wanted to prepare students to critically examine the events of the movement and the actions of the movement's leaders. Mr. Sinclair thought studying Kohlberg's stages would help students understand the rationale and moral judgments underlying the actions of these activists. In keeping with his aim of relating the curriculum to the students, he wanted students to connect this understanding to "the choices they make in their own lives" as citizens.

Mr. Sinclair was familiar with Parker's (2003) discussion of Kohlberg's stage theory of moral development to explain the concept of justice (pp. 54–75). Kohlberg's theory consists of six stages (obedience and punishment, selfishness, "good boy/girl," law and order, social contract, and principle conscience) and is divided into three levels (pre-conventional, conventional, and post-conventional). Those at the pre-conventional level are rigidly oriented to obedience and punishment avoidance, while those who reason more conventionally move beyond morality to laws that maintain group welfare and social welfare. Those who reason in post-conventional ways, on the other hand, figure out which laws are just and which could legitimately be broken by moving toward an individualized concept of justice (Kohlberg, Levine, & Hewer, 1984; Parker, 2003). The students discussed their viewpoints on a number of scenarios, provided by Mr. Sinclair, by determining when it was right to break the law. Such pedagogy enabled students to see that breaking the law could be justifiable, if the law was unjust; for example, Gandhi breaking the salt laws of British colonial India. As they discussed these scenarios, Mr. Sinclair incorporated Kohlberg's theory to show how the Civil Rights Movement leaders could not just be classified as law-breakers, but instead met the criteria for post-conventional stages of moral development. Using psychological theory as a lens, the teacher tried to show students the basis for political action against injustice that was illegal yet morally legitimate.

After these activities, Mr. Sinclair led his students in an in-depth examination of certain aspects of the Civil Right Movement through text-based discussions and inquiry-based lessons. In these lessons, the students analyzed various photographs and texts from major CRM events, such as the Jim Crows laws, Selma to Montgomery march, and Birmingham bus boycott. He selected materials from various sources including textbooks, magazines, and primary sources and newspapers.

The final part of the unit revolved around deconstructing Dr. Martin Luther King, Jr.'s *Letter From Birmingham Jail*. This letter was written to religious leaders by Dr. King addressing the charges that he was an outside agitator after he decided to get involved in Birmingham. Reading and discussing this letter might enable students, by exploring one another's interpretations, to understand how King distinguishes between just and unjust laws (Parker, 2003). Mr. Sinclair explained why he used this letter in our second interview:

> This is a way to make a connection between psychology and U.S. history. King is a good example because he is probably taught every year. I am trying to get them to understand the words, the background. He just didn't make it up out of thin air—it was tied to Kohlberg's stages of moral development. The letter was something that was well thought out. It had a purpose.

Mr. Sinclair had an explicit goal in mind as he designed this curriculum, which was to educate students to become "just citizens." Such citizens make it their duty to protect both just institutions and to prevent injustice while refraining from harming or exploiting others (Parker, 2003). He believed that using such examples would enable his students to understand the concept of justice that King embodied.

Lesson on King's Letter From Birmingham Jail: *Understanding
the Context for Illegal Political Action for Justice*

Martin Luther King, Jr.'s *Letter From Birmingham Jail* is an exemplar of enlightened political engagement that shows King's "reasoning about justice
and democracy" (Parker, 2003, xix). Mr. Sinclair involved his students in
an examination of the famous document. In order to help them understand its significance, he spent the first two days of this three-day lesson
teaching the class about critical events leading up to King's arrest in Birmingham. The following is an overview of the lesson:

> *I. Intro:* Inquiry activity about the events depicted in the film *"Missis-
> sippi Burning"*
>
> *II. Build-Up:* Elizabeth Eckford and her reflections about integration;
> History of Birmingham and King's involvement; Spike Lee's documen-
> tary *"Four Little Girls"*
>
> *III. Text-based Seminar:* Analysis of the *Letter From Birmingham Jail*
> through three questions:
> 1. How does Dr. King respond to being called an "outside agitator" in
>   Birmingham?
> 2. How does Dr. King respond to charges that his followers were break-
>   ing the law?
> 3. How does Dr. King feel about being labeled an "extremist" by his
>   critics?

Mr. Sinclair began this lesson with an introductory inquiry activity. The
students watched a PowerPoint slide presentation of eight photographs
from events after the 1964 disappearance and murder of three civil right
workers (James Chaney, Andrew Goodman, and Michael Schwerner) in
Philadelphia, Mississippi. He told the class: "Think of W questions: who,
what, why, where, and when. Look at the pictures and think of these questions. All of the pictures relate to a specific incident. All the pictures were
taken within four months of each other."

The students examined the first photograph of two African American
women, one White woman, and an African American man in dark clothing
leaving a building, after the funeral of one of the civil rights workers killed

in Mississippi. The students then answered the W questions in their journals before sharing their answers with the class. Students responded:

"It could be Martin Luther King's/Malcolm X's wives"
"The woman in the middle looked like Joan Crawford"
"The people were at a funeral, for JFK"
"The middle woman might be JFK's wife"
"It could be a courthouse because somebody was sentenced to death/life in prison and they were crying"
"They could be there for Medgar Evers"

Mr. Sinclair recorded every student answer using the speaker notes box in PowerPoint and projected these answers on the overhead screen.

This process continued for seven more photographs, and then Mr. Sinclair directed the class: "In your journal, come up with a hypothesis of what these slides have in common." As students worked on this task, he showed the eight slides again. After the students completed this task, Mr. Sinclair reviewed each slide in detail and explained the larger event students examined in order to provide the background information they needed for the unit.

Build-Up. To start the next period, Mr. Sinclair reviewed the eight pictures from the previous lesson. After this review, he posted a web page showing the chronology of events from the trial of those involved in the murder of the three civil rights workers in Philadelphia, Mississippi. He pointed out the major figures involved, such as Medgar Evers. During this examination, he referred to the historical tension between African Americans and Whites in the southern U.S., going back to the importation of slaves for labor, the Civil War, and Reconstruction.

Next, Mr. Sinclair projected a slide of an African American girl, Elizabeth Eckford, with books in her hands, being yelled at by several White men and women as she walked.[1] Students interpreted it drawing on details from the photograph: "They don't like her," "She's going to school, could get beat up." Mr. Sinclair again posted their answers on the screen before reviewing the history of desegregation at Little Rock's Central High School. During this review, one of the students pointed out that the White woman heckling Elizabeth Eckford, Hazel Bryan Massery, publicly apologized for her actions and admitted that racial segregation was wrong. Mr. Sinclair added "Elizabeth Eckford now questions whether it (the fight for desegregation) was worth it because of rising segregation today."

To illuminate his point and to connect the past with the present, he began an inquiry lesson on Homestead's current housing and school segregation, which the students investigated using figures found on Web sites of local newspapers, the city government, and the school district. Students, in groups of four, studied the demographic information on four parts of the city (north, south, east, and west) before the Civil Rights Movement and compared the data with similar figures from the year 2000. Based on this investigation, several groups discovered that certain parts of the city, particularly the Westside, had similar percentage of African American residents both before the Civil Rights Movement and in the year 2000.

This atypical activity stands out because social studies teachers, for the most part, do not teach segregation as an ongoing phenomenon in U.S. society. Instead, U.S. history lessons on segregation usually focus on how the *Brown* decision ended the "separate but equal" doctrine for public schools (Bell, 1992 & 2004; Hess, 2005). Mr. Sinclair, rather than relying on "official knowledge," pushed his students for more active citizenship by examining segregation in their own city and neighborhoods and asking if and how students should continue to fight for desegregation. He asked students to consider the socioeconomic approach to justice, which analyzes the interaction of values, knowledge, history, and social positions and situations in which people live, such as race, social class, and so on (Parker, 2003). This inquiry lesson enabled students to explore the underlying socioeconomic causes of segregation in Homestead by looking at, for example, where the jobs were located, where public transportation was available, and where public services were located. Students were asked beyond explanation of prejudices and actions of fellow citizens. Through this lesson, Mr. Sinclair added to the individual conceptions of justice presented through MLK, Jr. with the societal conception of justice by exploring the ideas presented by Marx, such as the social and class positions and situations (race, class, gender, sexual identity, religion) that people actually live in (for an in-depth discussion of both conceptions of justice, see chap. 4 of Parker, 2003).

Finally, Mr. Sinclair told students that they would study Martin Luther King, Jr.'s *Letter From Birmingham Jail*, but he wanted them to further understand its context first. Because he placed importance on using multimedia to hook his students, Mr. Sinclair showed several minutes from Spike Lee's documentary *"Four Little Girls,"* which focused on the 1963 bombing of the 16th Street Baptist Church in Birmingham, Alabama, an attack that left four African American girls dead. After the showing, Mr. Sinclair high-lighted several facts from the documentary to help them remember the situation in Birmingham: Spike Lee juxtaposed white and black view-points, Birmingham was referred to as "Bombingham," and the only inte-grated things in Birmingham were the streets, sewers, and water. Mr. Sin-clair then concluded the unit through a deconstruction of Dr. Martin Luther King, Jr.'s *Letter From Birmingham Jail.*

Text-based Seminar. Mr. Sinclair handed out an instruction sheet for their study of *Letter From Birmingham Jail* with the following background in-formation: "This twenty-page letter was written while King sat in a jail cell in Birmingham, Alabama. He had been arrested after leading a march pro-testing segregation. The letter was written in response to eight White Christian and Jewish clergymen who objected to Dr. King's activities. Mr. Sinclair reminded his students, "Dr. King was not from Birmingham and the black community was split. Remember, Booker T. Washington and W. E. B. DuBois had debated these ideas and DuBois was still alive."

The students began preparing for their seminar in three ways. First, they focused on three questions as they read the letter: How does Dr. King respond to being called an "outside agitator" in Birmingham? How does Dr. King respond to charges that his followers were breaking the law? How does Dr. King feel about being labeled an "extremist" by his critics?

Second, students prepared double-entry drafts in which they did the following: (1) Listed quotes in "Quotes" column that were interesting, that they agreed or disagreed with, or that helped clarify Dr. King's ideas better and, (2) Listed five-sentence minimum responses about what the quote means to them, how they can identify with the quote, or why they agreed or disagreed with the quote.

Third, they worked in teacher-selected groups of four to discuss the letter. In addition, they answered two questions: How does King justify breaking laws? And according to King, how is it that a law-breaker can be expressing the highest respect for the law?

Finally, Mr. Sinclair began the text-based seminar by asking students if they had any questions about the text. After answering several questions, he pointed out "no one knows for certain 'The Answer,' that's why we need the discussion." Then, Mr. Sinclair asked the opening question, "King is re-ferred to as an outsider. How does he react to it?" Students immediately an-swered and started talking about the letter. Mr. Sinclair interjected ques-tions if there was prolonged lull in the seminar. The students discussed many related subjects within the general context of "doing the right thing," such as discrimination against homosexuals, Hitler, the Bible, free speech, and racial justice. All students participated and the seminar lasted the rest of the period.

This text-based seminar on *Letter From Birmingham Jail* serves as an example of a discussion to help students understand the issues, values, and ideas raised by the letter. Such a lesson was designed to ensure that students could comprehend the text of the letter as well as the rationale for King, Jr.'s writing the letter. Parker (2003) calls such seminars forums in which democracy and difference can be experienced directly by students because students interact with each other across difference (defined across many categories), engage in competent public talk, and express honest viewpoints and the practice receptive listening. Thus, Mr. Sinclair's seminar is an example of multicultural democratic education in which students engaged in democratic education across racial, gender, and socioeconomic lines.

Teaching for Social Justice with Marginalized Students

Mr. Sinclair told me he decided to become a teacher because he wanted to do something about inequality in U.S. society, and believed that teaching was a powerful way that he could make a difference. Although this study cannot draw conclusions about the impact of his curriculum and pedagogy, it points to elements of it that serve as important examples of how teachers can aim to empower marginalized students and educate them to be citizens in a multicultural democracy. These elements include inclusive pedagogy, a diverse learning community, critical thinking, discussion, and transformational knowledge.

Mr. Sinclair's inclusive pedagogy, in which student input was welcome, was important for his class. During informal conversations with Mr. Sinclair and the students, they said that a "lack of voice" served as a major factor in students' lack of connection to traditional schools. This meant that students were not given a chance to show what they knew or could do; instead they were negatively assessed because they did not provide the right answers or behave correctly. Mr. Sinclair's pedagogy, on the other hand, enabled students to have voice through lessons in which students were not expected to have the right answers. Instead, the emphasis was on active participation as students expressed their ideas and develop "voice."

The teacher created a safe space—an "open classroom climate" (Dilworth, 2000; Hahn, 2001; Torney-Purta, 2002), which had not been previously provided.

In order to create this safe space, Mr. Sinclair developed a sense of community in his class. Building of community means teachers create a climate of mutual respect to help students build positive relationships, resolve conflicts, and develop group problem-solving skills (Browing, Davis, & Retsa, 2000; Nelsen, Lott, & Glenn, 2000). To build community, for example, students are encouraged to engage in discussion and interact socially with other students from different racial, ethnic, cultural, and language groups, to build understanding. To do this, teachers can structure interracial cooperative groups that enable students from different racial and ethnic groups to become acquainted as individuals (Banks, 2001). This is important because, as Dewey (1916) stated, it is by associating and resolving issues with people whose views are different from one's own that democracy is learned.

Several empirical studies provide evidence that building of community is connected to democratic values in classrooms. In their study of elementary students, Schaps and Lewis (1997) report that increases in sense of community are linked to concern for others and democratic values. Further, when teachers build communities in schools and classrooms, students begin to experience what it means to be compassionate, involved citizens (Wood, 1990). Students who participate in community building that, for example, emphasizes egalitarian participation and resolution of conflict by discussion and empathy for others, learn the skills to conduct themselves in the wider democratic society (Le Tendre, 1999).

Mr. Sinclair created a comfortable classroom environment that had a very strong sense of community and diversity. This was partly helped by the fact that these students had been part of a cohort for the past three semesters. To build community, he used activities and discussions that helped students see each other as individuals, rather than representatives of larger groups, with the goal of understanding each other. For example, during the text-based seminar discussion, he frequently referred to where the students lived and attempted to tie the curriculum to their family, friends, or work life. This was important because these students lived in many different neighborhoods in the city of Homestead. They came from various cultural, racial, and socioeconomic backgrounds and, for the most part, did not socialize with others outside of this class because of work and family obligations.

Mr. Sinclair said he wanted to stress the importance of this class as "a public space where they get together with others to learn." The manner in which the teachers created open and safe classroom climates is important to promoting students' positive perceptions of their experiences (Dilworth, 2000). Because of his methods, students were exposed to a variety of perspectives that moved beyond stereotypes and allowed them to see each other's personal stake in the issue at hand. For example, students sometimes asked others who tended to be vocal to be quiet to make sure all of their peers had a chance to speak. They were even interested in hearing opposing viewpoints. Through discussion, they strived to learn from each other. Mr. Sinclair explicitly expected students to provide their informed opinions without fear of disagreement with others. The goal of discussions was to examine an issue thoroughly to better understand it and differing perspectives on it. He told me, "It's important for students to have their own ideas, but it's also important to see the other side to better understand it. Without seeing the other side, as Gandhi stated, democracy isn't happening."

While Mr. Sinclair's pedagogy provided a safe space for students to have voice and become active participants, these marginalized students may not have such spaces as citizens upon graduation. The lack of safe spaces can be explained by the ongoing inequalities and discrimination which create significant impediments in civic engagement among low-income and minority youth (Camino & Zeldin, 2002). Mr. Sinclair's inclusion of critical thinking and sociological conceptions of justice played an important role in the enactment of multicultural democratic education.

Critical thinking may be defined as a process of actively and skillfully conceptualizing, applying, analyzing, synthesizing, or evaluating information gathered from, or generated by, observation, experience, reflection, reasoning, or communication (Scriven & Paul, 1996). Several studies provide evidence that an emphasis on critical thinking may contribute to democratic understanding and attitudes among students. Torney, Oppenheim, and Faren (1975) found that students in nine countries who engaged in critical thinking activities, such as discussion of issues, were politically knowledgeable and held less authoritarian attitudes than their peers who did not. In a more recent study, Hahn (2001) found that practice in decision-making after exposure to various viewpoints is essential to develop the knowledge, abilities, and values needed for democratic life. Moreover, civic action, if it does not grow out of informed decision-making, may reinforce political naiveté or apathy (Hahn, 2001). Civic action based on critical thinking, however, has the potential to engage citizens working to improve society.

Mr. Sinclair aimed to advance critical thinking in several ways. He told me that he wanted to foster informed students "who see that there's more than their opinion on something." For example, he included viewpoints from both Whites and African Americans while studying both the events surrounding the 1964 murder of civil rights workers in Philadelphia, Mississippi and desegregation. By incorporating Elizabeth Eckford's current sentiments about integration, he provided students with a critical (in two senses of the word) perspective as students studied the fight for desegregation. Mr. Sinclair wanted to promote examination of issues from many viewpoints, which he felt was essential to democratic living for his students. His rationale reflects the research on issues-centered teaching in social studies, which enables students to develop advanced intellectual abilities (Ochoa-Becker, 1996) and move beyond relativistic notions of truth (Evans, Newmann, & Saxe, 1996). In short, this issues-centered pedagogy enabled Mr. Sinclair to emphasize reasoning and informed decision-making (Engle, 1996).

Second, Mr. Sinclair also used discussions to promote critical thinking. Discussion is one method that facilitates critical thinking because it encourages participants to present and examine multiple perspectives on an issue. Discussion, as defined by Dillon (1994), is "a particular form of group interaction where members join together in addressing a question of common concern, exchanging and examining different views to form their answer, enhancing their knowledge or understanding, their appreciation or judgment, their decision, resolution or action over the matter at issue" (p. 8). Moreover, social studies educators (Engle & Ochoa, 1988; Hahn, 1998; Harris, 2002; Hess, 2002; Oliver & Shaver, 1966; Parker, 1996; Rossi, 1995) also support discussion as a pedagogical method for a variety of reasons, including:

- It can help young people develop the group discourse skills and dispositions necessary for participatory citizenship;
- It enhances critical thinking;
- It deepens understanding of important democratic issues and concepts;
- It develops a more democratic classroom community; and
- It influences future political participation.

Anand R. Marri

Mr. Sinclair's choice of the text-based seminar on *Letter From Birmingham Jail* serves as an example of his use of discussions to promote critical thinking. His students held a number of strong opinions, but were respectful of other's ideas. Several students believed that King should not have broken the law the way he did and, instead, should have waited for the support of the larger African American community in Birmingham. Others felt differently, stating that he did the right thing by drawing attention to the injustice in Birmingham. By connecting these students' sentiments to conceptions of justice, the teacher also enabled students to see the difference between individual conceptions of justice, as illustrated by Kohlberg, and societal conceptions of justice, as illustrated by Marx. Mr. Sinclair provided a platform for them to exchange informed viewpoints in order to better understand the text and the issues raised by the text.

Mr. Sinclair mentioned, both in class and during interviews, that students needed to be able to understand "multiple perspectives and other's viewpoints" to better think for themselves and discussions facilitated this outcome. His own pre-service and in-service training enabled him to implement discussions in his classrooms. Mr. Sinclair knew that students would disagree with each other, but he wanted them to know that "disagreement is okay." For example, during the text-based discussions and other classes, students did not make personal attacks on those they disagreed with. Instead, they attacked the perspectives that were being presented or asked for more evidence to better understand the point being made. These students also supported their own points with evidence from the unit. This disagreement enabled students to compare evidence and viewpoints, and in the end, make informed choices, as evidenced in the seminar and classroom discussions during the course of my observations.

Teaching for informed citizenship aimed at working for social justice involves teaching both mainstream and transformative knowledge and skills (Parker, 2003; Wade, 2001). "Most of the knowledge that constitutes the established canon in the nation's schools, colleges, and universities is mainstream academic knowledge" (Banks, 1995, p. 393). Mainstream academic knowledge and skills provide students with the "codes of power" (Delpit, 1988) that students need to thrive in schools, colleges, and universities. Codes of power are usable knowledge and skills that enable students to communicate effectively in standard literary forms. For example, students are knowledgeable about the Bill of Rights and Jim Crow laws, and learn the skills to write an effective essay with a thesis statement and supporting evidence, and learn how to conduct research using the Internet.

Mainstream academic knowledge and skills are necessary but not sufficient for social justice. "Transformative academic knowledge consists of concepts, paradigms, themes, and explanations that challenge mainstream academic knowledge and that expand the historical and literary canon" (Banks, 1995, p. 394). Content is presented that challenges the notion that traditional interpretations are universalistic and unrelated to human interests (Collins, 1990; Crocco, 2003). Transformative academic knowledge and skills emphasize the content and skills that question and critique the standard views accepted by the dominant society. For example, students learn that Rosa Parks was not just a tired seamstress who decided to sit-in at the front of bus. Rather, they learn that she trained at the Highlander School and her actions were part of a larger planned action in the fight against segregation.

Mr. Sinclair's strength lay in incorporating transformational knowledge in his curriculum. He stressed critical perspectives by, for example, looking at the fight for desegregation. In his teaching about the Little Rock Nine, Mr. Sinclair pointed out that segregation in the United States was not just a historical event as it is commonly referred to in most U.S. history textbooks. To overcome this misconception, he included Homestead's housing statistics highlighting race/ethnicity for four parts of Homestead before the CRM and in the year 2000. Mr. Sinclair also had students read a newspaper article that focused on the graduation rates of students of color in the district and surrounding communities. Finally, Mr. Sinclair incorporated Elizabeth Eckford's comments that questioned whether the fight for desegregation was worth it. He aimed to show how segregation continues to be a current issue facing citizens today and did not end with the victories of the Civil Rights Movement.

Mr. Sinclair emphasized multiple perspectives representing different racial, socio-economic, and gender groups within the course content to make it more complete. For example, when discussing Dr. King's letter, he provided comments from a variety of groups, such as African Americans who lived in Birmingham, other African American community leaders, whites from Birmingham, and the KKK. He said that in a democracy "all voices should be heard." In working toward this goal, Mr. Sinclair also highlighted the critical thinking and historical understanding. Mr. Sinclair connected the curriculum to current issues and events in order to have students examine the larger concepts. For example, when discussing the question of responsibility for helping others in light of MLK, students analyzed local issues such as the increasing of homelessness in Homestead. They addressed this question through a local context of the problem. For example, in which part of the city are the most homeless persons found? What resources/services are available for Homestead's homeless? What help is available for homeless teen-agers, both in and out of school? By exploring such questions, students came to examine the context and the implications of persistent problems.

Mr. Sinclair aimed to help students work toward historical understanding of the bigger picture by using the curriculum to address essential questions. One essential question for this unit was "What were the reasons and effects of Dr. King's *Letter From Birmingham Jail*?" Another was "Why was the death of the three civil rights workers in Philadelphia, Mississippi so important to the CRM?" Through these questions, students analyzed the Civil Rights Movement by examining the larger context of the events. Mr. Sinclair taught them that these events were not typical, the entire nation was not behind the Movement, and the Movement did not have a single unified idea behind it. Instead, he taught that a variety of perspectives played a role in it, along with the context of the time period. Mr. Sinclair said that he aimed to go beyond the "well this happened then and this happened then" method of teaching history because students found this approach boring and not worthwhile. Mr. Sinclair wanted his students to see the complexity in studying and learning history.

While Mr. Sinclair stressed transformative academic knowledge, he limited the emphasis on mainstream academic knowledge. For example, in the debriefing of the eight pictures in the PowerPoint presentation, Mr. Sinclair presented with it a history of the events and the persons in the pictures. The information taught was similar to the content in found in many textbooks. Students were only held responsible for this content through their writing assignments and were not tested on this knowledge through exams, as they would be in most U.S. history classrooms.

Because Mr. Sinclair did not stress mainstream academic knowledge, his students were not prepared with established canons of most U.S. history courses. For example, during discussion preparation and group work time, students asked numerous informational questions about CRM content, such as the Civil Rights laws, Plessy v. Ferguson, and the role of the NAACP. Normally, this content would have been taught in other more mainstream classrooms and students would have been familiar with the content. However, Mr. Sinclair did not emphasize nor make his students responsible for such mainstream content.

Mr. Sinclair's choices about content did not prepare his students with some of the "codes of powers" they needed for informed and active citizenship. According to Delpit (1995), "codes of power," such as ways of talking, ways of writing, ways of dressing, and ways of interacting, serve as rules for participating in power. Gee (1999), similarly, calls these the actions, interactions, symbols, beliefs, etc. to produce, reproduce, sustain, and transform a given "form of life" or discourse (p. 7). Thus, success in these institutions—such as school and the workplace—requires the acquisition of these norms of power. Getting actions, words, and interactions "right" in the discourses of school and work means that people are able to "pull off" being a good student or worker (Gee, 1999). Being explicitly taught these codes makes acquiring power easier (Delpit, 1995). Unfortunately, Mr. Sinclair's pedagogy did not emphasize some of these codes needed for active and informed citizenship.

The choices Mr. Sinclair made reflect the dilemma faced by many teachers who aim to teach for engaged citizenship. Mr. Sinclair chose between extensive coverage of the Civil Rights Movement and in-depth analysis of MLK, Jr.'s rationale and action. Given the students in his classroom, he chose to prepare "just citizens" (Parker, 2003) by helping them understand both individual and group conceptions of justice. Such a clear goal, according to Mr. Sinclair, made his sacrifice of mainstream academic content and skills justifiable. However, Mr. Sinclair also recognized that his students would be at a disadvantage in a U.S. History course at the postsecondary level because of their lack of mainstream academic knowledge and skills.

Implications

The ultimate goal of this research is to uncover ways in which to transform a marginalized student population into a thoughtful, active, and effective citizenry. As a first step, I have investigated one example of multicultural democratic education designed to help students become thoughtful, active, and justice-oriented citizens. Teacher educators may want to share the practices from this study with pre-service teachers to think about the purpose of teaching about and for democracy in complex ways. This may help pre-service teachers grasp the reality that teaching students to become thoughtful, active, and justice-oriented citizens in these diverse United States is a challenging enterprise that requires intellectual understanding, skill, intense preparation and a focus on purpose. The challenge becomes more complex as teachers work with marginalized students. However, this challenge is crucial because education for democracy must address the needs of all citizens, especially those who are marginalized.

At the same time, such an example will hopefully inspire teachers to believe that it is possible and worthwhile. Such work involves facing dilemmas and making choices with a clear sense of purpose. For Mr. Sinclair, his goal was to prepare "just citizens" (Parker, 2003) and he made the necessary choices to meet that goal. By doing so, in his work with marginalized students in an alternative school, Mr. Sinclair exemplified the kind of citizenship envisioned in the model of multicultural democracy.

Note

1. This is a famous picture of Elizabeth Eckford, 15, and one of the "Little Rock Nine," being heckled by Whites as she walked to Central High School in Little Rock, Arkansas.

References

Apple, M. (1993). Constructing the "Other": Rightist reconstructions of common sense. In C. McCarthy & W. Crichlow, (Eds.), *Race, representation and identity in education* (p. 24–39). New York: Routledge.

Ball, A. (2000). Empowering pedagogies that enhance the learning of multicultural students. *Teachers College Record, 102*(6), 1006–1034.

Banks, J. (2001). Citizenship Education and Diversity: Implications for Teacher Education. *Journal of Teacher Education, 52*(1), 5–16.

Banks, J. (2003). Series foreword. In W. Parker, *Teaching democracy: Unity and diversity in public life.* New York: Teachers College Press.

Bell, D. (1992). *Faces at the bottom of the well.* New York: Basic Books.

Bell, D. (2004). *Silent covenants: Brown v. Board of Education and the unfulfilled hopes for racial reform.* New York: Oxford University Press.

Browning, L., Davis, B., & Resta, V. (2000). What do you mean "think before I act"? Conflict resolution with choices. *Journal of Research in Childhood Education, 14*(2), 232–238.

Camino, L., & Zeldin, S. (2002). From periphery to center: Pathways for youth civic engagement in the day-to-day life of communities. *Applied Developmental Science, 6*(4), 213–220.

Collins, P. (1990). *Black feminist thought: Knowledge, consciousness, and the politics of empowerment.* Boston: Unwin Hyman.

Crocco, M. (2003) Dealing with difference in the social studies: A historical perspective. *International Journal of Social Education, 18*(2), 106–126.

Delpit, L. (1988). *The silenced dialogue: Power and pedagogy in educating other people's children.* Harvard Educational Review, 58, 280–298.

Delpit, L. (1995). *Other people's children: Cultural conflict in the classroom.* New York: The New Press.

Dewey, J. (1916). *Democracy and education.* New York: Macmillan.

Dillon, J. (1994). *Using discussion in classrooms.* Buckingham, England: Open University Press.

Dilworth, P. (2000). *Multicultural content integration in social studies classrooms.* Unpublished doctoral dissertation, Emory University.

Engle, S. (1996). Foreword. In R. Evans and D. Saxe (Eds.), *Handbook on Teaching Social Issues—NCSS Bulletin 93* (pp. v–viii). Washington, DC: National Council for the Social Studies.

Engle, S., & Ochoa, A. (1988). *Education for democratic citizenship.* New York: Teachers College Press.

Epstein, T. (2000). Adolescents' perspectives on racial diversity in United States history: Case studies from an urban classroom. *American Education Research Journal, 37*(1), 185–214.

Evans, R., Newmann, F., & Saxe, D. (1996). Defining issues-centered education. In R. Evans and D. Saxe (Eds.), *Handbook on Teaching Social Issues—NCSS Bulletin 93* (pp. 2–5). Washington, DC: National Council for the Social Studies.

Freire, P. (1990). *Pedagogy of the oppressed.* New York: Free Press.

Gay, G. (1997). The relationship between multicultural and democratic education. *The Social Studies, 88*(1), 5–11.

Gee, J. (1999). *An introduction to discourse analysis: Theory and method.* London: Routledge.

Grant, S. (2001). An uncertain lever: Exploring the influence of state-level testing in New York State on teaching social studies. *Teachers College Record, 103*(3), 398–426.

Grant, S. (2003). *History lessons: Teaching, learning, and testing in U.S. high school classrooms.* Mahwah, NJ: Erlbaum.

Hahn, C. (1998). *Becoming political.* Albany: State University of New York Press.

Hahn, C. (2001). Democratic understanding: Cross-national perspectives. *Theory into Practice, 40*(1), 14–22.

Harris, D. (2002). Classroom assessment of civic discourse. In W. C. Parker (Ed.), *Education for democracy: Contexts, curricula, and assessments* (pp. 211–232). Greenwich, CT: Information Age Press.

Hess, D. (2002). Discussing controversial public issues in secondary social studies classrooms: Learning from skilled teachers. *Theory and Research in Social Education, 30*(1), 10–41.

Hess, D. (2005). Moving beyond celebration: Challenging curricular orthodoxy in the teaching of Brown and its legacies. *Teachers College Record, 107*(9), 2046–2067.

Kohlberg, L., Levine, C., & Hewer, A. (1984). The current formulation of theory. In L. Kohlberg (Ed.), Essays on moral development (Vol. II). *The psychology of moral development: The nature and validity of moral of moral stages* (pp. 212–319). San Francisco: Harper & Row.

Le Tendre, G. (1999). Community-building activities in Japanese schools: Alternative paradigms of the democratic school. *Comparative Education Review, 43*(3), 283–310.

Lightfoot, S. (1983). *The good high school.* New York: Basic Books.

Marri, A. (2003). Multicultural democracy: Toward a better democracy. Intercultural Education, *14*(3), 263–277.

Marri, A. (2005). Building a framework for classroom-based multicultural democratic education (CMDE): Learning from three skilled teachers. *Teachers College Record, 107*(5), 1036–1059.

Miles, M., & Huberman, A. (1984). *Qualitative data analysis: A sourcebook of new methods* (2nd ed.). Thousand Oaks, CA: Sage Publications.

Nelsen, J., Lott, L., & Glenn, H. (2000). *Positive discipline in the classroom* (3rd ed.). Rocklin, CA: Prima Publishing.

Ochoa-Becker, A. (1996). Building a rationale for issues-centered education. In R. Evans and D. Saxe (Eds.), *Handbook on Teaching Social Issues—NCSS Bulletin 93*(pp. 6–12). Washington, DC: National Council for the Social Studies.

Oliver, D., & Shaver, J. (1966). *Teaching public issues in the high school.* Boston: Houghton Mifflin.

Parker, W. (1996). "Advanced" ideas about democracy: Toward a pluralist conception of citizen education. *Teachers College Record, 98*(1), 104–125.

Parker, W. (2003). *Teaching democracy: Unity and diversity in public life.* New York: Teachers College Press.

Rossi, J. (1995). In-depth study in an issues-oriented social studies classroom. *Theory and Research in Social Education, 23*(2), 88–120.

Schaps, E., & Lewis, C. (1997). Building classroom communities. *Thrust for Educational Leadership, 27*(1), 14.

Scriven, M., & Paul, R. (1996). *Defining critical thinking: A draft statement for the National Council for Excellence in Critical Thinking.* [Online 2003]. Available: www.criticalthinking .org/University/univclass/Defining.html

Torney, J., Oppenheim, A., & Faren, R. (1975). *Civic education in ten countries: An empirical study.* New York: Halstead Press.

Torney-Purta, J. (2002). The school's role in developing civic engagement: A study of adolescents in twenty-eight countries. *Applied Developmental Science, 6*(4), 203–212.

Wade, R. (2001). Social action in the social studies. *Theory into Practice, 40*(1), 23–28.

Westheimer, J., & Kahne, J. (2004). What kind of citizen: The politics of educating for democracy. *American Educational Research Journal, 41*(2), 237–269.

Wood, G. (1990). Teaching for democracy. *Educational Leadership, 48*(3), 32–37.

CHAPTER 4

Urban Youth and the Construction of Racialized and Classed Political Identities

Kysa Nygreen

Scholars of democratic citizenship education have long explored the processes through which individuals come to see themselves as democratic citizens. In order to better understand what kinds of educational experiences can enable or facilitate greater levels of civic engagement, researchers have examined why some people engage in political action at particular times and in particular ways—and why some do not. Drawing insights from cultural anthropology, this chapter begins with the assumption that political agency is tied to a sense of personal or collective political identity, through which individuals come to identify themselves as particular kinds of political subjects (Gregory, 1998; Holland, Lanchicotte, Skinner, & Cain, 1998). This chapter offers a close examination of the processes through which young people construct, revise, and enact various individual and collective political identities. In particular, it highlights the role of race and class in the construction of youth political identities.

At the center of this chapter are three young adults (age 16–19) who were students and graduates of a high-poverty, urban continuation high school in California. These youth were involved in a participatory action research (PAR) project, which culminated in a youth-led social justice class. They designed and taught this class once a week for one semester as part of a regular U.S. Government course for 11th and 12th grade students at their high school. In this chapter, I draw on ethnographic data collected from the project to examine how these three young adults constructed individual and group political identities as they worked together to design, teach, and reflect on their youth-led social justice class. My analysis is based on three research questions:

1. How did the youth articulate the nature and role of political institutions in shaping their lives and the lives of others like them?
2. How did the youth articulate *their own role as agents* in shaping political institutions?
3. How did the youth act on this understanding by representing themselves as various "kinds" of political subjects?

In answering these questions, I illustrate how the three focal youth positioned themselves as members of subordinated social groups, which were defined by race and class. Secondly, I show how they constructed and enacted a shared political identity as *educators* through the process of teaching a youth-led class. Throughout the chapter, I examine the narratives or discourses they drew on to position themselves as particular kinds of political subjects—whether victims of oppression or agents of social change. This chapter does not attempt to evaluate the accuracy of the youth's political beliefs, or to assess the effectiveness of the project as a civic education effort. Instead, the aim of this chapter is to convey the processes through which a particular group of youth articulated and enacted various political identities, in order to contribute to sociocultural theories of identity formation and youth political agency.

Theoretical Framework: Political Identity

The framework of political identity used in this chapter is rooted in sociocultural theory and ethnography, a perspective that focuses on the subjective experiences, interpretations, and locally-constructed knowledge of participants. In contrast to the more common use of tests and surveys to measure civic knowledge and engagement, a sociocultural approach investigates the processes through which young people construct their own political interpretations or meanings (Bhavnani, 1991; Epstein, 1998, 2001; Flanagan & Gallay, 1995; Kirshner, Strobel, & Fernández, 2003; O'Connor, 1997; Rubin, 2007; Seixas, 1993; Stevick & Levinson, 2007). By focusing on processes and practices of meaning-making in particular local contexts, the sociocultural perspective both complements and complexifies the existing research literature on youth civic engagement (Stevick & Levinson, 2007).

This chapter focuses on the processes of youth political identity formation. Rather than viewing "identity" as static or fixed—something that exists inside an individual's head or on their body—I conceptualize identity as a fluid and active concept, what we might think about as an ever-shifting *practice of identification* (see, for example, Bettie, 2003; Gee, 2001; Gregory, 1998; Holland et al., 1998). Gee (2001) offers a useful definition of identity as a way of "acting and interacting as a certain 'kind of person'" (p. 99). He explains: "All people have multiple identities connected not to their internal states but to their performances in society" (p. 99). In this chapter, I define *political* identity as the dimension of identity that informs and governs political action. Following Gee's notion of identity as a way of "acting and interacting as a certain 'kind of person,'" I conceptualize political identity as a way of acting and interacting as a certain "kind" of political subject—be it a responsible voter, victim of oppression, teacher of social justice, or engaged agent of social change. Although political identities are fluid and shifting (like all identities), I begin from the theoretical assumption that they are shaped by and rooted in a subjective sense of "who we are" in relation to political structures and institutions. For this reason, my research questions focus on the ways in which youth conceptualize and articulate the role of political institutions in shaping their lives, and their own role as agents in shaping political institutions.

This study of youth political identity formation is grounded in the theoretical claim that identities are constructs which mediate political agency (Bettie, 2003; Gregory, 1998; Holland et al., 1998). Articulating this relationship between identity and agency, cultural anthropologists Holland, Lachicotte, Skinner, & Cain (1998) explain: "Identities are hard-won standpoints that, however dependent upon social support and however vulnerable to change, make at least a modicum of self-direction possible. They are possibilities for mediating agency" (Holland et al., 1998, p. 4). In a similar vein, Gregory (1998) argues that a precondition for politics is a temporary "fixing" of our ever-shifting identities. In this framework, identities are conceptualized as positions from which individuals act when they engage in democratic publics or take action to change the social conditions of their lives. Thus, by understanding the processes of political identity formation, we can better understand how young people might come to see themselves as democratic citizens, and why they may (or may not) participate in civic life at particular times and in particular ways.

A final point about identity which I take from socio-cultural theory is the idea that identities are not formed in a vacuum. Our identities are shaped in part by our lived experiences, but they are also shaped by the narratives we use to explain and interpret those experiences; we draw from pre-existing discourses or shared meaning systems to make sense of our experience and to position ourselves as particular kinds of people. Bettie (2003) explains: "Discourses, or public meaning systems (political, social science, popular culture, etc.), are the material for identity formation. We deploy these discourses to construct our identities but from a limited range of options. Consequently, some identities are readily made possible while others are not" (p. 54). In short, identity formation occurs in the context of, and in dialogue with, the social and cultural worlds we inhabit. The discourses that are readily available to us offer possible ways to inter-pret and explain our lived civic experiences, making some political iden-tities (or subjectivities) more likely or accessible to us than others. In this chapter, I define *civic experiences* as any lived experience through which we come in contact with state or public institutions, political processes, or structures of political power.

Some scholars have argued that marginalized youth are more likely than privileged youth to draw on "counter-narratives" (Giroux, Lankshear, McLaren, & Peters, 1996) or "vernacular histories" (Barton & Levstik, 1999) to explain and interpret their civic experiences (see also Bhavnani, 1991; Epstein, 2001; Ladson Billings, 2004; Rubin, 2007; Sánchez-Jankowski, 2002). According to these authors, low-income youth and youth of color are likely to experience or witness "disjuncture" (Rubin, 2007) between the ideals and realities of U.S. democracy. In contrast to a domi-nant discourse portraying U.S. democracy as fair, open, and equal, margi-nalized youth directly confront and experience the effects of institutional-ized racism, limited economic opportunities, political disenfranchisement, and (often) police harassment or brutality. In order to make sense of these disjunctures, youth may draw on vernacular histories rooted in community-based knowledge, which diverge from (or contradict) the dominant dis-course of U.S. democracy. However, it is important not to generalize about all marginalized youth on the basis of these studies, as other schol-ars have written about marginalized youth who *do* identify with aspects of the dominant discourse of U.S. democracy (Barton & Levstik, 1999; Mac-Leod, 1995; O'Connor, 1997). Barton and Levstick found, for example, that African American middle school students embraced the dominant narrative of U.S. history as a steady march of progress toward greater equality and expanded equal rights, even while critiquing instances of discrimination.

The lesson we might take from these conflicting findings is that neither our civic experiences alone, nor or our positions within social hierarchies, can determine the political subjectivities and perspectives we develop. Youth with similar civic experiences and positionalities may interpret them in very different ways; their interpretations are shaped in part by the shared meaning systems or discourses to which they have access, as well as those which are valued within their peer groups, homes, and communities. At the same time however, we cannot say that discourses *determine* political identities. In fact, we will see in this chapter how the very same narratives (and counter-narratives) can be employed to support very different political identities and forms of political agency.

Research Context and Methods

The context for this study was a youth-driven participatory research project that involved students and graduates from "Jackson High,"[1] a high-poverty, urban, continuation high school in California. A continuation high school is a school to which students are involuntarily transferred due to poor academic performance; thus, all Jackson students can be described as low-scoring.[2] Of approximately 130 Jackson students at the time of this project, about 80% qualified for free or reduced-priced lunch, 75% were African American, and 97% were students of color.[3] These numbers suggest that, by and large, Jackson students occupied subordinate positions within multiple social and educational hierarchies. Prior to initiating this research, I worked as a classroom teacher at Jackson High and later as a volunteer tutor, mentor program coordinator, and regular substitute teacher. This study of youth political identity emerged through my experience working at the school site and the relationships I maintained with current and former students.

The study used a combined research approach that integrated aspects of participatory action research (PAR) and ethnographic data collection. In choosing this method, I was informed by a growing number of educational scholars who have integrated forms of participatory inquiry with ethnographic or qualitative research, in order to "foreground the engagement of those most affected by unequal schools and social policy" (Oakes, Rogers, & Lipton, 2006, p. 39) in the production of knowledge about, and the quest for solutions to, the persistent patterns of educational inequality that characterize U.S. public education (e.g., Collatos & Morrell, 2003; Dyrness, 2004; Fine, Roberts, & Torre, 2004; Oakes et al., 2006). Participatory action research (PAR) is a process in which marginalized groups, who are negatively impacted by a particular social problem or issue, undertake systematic inquiry about its underlying causes and potential solutions (Hall, 1992; Maguire, 1987; Park, 1993). Through this inquiry process, PAR aims to inspire and facilitate collective political engagement, and ultimately, to empower these groups as political actors in ways that can translate to other arenas of political action. Because these are also the goals of democratic citizenship education, it can be argued that the methods employed in this project were congruent with the area being studied. Rather than observe democratic citizenship education from a distance, this project aimed to implement a modest case study in which the production of new knowledge and its translation into practice were a simultaneous and mutually-reinforcing process. In addition to the goals of democratic citizenship, PAR seeks to produce new and critical knowledge by incorporating the voices and perspectives of those previously silenced or marginalized within academic research (Fine, 1994; Maguire, 1987; Oakes et al., 2006). In this way, PAR is a fitting complement to ethnography, a more traditional research method that seeks to uncover and give voice to the locally-constructed knowledge and perspectives of research subjects—often those from marginalized and underserved communities.

With these understandings of PAR and ethnography in mind, I invited three recent graduates of Jackson High to join me in developing a youth-driven project to investigate the issue of educational inequality and its impacts for Jackson students. The group was named Participatory Action Research Team for Youth (PARTY). For two school years, PARTY members attended weekly two-hour meetings, held first at a local college campus and later at my own home. In addition to myself, eight youth participated in PARTY for varying lengths of time, including four young women and four young men. The youth members ranged in age from 16 to 19[4] and included White, African American, Filipino, and mixed-race (Latino/African American) youth. All of the youth participants were working-class or poor, and came from families that could be described as "educationally disadvantaged": Five had siblings or cousins who had attended or would attend the same continuation high school; none had any close friends or family members with experience at a four-year college or university. I was 26 years old when the project started, and a white woman from a family that could be described as "educationally privileged."[5]

In its first year, PARTY members attended weekly meetings in which we discussed current events, learned about different research techniques, developed and analyzed a survey of Jackson students, and conducted interviews of Jackson students and teachers. Based on this work, PARTY members chose to develop and teach a class at Jackson High on the topic of social justice. The stated aim of the class, which came to be known as the "PARTY class," was to foster greater political awareness and engagement among Jackson students. The group gained permission from the U.S. Government teacher to lead one class per week for one semester, in a U.S. Government course for 11th and 12th grade students. Three PARTY members—D, Suli, and Leila[6]—taught the PARTY class and continued to meet each week to reflect on their teaching and plan upcoming classes. As a participant observer in the project, I took detailed field notes and analytic memos after each weekly PARTY meeting. Second, meetings were audio-taped and transcribed, enabling me to capture longer quotes and conversation dynamics among the youth participants and myself. Third, I conducted and transcribed semi-structured interviews with each PARTY member. Fourth, I observed the weekly youth-led PARTY class and conducted interviews with eight students in the class. Finally, I maintained close working relationships with each of the youth participants and spent hours each week talking on the phone or hanging out with them individually or in smaller, informal groups. These relationships and the time spent together informally enhanced my understanding of the "official" data gathered, and significantly shaped my analysis of the findings.

The method of data analysis involved inductive thematic coding of field notes, meeting transcripts, interview transcripts, and written artifacts collected during the project (such as lesson plans and handouts from the PARTY class, or news articles brought to PARTY meetings for discussion). Working from these documents, I used the constant comparative analysis method (Glaser & Strauss, 1967) to generate codes and categories of analysis. Additionally, using the audio transcripts from weekly PARTY meetings, I conducted line-by-line conversation analysis to explore how the youth defined, articulated, and constructed meanings of social justice and political engagement in the context of weekly PARTY meetings. Data were triangulated by comparing field notes, meeting transcripts, interviews, written artifacts, and classroom observations against each other. Finally, I conducted member checks by sharing my analytic memos and all drafts of writing about the project with the youth PARTY members, throughout the two years of the project and the following year of writing up the results. Through several iterations of what would become a doctoral dissertation, I received and incorporated feedback from the three focal PARTY members.

The PARTY project was simultaneously an educational intervention and a context for ethnographic data collection. This combined model resembles what Oakes and Rogers (2006) have called "social design experiments"; these are educational interventions undertaken for the purpose of generating new knowledge while, simultaneously, engaging participants in social inquiry and action. In writing up the findings of these social design experiments, Oakes and Rogers explain:

> We do not offer our examples as exemplary (or even replicable) cases of equity reform success. Rather, these are carefully grounded narratives that convey the personal experiences of the participants—the identities, histories, and ongoing works of students and teachers—as they seek to disrupt inequitable social environments. (42)

In this chapter, I offer my analysis of the PARTY project in much the same spirit: PARTY was a small and modest project with limited impact, not a "model" to be emulated or replicated. Likewise, PARTY members are not to be seen as "representative" samples of Jackson students or low-scoring urban youth more generally. Instead, the project provided a context for investigating and illuminating how individual and group political identities were negotiated in practice. By working closely *with* the youth on a shared and multi-faceted project of this nature, I was able to gain a richer understanding of the ways in which they defined, articulated, and enacted various political perspectives and identities over the course of the two-year project and beyond. These ethnographic findings serve as the basis of the arguments advanced in this chapter.

Racialized and Classed Political Subjects

My first research question addressed the ways in which PARTY members interpreted the role of political institutions in shaping their lives and the lives of others like them. In this chapter, I focus my analysis on the three PARTY members who designed and taught the social justice class. These were: D, age 20, an African American young man and high school graduate; Suli, age 20, a biracial (Latino and African American) young man and high school graduate; and Leila, age 17, a White young woman and high school junior. Weekly PARTY meetings were a place in which these three young adults tried on, tested, and revised their theories of government and its role in shaping their lives. Through an analysis of their interactions and conversations in these meetings, I illustrate how the youth constructed individual and group political identities as members of subordinated race/class groups, and how they framed these groups as oppositional to both the government and to dominant social groups. I show how these racialized and classed political identities were produced through and informed by group members' casual conversations about current events, their lived civic experiences, and the narratives (or counter-narratives) they employed to interpret their experiences.

Casual conversations about current events, a routine practice in PARTY meetings, were one of the avenues through which the youth constructed and articulated their emerging political identities. Oftentimes, a conversation about the news was already underway before PARTY members even arrived at the meeting. In one typical PARTY meeting, for example, D and Suli arrived a few minutes early. Even before they entered the room, D's voice was audible as it carried through the hallway: "Man, he didn't answer *none* of them questions!" exclaimed D, his voice conveying frustrated anger. D was referring to President Bush, who had given a televised speech the previous night. As the two young men plopped themselves down on opposite sofas, D continued narrating to Suli without a pause. "And I'm sitting there thinking to myself: *Iraq* didn't do it [carry out the September 11, 2001 attacks]! Iraq didn't do it!" Suli listened with wide eyes and careful attention, as if captivated by the unraveling story. "Then when the reporter asked about North Korea, he was like"—D suddenly switched into a voice that impersonated President Bush's inflection and Texas accent—"Yeah, we've been talking to them [North Korea], and we're gonna *peacefully* talk to them. And don't get us wrong, war is our last resort." D broke from his impersonation of President Bush and exclaimed: "Come on, man! War is your *first* resort!"

At the time of this meeting, the U.S. was on the verge of a war in Iraq. The official justification for war was the claim that Iraqi leader Saddam Hussein possessed Weapons of Mass Destruction (WMD). But a possible war in Iraq was also framed as part of the larger War on Terrorism, and members of the Administration made public statements implying a connection between Saddam Hussein and the terrorist attacks on the World Trade Center on September 11, 2001. A well-publicized poll at the time found that 69% of Americans believed it was at least likely that Saddam Hussein was involved in the September 11 attacks (Milbank & Deane, 2003); however, no connection was ever established. Thus, D's insistence that "Iraq didn't do it!" reflected a level of "political knowledge," on at least one important political fact, that surpassed nearly 70% of Americans at the time. As D continued his review of the President's speech, he noted a possible double standard in U.S. foreign policy: Although Iraq's alleged WMD served to justify a pre-emptive war, the same argument did not apply to North Korea, a country also believed to possess WMD. D asked: "Why [are] they not on Korea? Seriously! North Korea's admitted, finally admitted, after years and years of not admitting, that 'We got it [a WMD], and we're not givin' it up. If y'all try to make us give it up, we're going to war.' Iraq ain't even said that!" he concluded, punctuating this last statement in a voice of exasperated frustration.

In a later PARTY meeting, after the U.S.-led invasion of Iraq and the failure to discover the alleged WMD, Leila commented in a meeting:

> Leila: You know what's funny? It's like, they were talking about the weapons, and then it's like, they haven't found any, and so now they changed it into like "we're freeing the Iraqi people." And it's just like, Why didn't anyone notice how that just totally switched around?
> D: They don't even want the UN [United Nations weapons inspectors] to come in. They want their *own* people to come in. That's why I think that they're gonna plant something. They'll be like [*feigning surprise*] "Oh look! We *found* something!
> Leila: Yeah, exactly!

D's suggestion that the U.S. government might plant a false weapon met with no shock or opposition from the others. His implicit lack of trust in political leaders was taken for granted by PARTY members. In the following week, D made fun of Americans who trusted politicians about WMD in Iraq. In a precise standard or "white" American accent, he mocked: "It *has* to be right! It *has* to be right! Our government wouldn't lie to us!" His impersonation sent Suli and Leila into a fit of laughter. Switching back to his regular voice, D concluded: "Shit! They got more reason *to* lie than *not* to lie!"

These represent only a few of many similar discussions in PARTY meetings about the U.S. role in Iraq and the War on Terrorism. These conversations illustrate that PARTY members did not simply report what they saw on the news, but engaged critically with the substance of news—for example, drawing a comparison between foreign policies with Iraq and North Korea, and identifying inconsistencies in the president's arguments. Their conversations also illustrate a deep lack of trust in the current presidential administration. Mistrust of the president and his administration was common at that time, particularly among opponents of the Iraq war, and the youth were certainly drawing from discourses that were readily circulated by these opponents in what was a very polarized and polarizing social period. However, D's comments suggest a mistrust that extends beyond individual politicians, to include a wider set of political institutions. He even went so far as to mock those Americans who took government authorities at their word, suggesting that those who believed "our government wouldn't lie to us" were naïve (and also, by way of his voice impersonations, he suggested they were probably white). This criticism suggests his view that lying is one thing the government does routinely. Here, we can also see how "the government" was depicted as a singular, faceless institution which was not to be trusted. This depiction of "the government" was frequently reproduced in PARTY meetings.

Mistrust of "the government" was reflected in the youth's narratives about the present as well as the past. For example, D wondered:

Why would God bless this country? This country was created off evil. Violence, death. How many Indians did they kill? They have no record. How many Black people did they kill? They have no record. How many Asians did they kill? They have no record. [. . .] That's why I say God wouldn't bless this country, because this country is evil.

In this statement, D articulated a historical narrative that put racial violence at the center of U.S. history and national formation. This view of

U.S. democracy runs counter to the master narrative most often taught in U.S. schools: a master narrative that depicts the government's role as *expanding* democratic rights, and of history as a march of progress toward greater and greater equality. Instead, he depicted the government's role as *maintaining*, rather than reducing, racial subordination and violence. And, he suggested that state-sponsored violence against racial minorities was a constant feature of U.S. history, rather than diminishing over the years.

Within the PARTY group, counter-narratives like this one were constructed, shared, and affirmed through talk. The youth drew upon these counter-narratives to interpret their varied civic experiences, particularly those that revealed disjunctures between the ideals and realities of U.S. democracy. For D and Suli, these civic experiences included their encounters with law enforcement and the criminal justice system. These encounters served as key points of reference when articulating an identity as members of subordinated racial groups. In one weekly meeting, from their relaxed positions on two couches, the three PARTY members flipped through an educational comic book designed to teach young adults about their rights if stopped by police or arrested, such as the right to consult a lawyer or not to consent to a search (Midnight Special Law Collective). Leila had acquired the book at an anti-war protest the preceding weekend, and brought it to the meeting to share with others. In the first story, a young African American man is arrested while waiting for a bus, for no apparent reason, and taken to the police station. After a search determines he has no drugs and very little money on him, he is nevertheless kept in jail overnight without knowing what he is charged with. As the three PARTY members read through the book in silence, Leila asked, "Does this stuff really happen?" Suli sat up on the couch—where he had been comfortably reading in a lying-down position—and looked at Leila, replying "What stuff?" Leila continued, "Like, the cops just picking people up for no reason." Both Suli and D looked inquisitively at Leila, as if waiting for her to elaborate on the question. She proceeded:

> Leila: Is it a little bit over exaggerated at all? Or do you think . . . I mean, I don't know.
> D: What?
> Leila: I mean it seems real ignorant of me to say that, but I don't really. . .
> Suli: What?

Leila: It seems really over-exaggerated. But then, cops do—
Suli: Cops picking you up for no reason?
Leila: Yeah. People getting arrested—
Suli: Do you want me to tell you a story?

Without waiting for a response, Suli embarked on a story about a time he was pulled over by an officer for making an illegal left turn. After he and his car were searched, Suli was taken to the police station and held several hours. His story provoked a slew of others about unfair arrests and harassment by police. D recalled a time he was stopped and searched "with guns pulled," and brought to the station for riding his bicycle at night without a light. Suli told of a time he was handcuffed and brought to the station for suspected robbery, and then released with no charges. Both recalled a night they were together, walking with a group of friends when a police officer "threw [their friend's] head into the gate," provoking the youth to call for an ambulance. As they told these stories, D and Suli emphasized that, from their perspective, they had done nothing to warrant this treatment except "fit the description" of a criminal. The young men relayed these stories with a combination of outrage and resignation. It was as if, despite their injustice, these kinds of events were taken for granted as normal and natural; they did not evoke the shock we might expect in response to clear violations of civil liberties and Fourth Amendment protections.

Conversations like this one illustrated the gap between PARTY members' experiences with and assumptions about law enforcement. To Leila (who is white and female), the events depicted in the comic book seemed almost too exaggerated to be "realistic," and she was uncertain whether to interpret the story as a *literal* example of a common occurrence or a symbolic illustration of an extreme case. Yet to D and Suli (who are black or biracial and male), there was nothing unrealistic about the story; they insisted that events like this occurred frequently and systematically. This episode from a PARTY meeting reveals some of the ways that race worked independently of class in structuring the youth's encounters with law enforcement and the criminal justice system. Much research suggests that D and Suli were not unique in this respect: In marginalized communities of color, police harassment and abuse are commonplace (Flanagan & Gallay, 1995; Kwon, 2006; Lopez, 2003; Pintado-Vertner & Chang, 2000; Rubin, 2007; Youth Force Coalition, 2000), and stories about these encounters are shared over and over among friends, families, and neighbors. For D and Suli, these stories were a key point of reference used to justify their mistrust of "the government" and to position themselves as members of subordinated racial groups.[7] Their belief that the government worked against their interests and the interests of others like them (defined as other members of subordinated racial groups), was continually reaffirmed and reproduced through the stories told about the criminal justice system.

Leila brought a different set of civic experiences and a different set of discourses to explain and interpret her experiences. In describing the role of government in shaping her life and lives of others like her, she often drew from a Marxist critique of capitalism. In PARTY meetings, for example, Leila asserted: "To have a rich, you have to have a poor, that's how capitalism works," and, from another meeting: "There needs to be a certain amount of poor people for capitalism to work. [. . .] The government, just all the way from the top to the bottom, it's just kind of racist and classist." Leila identified herself as a member of the working class, and claimed in an interview that "We could do *so much* if we could just unite. I mean, we're all workers, we're all the working class. We could really shut the system down." Leila's self-identification as a member of the "working class" is unique given the lack of a public discourse on class in U.S. society (Bettie, 2003). Rather than drawing from her lived civic experiences, Leila often cited her friends as the source of her political perspectives and theories. She described herself and her friends as activists who were committed to animal rights, veganism, and (in some cases) anarchism. During the project, Leila also became involved in the growing anti-war movement and attended several anti-war protests with her friends (who, she claimed, were mostly white and out of high school). Leila's exposure to counter-hegemonic political ideologies through her friendship group—and her growing involvement in the anti-war movement—provided an analytic framework for making sense of her lived experience as a working class girl.

Despite their many differences, Leila echoed Suli and D by identifying herself as a member of a subordinated social group, and depicting the government as a singular and powerful institution working against her interests and the interests of others like her (defined as other members of the working class). I do not mean to suggest that the experiences of race and class subordination are equivalent or that they were interpreted as equivalent within the PARTY group. Instead, I argue the youth *constructed* a shared group identity within the context of their participation in PARTY.

This was achieved through their use of discourses that both recognized difference and affirmed common interest; by drawing from these discourses they positioned themselves, collectively, as members of *subordinated social groups* in opposition to the government and to dominant social groups. Where they found common ground, it was in their portrayal of government as a singular and powerful institution that worked against their interests and the interests of others like them: "Others like them" were defined, implicitly, as other members of subordinated social groups, delineated by race and/or class. In this way, the youth constructed and affirmed a collective identity as racialized and classed political subjects.

Constructing a Political Identity as Educators

As we saw in the previous section, PARTY members conceptualized political institutions in the singular, as "the government," and described this entity as a powerful agent that worked against their interests and the interests of others like them. But how did they conceptualize their own agency within this structure? In this section, I illustrate how PARTY members constructed a group political identity as *educators*—an identity that was informed by their use of counter-narratives to describe the role of the government and social movements in shaping the course of U.S. history. Although each PARTY member brought his or her own unique motivations for teaching, they all portrayed the PARTY class as an act of political engagement, and discursively connected it to a larger goal of social change. Yet, their political identities were shifting and fluid, and PARTY members easily fluctuated between positioning themselves as empowered agents of social change and powerless victims of oppression. In either case, however, they employed the same historical counter-narratives about the nature and role of the government in shaping U.S. history and society. Whether identifying as change agents or as victims of oppression, the group members consistently reproduced and reaffirmed their individual and collective political identities as racialized and classed political subjects, positioned in opposition to the government and to dominant social groups.

When they chose to teach a social justice class at Jackson High, PARTY members portrayed this activity as an act of political engagement. The class was not (at least not explicitly) intended to raise students' academic achievement or their commitment to school success. Instead, PARTY members described it as a political intervention meant to build solidarity with, and inspire civic engagement among, other members of subordinated race/class groups like themselves. In articulating their goals for the class, PARTY members discursively linked their teaching to their own historical understandings of social change, and they reiterated their identities as racialized and classed political subjects. This was especially the case for D and Leila, who each articulated well-developed counternarratives about the government's role in history and society when they talked about their role as educators in the PARTY class. For example, when asked in an interview what he wanted students to learn in the class, D responded:

> I want to teach [students] that it's power in numbers. If you come, millions and millions and millions, they not gonna be able to stop us, even the National Guard. If *everybody* in this country believed in *one* thing, and actually stepped up the plate, we're unstoppable. Even if minorities just come together. And, we just on different sides, minorities and then high class rich people, they're on the other side. We're unstoppable! Nothing can stop us! That's what Martin Luther King was preaching, that it's power in numbers. That's why he actually started all them walks and protests and all that.

In this statement, D situates the PARTY class as part of a larger struggle for collective social change. He identifies himself and students as members of a subordinated racial group that stood in opposition to the government and to "high class rich people," and he articulates a theory of change based on the "power of numbers"—the idea that change comes through mass social movements in which members of subordinated racial groups ("the minorities) struggle *against* the government and dominant social groups ("high class rich people" protected by the National Guard). He draws on his own historical understanding of the Civil Rights Movement, conjuring a mythical image of Martin Luther King Jr. as the individual who "started" its many walks, protests, and demonstrations.[8] Later in the same interview, D elaborated further on this goal:

> D: I'll teach them [students]. And that's the only way the cycle will keep going. That's the only reason why we actually know Martin Luther King and Malcolm X and every other Black activist and White

activist, because somebody taught them. They decided to *talk*, and tell other people. And if people keep on doing that for another hundred years, we *will* see some change.

Once again, D conjures the images of Civil Rights leaders Martin Luther King and Malcolm X—both African American men like himself—and symbolically associates them with his own role as educator in the PARTY class. He situates the PARTY class within a long historical tradition of popular education, and claims that if this cycle of teaching and learning continues, the world will eventually have to change.

Like D, Leila expressed a well-developed counter-narrative about social movements as an engine of change to contextualize her role as educator in the PARTY class. For example, when asked in an interview what she wanted students to learn in the class, Leila explained: "I want [students] to know that we really do, like, the lower class people really do have the power. If everyone would just work together, we could shut the system down. We really could." In this statement, Leila identifies herself and students collectively as members of the working class. Like D, she emphasizes that this subordinated social group has the real power to change society even if they are positioned on the bottom of the sociopolitical hierarchy. Both Leila and D constructed their role as educator to mean raising the consciousness of subordinated race/class groups (of which they were members), in order to inspire them toward political engagement. Additionally, they both defined political engagement collective action, undertaken by subordinated social groups, to mean struggle *against* "the government" or "the system," rather than working within its structures and institutions.

In contrast, Suli offered shifting and uncertain statements of his goals for the class. At times he emphasized his desire to teach students how to participate within existing political institutions, such as learning how to vote or attend and speak at a city council meeting. At other times he emphasized the psychological benefits of providing students with a positive learning experience. He claimed, for example, "My main goal for teaching is like, they [students] will see us and be like "OK they gave us all this information and now I'm gonna use it.'" To explain how he thought students might use the information from class, Suli offered that "they might know how to vote, [which is] something that they wouldn't necessarily look at before." (However, it should be noted that the PARTY class never offered explicit lessons to help students understand how to register and vote, or how to choose from among different candidates or parties.) Suli also mentioned that he wanted students to see that "everything can change," and cited the PARTY class itself as an example of change that was already occurring. Despite the different motivations for teaching they expressed during interviews, in meetings the PARTY members constructed one *shared* goal for the class: "voicing opinions." The ability to formulate and voice political opinions emerged as a clear and simple goal that every PARTY member could identify with. Referring to students, Suli explained: "they've *got* opinions, but sometimes they just don't voice it. They might think these topics we're talking about don't affect them. But they *do* affect them. And [in the PARTY class] they might start to see that."

In general, then, PARTY members articulated the role of educator as a political identity and described their teaching of the PARTY class as a form of political engagement. They embraced their role as educators and framed it as a *politicized* identity in the sense that educating students was explicitly aimed at generating social critique and change. Yet, although they identified themselves as agents of change—and took action in the form of educating to bring about social change—their political identities remained fluid and shifting throughout the two-year project. At times, PARTY members individually and collectively expressed a sense of social responsibility and political agency *as* racialized and classed political subjects. At other times, they expressed sincere doubts about the possibility of changing an entrenched system of inequality, and identified themselves as victims situated at the bottom of multiple social hierarchies. In either case, however, the youth drew from the same well of narratives and counter-narratives about the nature and role of the government in shaping their lives and U.S. society. These same narratives were readily employed to justify taking action as well as to justify inaction.

For example, in one PARTY meeting I posed the question of whether the class should incorporate more positive or inspiring examples of social change. My suggestion came in response to a student comment, who had claimed the PARTY class made him "depressed" due to its focus on social problems and inequalities. D quickly pointed out: "If they're feeling depressed that just means they're sucking up the knowledge that we're giving them!" Leila and Suli agreed that feeling "depressed" was a good sign because it indicated students were learning and "paying attention" in the class. Still, I pushed them to include some lessons on "positive examples of social change" to balance out the curriculum. Leila agreed and suggested the next class be "positive." The following exchange ensued:

> D: What is positive?
> Leila: What?
> D: What is positive?
> Leila: Making your word, like, making yourself heard.
> Suli: What was the result of it?
> Leila: Being on the front page of the newspaper, that's positive 'cause that's giving information to the people.

In this exchange (Leila explained later in the meeting), she was referring to the anti-war protests that were a regular feature in U.S. cities across the country (and in which she had participated). For her, these protests were an example of positive change because people were making their voices heard and even making it into the newspapers. Yet Suli was not convinced that protest alone was an example of positive change. He pressed Leila by asking her, "What was the result of it?" Indeed, despite an unprecedented level of protest both within the U.S. and internationally—and despite Leila's attendance at anti-war marches, demonstrations or vigils nearly every week—the U.S. had entered a war in Iraq; the protests appeared to have made no difference in shaping actual policy. Leila suggested that being in the newspaper provided validation of the protesters' cause and a public record of their dissent, therefore representing an example of positive change. D and Suli were not convinced, however. Suli responded: "Real talk, I don't see nothing positive in my neighborhood. All I see is crack-heads walking back and forth."

In this conversation, Leila made an unsuccessful attempt to convince D and Suli that collective protest offered an inspiring example of social change. In asking "what is positive?" the two young men suggested that there were no positive examples of change and, instead, students in the PARTY class *should* be depressed about what they were learning. Yet D's insistence that current large-scale political protests were unimportant seemed to be in stark contrast to his previous statements about the importance of collective action and his repeated references to the Civil Rights Movement as an inspiration for his teaching. His contrasting position on anti-war protests could be a result of the anti-war movement's racially white public face. Indeed, the predominantly white representatives of the anti-war movement were not consistent with D's depictions of collective action undertaken by "all the minorities" coming together against "high class rich people." The anti-war movement offered no clear model for him to engage *as* a racialized African American political subject *for* a racially defined political cause. While in other moments, D supported and identified with African American celebrities who spoke out against the war, including actor Danny Glover and the hip-hop group Black Eyed Peas, he also noted that their capacity to "voice their opinions" was a result of their being rich and famous, and cited this as the reason that he wanted to become a rapper himself. He seemed to suggest that only by gaining celebrity status could he, as an African American male, exercise meaningful political voice. Until he became a famous rapper, there was nothing he could do and no way to politically engage.

In another PARTY meeting, Leila argued that people who are not "being active in society" had no right to complain about it. Suli concurred: "Same thing for people that don't vote. How [are] you gonna not vote, and then be mad about all that's going bad?" To this, D argued back: "Man, that's built up over *years!* They feel that it's no point in voting . . . and it's true!" Here, D suggests that voting is pointless because the problems in society are "built up over years." If these problems are rooted in deep historical inequalities and systemically entrenched, then casting a vote within the current system is an insufficient way to make any real difference. Still, Suli challenged D: "But if you didn't voice your opinion though, then how can you really be mad?" D shot back angrily: "I'd rather *voice* my opinion than go vote!" The question raised through this exchange was whether voting constituted a means of exercising political voice: Was voting an avenue for expressing political opinions? Or was voting simply an expression of buying into a system which was inherently flawed?

In response to D's comment, Leila claimed, "I feel to a certain extent there is no point to [voting] because there's so many scandals within it," and recalled the disenfranchisement of many African American voters during the 2000 presidential election in Florida (and elsewhere). The youth had witnessed this election when they were old enough to understand what it meant and it was still very present in their collective historical memory. I asked the group whether encouraging voting should be a learning goal for the PARTY class, and Suli acknowledged: "I know the majority of people in the [PARTY] class aren't, even with the knowledge that we're giving them and them having an opinion, still aren't gonna vote." D responded: "How [are] we gonna teach them to vote when *we* don't vote?" "Yeah, I didn't vote either!" Suli admitted.

In this conversation, PARTY members struggled to define exactly what forms of political engagement they should seek to promote in their role as educators. They expressed a collective ambivalence about the role and potential of voting in elections as a means of exercising political voice. Even Leila, who typically supported voting most vocally in the group, expressed her own doubts about whether there was "a point" to voting, given the inherent inequalities she perceived in the election system. It is important to point out that each of youth's positions on voting and other forms of political engagement remained fluid throughout the project; for example, in a different meeting D claimed that "once [students in the PARTY class] actually analyze the knowledge, they'll know that voting *is* the only way to change." However, in this particular conversation, PARTY members accepted it as normal and natural that "the majority of people in the class aren't [. . .] gonna vote," and they exhibited a degree of resignation about the slim possibilities of change—a stark contrast from earlier claims that "the people have the power." To justify their resignation, they employed the same historical counter-narratives that also inspired their commitment to social action: emphasizing the social inequalities that have been "built up over years" and the systematic nature of racial inequalities built into democratic elections in the U.S. These same historical counter-narratives were used, at times, to inspire a commitment to political action and, at other times, to justify inaction. In short, their interpretations of the government's role in shaping past and present U.S. society were readily employed to support very different forms of political agency.

Conclusions and Implications: Identity, Agency, and Democratic Citizenship Education

Much research on civic attitudes and engagement measures students' responses to direct questions elicited at one point in time—whether through a survey, test, or interview. Even longitudinal studies that may follow students over a longer time period of time can only capture their responses to a direct question at the moment in which the question is posed. While such studies continue to generate important insights about overall levels and kinds of civic attitudes and engagement, they do not help us understand the messy processes through which young people negotiate and interpret their lived civic experiences, or how they wrestle with political contradictions in the context of their everyday lives. In contrast, the PARTY project engaged a small group of urban youth for a period of two school years, and used ethnographic data collection procedures to capture how they wrestled with political questions in the real-life context of developing, teaching, and reflecting on a youth-led class. This ethnographic approach allows us to illuminate the complexities of youth's political perspectives and the inconsistencies between how they respond to direct interview questions, and how they behave or talk in other local and lived social contexts. It also illuminates the shifting and fluid nature of political identities, enabling us to understand how seamlessly and quickly individuals may shift from one subjectivity to another.

The three PARTY members who were the focus of this study constructed a collective political identity as racialized and classed political subjects. In articulating the role of political institutions in their lives, the youth identified themselves as members of subordinated race/class groups, and positioned these groups in opposition to the government and to dominant social groups. In general, the youth depicted "the government" as a powerful and unitary agent that worked against their interests and the interests of others like them, and their mistrust of government incorporated both politicians and political institutions generally. The youth drew primarily on counter-narratives to interpret their lived civic experiences as marginalized low-income youth and/or youth of color. These counter-narratives framed the government's role as *maintaining*, rather than *reducing*, social inequalities, and served to strengthen and affirm the youth's political identities as racialized and classed political subjects and educators. This chapter has argued that such counter-narratives sometimes led the youth to identify as powerless victims for whom political engagement was pointless and meaningless. But at other times, the youth drew from identical counter-narratives to identify themselves as empowered agents of social change. In both cases, however, the youth consistently used language to reaffirm, for themselves and others, a subjective sense of themselves as racialized and classed political subjects.

It is important to emphasize that I do not claim these racialized and classed subject positions were fixed within the individual PARTY members. My analysis in this chapter examines only what occurred *in the context* of the PARTY group, as manifested through weekly PARTY meetings and individual interviews about the project. Within this specific context, I argue the youth participants constructed and consistently reaffirmed a shared group identity as racialized and classed political subjects, and I seek to illustrate *how* this collective identity was produced and reinforced through the youth's use of language. In addition, I explore the ways in which this collective identity informed the exercise of political agency within this particular context. I conclude that both a stance of powerlessness as well as a stance of empowerment or activism were possible outcomes of their racialized and classed political identities. I show how the youth easily shifted between these two stances while drawing from the same well of narratives and counter-narratives about the relationship between political institutions and their own lives.

I maintain the possibility that each of these youth would have behaved differently if the composition of group members had been different. I also hold that D, Suli, and Leila quite certainly exhibited different political identities within the different contexts of their lives—whether their workplaces, schools, homes, or friendship groups. This study did not attempt to trace their shifting identities across these different contexts, but rather to examine one particular context in detail, in order to shed light on the processes through which political interpretations are constructed and negotiated through language and dialogue. This chapter's focus on youth political identity is grounded in the theoretical assumption that identities—despite their fluid and shifting character—are constructs which mediate political agency. By illuminating the processes through which young people create, revise, and negotiate distinct political identities, we will be better equipped to design educational experiences that enable or facilitate more active forms of political agency.

Notes

1. A pseudonym.
2. I choose the term *low-scoring* instead of the more common *low-achieving* to highlight that the basis of this label is past performance on school-based assessments, rather than other kinds of achievements.
3. Figures are rounded to protect the anonymity of the school.
4. Ages at the start of the two-year project.
5. My own multiple privileges compared with the youth members was critical in shaping the nature of research process and my relationships with youth. Space limitations prevent me from elaborating on these relationships here.

6. Pseudonyms.
7. Law enforcement and the criminal justice system are points of contact between many young people and the state. Other scholars have argued that a pattern of hostile relations with law enforcement within low-income communities of color serves as the basis of deep (and justified) mistrust of government institutions (Flanagan & Gallay, 1995; Lopez, 2003; Rubin, 2007; Sánchez-Jankowski, 2002).
8. This historical understanding of the Civil Rights Movement overemphasizes the role of individual leaders or heroes like Martin Luther King, Jr., and downplays the role of ordinary citizens and local-level community organizers; it was these latter groups who, for the most part, carried out the necessary work of movement-building that initiated the Civil Rights Movement (Payne, 1995). D's Civil Rights narrative, which elevates the role of individual leaders and erases the role of community organizing and movement-building, reflects the dominant discourse about the Civil Rights Movement as well as most mainstream approaches to teaching about the movement in schools (Menkart, Murray, & View, 2004; Payne, 1995). A more detailed analysis of Civil Rights narratives expressed in the PARTY group, and their inherent contradictions, is beyond the scope of this chapter.

References

Barton, K., & Levstik, L. (1999). It wasn't a good part of history: National identity and students' explanations of historical significance. *Teachers College Record, 99*(3), 478–513.

Bettie, J. (2003). *Women without class: Girls, race, and identity*. Berkeley: University of California Press.

Bhavnani, K.-K. (1991). *Talking politics: A psychological framing for views from youth in Britain*. Cambridge: Cambridge University Press.

Collatos, A., & Morrell, E. (2003). Apprenticing urban youth as critical researchers: Implications for increasing equity and access in diverse urban schools. In B. Rubin & E. Silva (Eds.), *Critical voices in school reform: Students living through change* (pp. 113–131). New York: Routledge Falmer.

Dyrness, A. (2004). *Speaking truth to power: Immigrant parents, progressive educators, and the politics of change in an urban school*. Unpublished doctoral dissertation. Berkeley: University of California.

Epstein, T. (1998). Deconstructing differences in African-American and European-American adolescents' perspectives on U.S. history. *Curriculum Inquiry, 28*(4), 397–423.

Epstein, T. (2001). Adolescents' perspective on racial diversity in U.S. history: Case studies from an urban classroom. *American Educational Research Journal, 37*, 185–214.

Fine, M. (1994). Dis-stance and other stances: Negotiations of power inside feminist research. In A. Gitlin (Ed.), *Power and method* (pp. 13–35). New York: Routledge.

Fine, M., Roberts, R. A., & Torre, M. E. (2004). *Echoes of Brown: Youth documenting and performing the legacy of Brown v. Board of Education with DVD*. New York: Teachers College Press.

Flanagan, C., & Gallay, L. (1995). Reframing the meaning of "political" in research with adolescents. *Perspectives on Political Science, 24*(1), 34–41.

Gee, J. (2001). Identity as an analytic lens for research in education. *Review of Research in Education, 25,* 99–125.

Giroux, H., Lankshear, C., McLaren, P., & Peters, M. (Eds.). (1996). *Counter narratives: Cultural studies and critical pedagogies in postmodern spaces.* New York: Routledge.

Glaser, B., & Strauss, A. (1967). *The discovery of grounded theory: Strategies for qualitative research.* Chicago: Aldine.

Gregory, S. (1998). *Black corona.* Princeton, NJ: Princeton University Press.

Hall, B. (1992). From margins to center? The development and purpose of participatory research. *The American Sociologist, 23*(4), 15–28.

Holland, D., Lanchicotte, W., Skinner, D., & Cain, C. (1998). *Identity and agency in cultural worlds.* Cambridge, MA: Harvard University Press.

Kirshner, B., Strobel, K., & Fernández, M. (2003). *Critical civic engagement among urban youth, Penn GSE perspectives on urban education* (Vol. 2).

Kwon, S. (2006). Youth of color organizing for juvenile justice. In S. Ginwright, P. Noguera, & J. Cammarota (Eds.), *Beyond resistance: Youth activism and community change* (pp. 197–214). New York: Routledge.

Ladson Billings, G. (2004). Culture versus citizenship: The challenge of racialized citizenship in the United States. In J. Banks (Ed.), *Diversity and citizenship education* (pp. 99–126). San Francisco: Jossey-Bass.

Lopez, N. (2003). *Hopeful girls, troubled boys.* New York: Routledge.

MacLeod, J. (1995). *Ain't no makin' it.* Boulder, CO: Westview Press.

Maguire, P. (1987). *Doing participatory research: A feminist approach.* Amherst, MA: Center for International Education.

Menkart, D., Murray, A., & View, J. (Eds.). (2004). *Putting the movement back into civil rights teaching.* Washington, DC: Teaching for Change.

Midnight Special Law Collective. *Know your rights comix.* Retrieved September 11, 2006, from http://www.midnightspecial.net/comic/issue1/en/page1.html

Milbank, D., & Deane, C. (2003, September 6). Hussein link to 9/11 lingers in many minds. *Washington Post,* p. A1.

O'Connor, C. (1997). Dispositions toward (collective) struggle and educational resilience in the inner city: A case analysis of six African-American high school students. *American Educational Research Journal, 34*(4), 593–629.

Oakes, J., Rogers, J., & Lipton, M. (2006). *Learning power: Organizing for education and justice.* New York: Teachers College Press.

Park, P. (1993). What is participatory research: A theoretical and methodological perspective. In P. Park, M. Brydon-Miller, B. Hall, & T. Jackson (Eds.), *Voices of change: Participatory research in the United States and Canada.* Westport, CT: Bergin & Garvey.

Payne, C. (1995). *I've got the light of freedom: The organizing tradition and the Mississippi freedom struggle.* Berkeley: University of California Press.

Pintado-Vertner, R., & Chang, J. (2000). *The war on youth.* Retrieved September 8, 2006, from http://www.arc.org/C_Lines/CLArchive/story2_4_01.html

Rubin, B. C. (2007). There's still no justice: Youth civic identity development amid distinct school and community contexts. *Teachers College Record, 109*(2).

Sánchez-Jankowski, M. (2002). Minority Youth and civic engagement: The impact of group relations. *Applied Developmental Studies, 6*(4), 237–245.

Seixas, P. (1993). Historical understanding among adolescents in a multicultural setting. *Curriculum Inquiry, 23*(3), 301–327.

Stevick, E. D., & Levinson, B. A. (Eds.). (2007). *Reimagining civic education: How diverse societies form democratic citizens.* Lanham, MD: Rowman & Littlefield.

Youth Force Coalition. (2000). *Schools not jails: A report on the northern california youth movement against proposition 21.*

CHAPTER 5

Service–Learning as a Promising Approach to High School Civic Engagement

Susan Root and Shelley H. Billig

Introduction

An informed, involved citizenry is essential to the sustainability of democratic societies. Researchers (e.g., Carnegie Corporation of New York and the Center for Information and Research on Civic Learning and Engagement, 2003; Patrick, 2003; Torney-Purta & Vermeer Lopez, 2006) have found that competent democratic citizenship has four prerequisites:

1. *Knowledge*, for example, an understanding of democratic principles, governmental and political institutions, major political and social issues;
2. *Skills*, such as the ability to analyze alternative positions on an issue, engage in wise deliberation, and use civic discourse and political action for one's own benefit and the greater good;
3. *Values and attitudes* needed for constructive engagement in political system and civic life, such as efficacy and tolerance; and
4. *Civic involvement and intentions to become civically involved*, for example in following the news, monitoring the performance of public officials, taking a stand on issues, or community service.

National assessments of students' civic knowledge and skills indicate that many youth arc failing to master these prerequisites. Results of the most recent National Assessment of Educational Progress (NAEP) civics assessment, for example, showed that only 32% of 12th graders scored at the proficient level or higher (Lutkus & Weiss, 2007). In a study conducted by UCLA, only 28% of entering college freshmen in the fall of 2000 expressed an interest in "keeping up-to-date on political affairs," down from 60% in 1966. Adolescents and young adults report less trust in the political system than older adults (Rahm & Transue, 1998).

Minority and disadvantaged youth perform even more poorly on quantitative indicators of civic development than their majority counterparts. For example, in recent studies, African-American and Hispanic youth scored lower on measures of civic knowledge, voting, voter registration, political discussion, political efficacy and trust than their white peers (Lopez, 2002; Lutkus & Weiss, 2007).

Schools represent an important agent for developing competent citizens, but currently face obstacles that challenge their ability to do so. Because of the No Child Left Behind Act of 2001, many teachers are reticent to address any subject matter other than reading and mathematics because they face strong accountability requirements for progress in these core subjects. Educational leaders have suggested that they may be more willing to address citizenship development if the strategies that allow them to are somehow connected to core academic subjects. Nearly half of all public schools in the United States and a third of all high schools have both sought and embraced an approach called service-learning that enables them to integrate the teaching of core subject matter while promoting civic engagement (Skinner & Chapman, 1999).

Service-learning is an instructional approach in which young people perform service to meet a real community need as a way of learning important curricular objectives. By providing this service, students learn about their roles and responsibilities in a democracy and how to become more civically engaged. By connecting the service to academic standards, teachers are able to help students acquire specific knowledge and skills needed to perform well on measures of accountability.

The purpose of this chapter is to present results from a national study of the impacts of service-learning on high school students' civic engagement. The data demonstrate that service-learning can be effective at revitalizing citizenship education, especially when particular design components are in place. The chapter begins with a discussion of service-learning, its potential for promoting civic engagement, and challenges associated with its adoption.

The study is then presented, first with an explanation of the methodology and then with findings and illustrations of best practice.

Service-Learning as a Promising Approach to Civic Development

The practice of service-learning typically requires students to engage in a cycle that includes preparation, action, reflection, and celebration/demonstration. *Preparation* refers to gathering information and planning a service activity. In the preparation stage, students typically conduct a community needs assessment and/or research to identify issues of concern to be addressed through the provision of community service. In high schools, young people frequently begin by brainstorming a list of social concerns, such as homelessness, pollution, illiteracy, transportation needs, voters' rights, or any other challenge that emerges. They conduct a needs assessment to supplement and focus their lists. Teachers serve as important facilitators in this process by helping students conduct research to understand the underlying causes of the issue and solutions that are realistic and doable in a certain amount of time. Students then plan *action*, wherein they determine what type of services they can provide to address the challenges that they chose for a focus. Sometimes students work within existing community agencies and sometimes they develop their own approaches. Often, students provide direct service, such as tutoring to children in low-performing schools, working with the elderly to collect oral histories about a community or event, or building a nature trail in a local park or a playground for a local elementary school. The types of service projects in which students can engage are virtually limitless.

Before, during, and after service, students engage in *reflection* activities. These activities may include journal writing, debriefing with other groups or community members, developing a research paper or debate topic, creating storyboards or videotapes of events, or producing nearly any type of oral or written product that conveys typically both a summary of what happened and a connection to cause/effect and feelings. Finally, students participate in *celebration and demonstration*, where they or others acknowledge the effort and show results, often in a public forum, such as an assembly or presentation to parents and community members.

Service-learning activities, by definition, have the framework of preparation-action-reflection-demonstration, but the practice of service-learning is not typically guided by a specific curriculum. Rather, it is more organic, promoting student-centered learning by having students determine the content of service, facilitated by teachers who oftentimes outline the planning and reflection activities. Service-learning thus takes multiple forms and has multiple potential outcomes, making it both appealing to young people and teachers because there is so much room for creativity.

Research on service-learning in K–12 schools has shown positive effects of participation on various elements of effective citizenship, including

- Concern for social issues (Metz, McLellan, & Youniss, 2000; Yamauchi, Billig, Meyer, & Hofschire, 2006);
- Respect for diversity (Melchior, 1999; RMC Research, 2005; Yamuchi, et al., 2006);
- Concern for others' welfare (Billig, 2000; Scales, Blyth, Berkas, & Kielsmeier, 2000);
- Commitment to service (Billig, 2001; Melchior, 1999; RMC Research, 2005).

However, studies also show that service-learning has a smaller impact on the acquisition of other civic competencies, such as knowledge of democratic principles or political institutions and processes (Walker, 2002). Some researchers have even expressed doubt as to whether service-learning, as currently constructed, is able to promote these outcomes. For example, according to Niemi (2000), many service-learning programs take a "decidedly nonpolitical, possibly even anti-political" stance. Kahne and Westheimer (2003) argued that service-learning programs may even interfere with civic development by failing to provide youth with an understanding of the structural sources of individual distress or the role of "collective efforts to improve policies and institutions" (p. 36).

The study presented here shows that service-learning can indeed be effective in promoting development of civic knowledge, skills, and dispositions. However, the study also indicates that educators must be deliberate in their designs in order for this to occur.

Case Studies

From 2003 to 2005, the authors and their colleagues conducted a quasi-experimental investigation of the impact of participation in service-learning on high school students' civic and academic engagement. Funded by the

Carnegie Corporation of New York, the research included multiple quantitative and qualitative measures of paired treatment and comparison groups.

Site Selection. Study sites were identified by nomination from state Learn and Serve directors, civic organizations, and literature reviews. Schools were selected to be in the sample if they

1. Focused on service-learning as a primary vehicle for teaching and learning of a specific subject matter;
2. Demonstrated at least some evidence that quality indicators, such as linkage to state content standards, regular reflection activities, and student voice, were in place; and
3. Were able to identify a matched comparison site with classrooms of students taking the same subject matter at the same grade level using a similar curriculum and with a similar demographic and achievement profile.

From the pool of sites meeting these criteria, the final sample comprised purposefully selected sites serving students with different ethnic and socioeconomic profiles, located in different types of communities (rural, suburban, and urban), and representing diverse regions of the country. The final sample for the study included

- Fort Myers, Florida: Academy High School 9th- through 12th-grade television production class, two 9th- through 12th-grade environmental science classes, a 9th- through 12th-grade art class matched with Dunbar High School 9th- through 12th-grade television production, environmental science, and art classes.
- Suburban Anoka-Hennepin, Minnesota: Anoka High School 12th-grade government and economics class and 11th-grade modern world history class matched with Coon Rapids High School 12th-grade economics and government class and 11th-grade world history class.
- Miami, Florida: Homestead Senior High School matched service-learning with non service-learning classrooms in 11th- and 12th-grade American government classes; Miami Coral Park Senior High School matched six service-learning with six non service-learning classes in 12-th-grade government and economics; the Miami Lakes Educational Center High School matched four service-learning with four non

service-learning classes in 11th- and 12th-grade world history and government; South Miami High School matched four service-learning and two non service-learning 11th- and 12th-grade American government classes; and Turner Technical Arts High School matched three service-learning and three non service-learning 11th- and 12th-grade English classes.

- Suburban Humble, Texas: Quest High School 12th-grade senior project class matched with Humble High School 12th-grade government class and 12th-grade economics class.
- Rural Coastal Towns, Oregon: Tillamook High School service-learning senior class matched with the senior class at Neah-Kah-Nie High School. The schools are located in the Tillamook, Oregon, school district and the Rockaway Beach, Oregon, school district, respectively.

RMC Research staff administered student surveys at these sites in the fall and spring of each year of the study. Survey subscales comprising 1 to 5 items each assessed several civic outcomes, including objective civic knowledge (based on the NAEP), self-reported civic knowledge, civic skills, community attachment, and civic engagement. Repeated measures hierarchical analyses of variance tested for overall differences between school or classroom pairs on subscales and individual items. For each statistically significant result, follow-up analyses of variance (ANOVAs) were conducted to determine which pairs were associated with the findings.

Effect sizes for statistically significant differences between school and classroom pairs are displayed in Table 5.1. Follow-up ANOVAs showed that service-learning students at Anoka High School, South Miami High School, and Quest High School made greater gains than comparison students on civic knowledge or self-reported civic knowledge subscales. Service-learning participants at Anoka High School also showed superior growth on the civic skill item, *I know how to work with others to solve a community* problem, while participants at South Miami High School increased more than comparison students on the civic disposition items, *Being informed about state issues is an important responsibility for everyone,* and *Being informed about local issues is an important responsibility for everyone.*

Data from these schools were selected for qualitative analysis in order to identify themes associated with their effectiveness in using service-

Table 5.1 Effect Sizes for Significant School Pair Effects for Student Outcome Subscales

Service-Learning Schools Comparison Schools	South Miami South Miami	Anoka Coon Rapids	Quest 10–12 Humble 10–12
Subscales			
Civic knowledge	.003	.044	.051
Self-reported civic knowledge	.040	.008	.084
Civic skills	.002	.014	.013
Community attachment	.000	.008	.083
Civic dispositions	.011	.005	.054
Efficacy	.017	.006	.000
Civic engagement	.015	.000	.043

Note. Effect sizes are expressed as partial Eta-squared.

learning for citizenship education. The following section provides a brief description of the schools at the time the study was conducted.

Anoka High School. Anoka High School is located northwest of Minneapolis. Its student population was 92%, White; 3%, Asian/Pacific Islander; 2%, American Indian; and 3% of other ethnicity. Fourteen percent of students qualified for free or reduced price lunch. Founded by a social studies teacher as part of a community improvement planning process, Anoka's service learning program had been in existence for 12 years. Students' service-learning projects involved global, national, state, or local issues, which were also pertinent to community improvement goals.

Quest High School. Quest is a magnet school of choice in Humble, Texas, near Houston. At the time of the study, 313 students were enrolled at the school, 87%, White; 7.5%, African American; 4%, Hispanic; and the remainder of other ethnic heritage. A key aim at Quest is to meet the needs of students who may not be successful in a traditional school setting. The curriculum emphasizes the application of knowledge and helps students learn how to learn; become academically prepared for postsecondary education, the workplace, or the military; and learn how to interact with the community. Service-learning has been adopted as an essential strategy in meeting these goals. As part of Quest's service-learning program, all students perform community service one day per week throughout each school year. They also enroll in a year-long senior seminar intended as a capstone to their earlier service-learning work.

South Miami High School. At the time of the study, 3,065 students attended South Miami High. Eighty-one percent were Hispanic; 10%, White; 9%, African American; and 1% of other ethnicity. Approximately 41% qualified for free or reduced lunch. Two social studies teachers partnered to implement service-learning at South Miami, under the auspices of Miami-Dade district's Bureau of Community Services. With a mission to "serve as a vehicle to provide meaningful community involvement efforts and programs which support the goals of Miami-Dade County Public Schools," the Bureau sponsors several districtwide initiatives each year, including community forums on issues of importance to Miami. The forums provide a thematic center for service-learning/advocacy projects in classrooms across the district, and bring students and community members together for discussion and action planning.

Qualitative data from these and other schools in the study were analyzed by RMC Research staff. Qualitative data collection methods included:

Teacher interviews. Teachers who implemented service-learning were asked how long they had been using service-learning, their reasons for adopting this approach, and the goals that service-learning allowed them to meet. Other questions elicited teachers' perceptions of the strengths and weaknesses of service-learning as a teaching method, and how using it had influenced their thinking about teaching and learning. A series of questions asked teachers about the perceived impacts of participating in service-learning on their students' civic knowledge, skills, and dispositions. Finally, teachers discussed facilitators and obstacles to their implementation of service-learning, whether they intended to use service-learning in the future, and if so, what things they would change.

Student focus groups. Focus groups composed of a convenience sample of 6 to 12 students were moderated by researchers at each site. Students were asked to describe their service-learning projects and explain how they chose them and with whom they had worked in the community. They discussed whether various academic activities, such as reading assignments, had been integrated into their projects. Students identified specific impacts, if any, of service-learning on their knowledge of federal and state government and their local community, civic skills, engagement in their communities, engagement in school, and relationships with other students. Students also identified the two most important things a person should do to be a good citizen in a democracy and whether they would participate in service-learning again if they had the opportunity.

Classroom observations. In spring 2004 and spring 2005, researchers observed an activity related to a service-learning project in each of the service-learning classrooms. Observations were for an entire classroom period and were coded to determine the presence of various design characteristics.

Findings

Qualitative data from the three schools were analyzed to surface themes associated with schools' and teachers' success in using service-learning to foster citizenship development. Findings revealed that the sites shared common components at each stage of the service-learning process including: research and advocacy (such as taking a stand on an issue in a public forum or writing persuasive letters), student voice (such as choosing the project, determining the actions to address the social issues identified, and/or leading the project), duration, cognitive challenge (such as the degree to which higher-order thinking skills were included in the design and reflection phases), and public demonstration of results. The components are discussed next in the context of the phases of service-learning.

Preparation Phase: Research, Advocacy, and Voice

At the three schools where quantitative measures showed that service-learning was associated with civic knowledge, skills, and/or dispositions, students' projects involved research on a public problem, followed by advocacy or taking a stand, specifically involving the promotion of a political or civic solution to a public problem. The structured opportunity that service-learning gave to students to publicly advocate for an issue helped them to acquire greater understanding of an issue, to develop better skills at communicating about and acting on an issue, and to develop positive dispositions toward social action. Students who engaged in advocacy experienced much stronger civic engagement outcomes than those who simply provided direct service with personal contact with those being served or those who provided indirect service, benefiting a population, but who did not participate in any advocacy activities.

For example, at Anoka High School, students worked in groups to identify an issue of concern to them. Students conducted research on their issue, including past governmental or community efforts to address it. They developed a written proposal for a solution. Students were then required to present their solution in a public venue and to attempt to implement a public solution. One group of students focused on the issue of traffic congestion in Minneapolis. After investigating the problem, they developed a proposal to bring a rail system to the north Minneapolis region. They presented their proposal to a state panel of legislators and officials involved with transportation issues.

At Quest High School, study participants were enrolled in the two-semester capstone sequence, Senior Exploratory Foundations and Senior Seminar. The Exploratory Foundations course focused on general international problems and the United States's role in those problems. Through their humanities and social studies class work, seniors studied global issues and participated in internships, which give them a better understanding of how issues are manifested locally. At the end of the semester, students chose one global issue about which they felt "passionate" for their service-learning project. In the follow-up to *Exploratory Foundations, Senior Seminar,* students developed sustainable action plans to address their global issue. Their action plans built awareness about a community need, and included research and an implementation plan that had the potential for lasting impact. They put their plans into action with the cooperation of a community partner. Throughout their projects, students maintained a portfolio, and at the conclusion of the year, students presented a summary of their research, plan, and progress to classmates, teachers, and school leaders.

At South Miami, service-learning students chose to sponsor a public forum for candidates for Miami's mayoral race. Students interviewed parents, peers, senior citizens, and residents from a primarily Hispanic area in the city to gain information about their concerns. They conducted research on the issues identified by citizens and wrote interview questions for candidates based on the results of their research. They also completed several activities to prepare for the candidate panel, such as engaging a television news show host as moderator, arranging a venue, and notifying the public. Finally, they wrote reflection papers explaining their positions on local issues and the candidate of their choice.

In each of these sites, students determined the civic issue that they would address, conducted research on their issue, and wrote and often presented something to others about their views and potential solutions to the civic issue. In doing so, students learned information-gathering skills, knowledge about a topic, persuasive writing, and presentation skills.

At all three schools where quantitative measures indicated that service-learning was associated with significant effects on civic outcomes, service-learning projects also included student voice or opportunity for student input into the selection, design, and implementation of projects. At these schools, young people chose their projects, planned and led the service activities, discussed the value of the projects and ways in which reflections would occur, and otherwise had ways to be heard and make choices. Voice was viewed as key to student investment in service-learning and ability to benefit from it. One teacher captured this idea succinctly: "Buy-in. They do have to buy into it. They have to find that it's a really exciting topic for them, and something they can relate to."

Another teacher noted that, although service-learning could contribute to students' sense of social responsibility, this responsibility would not emerge without the "freedom" to choose a personally important issue and invest it with enthusiasm.

> It's that freedom to select an object for their passion. They start feeling a sense of responsibility because . . . nobody wants to work on a project initiated and designed by someone else. . . . You have to confront them with the challenge. . . . Which part of the American dream do they want to take on?

Another teacher emphasized the obligation to empower students to express their views and apply their talents and skills as citizens in the here-and-now, rather than later.

> Kids are able to be leaders right now. We're always building leaders, but they're actually getting to be that now. I think in empowering kids to do that, we're building skills and behaviors that are long lasting.

Having a sense of voice helped students internalize the importance of civic action. One student reflected on his/her experience, saying:

I think I've changed a lot. Like before, I didn't really . . . care enough to do something about current legislation and the current situation. And now not only do I care about it, but I want to like shout it from the rooftops, you know?

Implementation Phase: Duration, Cognitive Challenge, Affective Community Connection, and Teacher Facilitation

At the three schools with positive civic outcomes, students' service activity was characterized by certain features, including duration of at least one semester, cognitive challenge, affective connection to the community, and teacher facilitation of student work.

Each school that made significant gains had extensive and intensive service-learning projects that lasted one semester to a year. The duration of projects appeared to provide students with time to grapple with tasks and think through the issues. As one teacher stated,

I think the length of the project is important. They've got to be long enough for the kids to really experience the process . . . for something to happen to them. . .

Effective teachers typically wove service-learning activities throughout the semester or year, giving students time to reflect deeply on each phase of the project and to get feedback from each other during the process.

In addition to designing activities of sufficient length, teachers at the three schools sought to construct service activities that created disequilibrium; that is, that forced students out of comfortable mindsets, social spheres, and activities, and into taking cognitive risks.

I feel that students really need learning experiences that make them do things that they have not done before. A weak education is one that takes what the kids are already good at and then they do it day after day, month after month. So we have to create a very safe environment in our classroom to try new things. . .

Each teacher designed cognitive challenges into the service activity by asking students to learn more about issues, investigate potential causes and solutions, weigh alternatives, resolve conflicts among themselves, consider how to persuade others, and manage complex tasks.

For one teacher, an additional aspect of cognitive challenge involved the service activity's ability to stimulate students to question their assumptions about society.

> For example, going to the Little Havana Senior Center impacted them tremendously. Just talking to the elderly and listening in a way that they may or may not listen to their grandparents. . . . They often come back and they're just stunned to learn that most of them are there because there's a hot meal and it makes them understand how serious the situation is in the country in terms of people truly not being able to cover their bills.

For other teachers, challenge was inherent in the ability of projects to prompt students to realize the complexity of social problems. One teacher captured the sentiment in this way:

> It's easy to talk about social action and what you are going to do to make changes and it's easy to talk about research and pick out . . . faults, but until you've actually lived it a little bit, you don't really understand it. That's why, you know, it is the kids for the first time probably really understanding the complexity and the difficulties of addressing social issues because they actually had to do that.

One teacher commented that challenging service projects were essential for helping students to develop skills for understanding and effective collaboration.

> You have to have deep, meaningful, high stakes tasks to move kids from superficial groupings to meaningful work. I think there's lots of casual socializing that occurs in a classroom, but if you want to move kids to work that really bonds them, and really makes them hone in on group skills and figure out what their own gaps are, you have to have those kinds of tasks.

As can be seen in these examples, service activities in these sites also engaged students affectively with their communities. Having direct contact with people in the community who were experiencing difficult life circumstances seemed to help students invest emotionally in an issue. As a result, students moved from a more egocentric way of viewing the world to one that enabled them to connect to larger issues, both in the community and more generally in society, and attached increased importance to their actions. Teachers also felt this affective engagement with the community was critical to students' ability to make the transition into adult citizenship. As one teacher stated:

> There (are) so many factors disconnecting our kids from the community. . . . It actually takes effort to build bridges and open windows. . . . Today's kids are falling into an abyss where they don't realize America is built on common ground, shared assumptions, community activism, and service to the republic. . . . (Through service-learning) they start to feel like, "This is my place where my people are, and I'm doing the work of my people."

One teacher felt that all service should be deliberately planned to connect students with people suffering the consequences of poor public policy decisions, since the experience would help students realize the ways in which their personal concerns intersected with wider social and political issues, and could clarify students' comprehension of the social world and themselves. He called this approach "grounding":

> We ground their autonomous learning experience by linking their personal micro-drama with the macro-entity. We start them at whatever level they're ready to enter and slowly their cognition gets clearer. . . . All this is only possible because of the affective component. So it's kind of a cool deal that their behavior is more focused, their affective domain is getting enriched with all kinds of passions, and their cognition is getting more accurate and moving up.

Teachers also felt that in affectively engaging with the community, students would form an ethical commitment to helping others, a commitment teachers viewed as foundational to democratic citizenship. One passionately committed teacher expressed this well:

> Service-learning is all about empowering students to do good work and learn something . . . in a meaningful way and then, in the end, be able

to sit back and see that they've made the world a little bit better. . . . What is it that we're instilling in our youth as their role in the world? I hope it's not to make money. I hope it's not to go fight in a war. . . . I hope it's not to have a nice home and nice cars or even to have a good family . . . I hope we're more than that—that we're about what's going on for everybody else. Service-learning aligns with that, because it brings a world that they would never know into their hearts, and they have to do something with that. They have to wrestle with it; they have to think about it and they have to perhaps try to do something about it.

Students' comments indicated that their service activities did serve this purpose and that they felt more connected to society and more committed to performing service in the future. One student enthused:

It made me want to go out and do more, like knowing that I have the ability to do that. I want to do different things and help out different people. . .

Skills at facilitating student participation were also apparent among teachers at the three sites. Students needed guidance as they tried to make sense of their experiences, understand the issues, and develop a plan for what to do to address community concerns. Students also needed support as they dealt with the emotional aspects of their experiences, the management of partnerships, and the understanding of how to be efficacious. One teacher described the role she played as a facilitator of student work.

This just takes that idea that teachers are facilitators of learning and opens it wide up. . . . I'm trying to get kids in contact with the right situation, so that things can happen so that they can learn.

Teachers identified several elements of successful facilitation. One essential requirement was to provide support while gradually relinquishing responsibility and control to students. A teacher described facilitation for this purpose in this way:

We stand behind them and make sure that things are going well. But they've done the contacts with the candidates. They've written the letters, they've written the invitations, they've done the press release to the newspapers. They're going to be greeters. They've put together the panel and have made up the questions. They've gone out and interviewed.

A second element involved providing students with the skills they needed to successfully complete their service projects and learn the core content expected of them. For example, one teacher stated:

> Service-learning is getting them out there in the community while we still have them in an educational environment. Teaching them how to do good research before they implement a project.

Teachers felt that when facilitation was optimal, all students, not just those with a history of high academic achievement, are able to succeed. One teacher described her moment of discovery:

> All of a sudden when you see them out in the community in a completely different role, you begin to appreciate the kids for their other intelligences that you never noticed before in the classroom. And that in itself . . . overall, helps the learning environment because that kid can have a chance to shine and feel good about who he is, and not just in front of you, but in front of his peers.

Students also described the importance of this facilitation for their growth.

> We're on a one-on-one level. That's why they call them facilitators and not teachers. They teach us, but they're facilitators; they help facilitate us in our journey. . . . I can call up the teacher and tell her what our plan is and just do it like professionally and not like I am a little kid . . .

Reflection Phase: Amount, Depth, and Civic Focus

Analyses of quantitative data for this study confirmed the significance of reflection, showing positive correlations between the amount of reflection and civic knowledge, self-reported civic knowledge, civic engagement, and efficacy (Billig, Root, & Jesse, 2005; Billig, Root, & Jesse, 2006). At the three sites in which service-learning was linked to more positive civic outcomes, both teachers and students reported engaging in continuous reflection before, during, and after the service activity.

Reflection activities at the sites where service-learning was associated with civic development also required students to engage in multiple, in-depth analyses of their projects. For example, in one classroom, students were required to complete a self-portrait based on their project in a format of the student's choice, such as a videotape, poetry, sculpture, painting, or other format, as well as a portfolio including all of the research project components, academic samples from each discipline, and a social action plan.

At a second site where students showed gains, reflection was intentionally designed to encourage students to consider the civic imports of what they had done and observed. The classroom observation provides an illustration of how this occurred.

American History Class

Class began at 9 A.M., with the teacher and 26 students present. The class had hosted a mayoral forum and the students were engaged in a reflection activity. The teacher started the class by saying: "Let's talk about what went on (with the mayoral forum). Which candidates did you like the best? Which questions did they answer well? Which did they not answer so well?" Several students responded to these questions, giving their opinions about whether candidates had monopolized the conversation, attacked others, or provided concrete answers to questions. One student noted, "I kind of liked the reverend because his answers were so simple until he began talking about religion." Another student agreed that this candidate's statements contradicted the constitutional separation of church and state. "Tying in religion and politics don't mix," the student said. Then others chimed in, some disagreeing. One student asserted the need to separate issues of church and state because people in the community have many different beliefs. The teacher asked, "Did any candidate stand out?" A student mentioned that one candidate discussed senior citizens, but wasn't specific. The teacher responded, "I think these are called 'glittering generalities,' where you say something that sounds really beautiful but had very little substance." The class continued to discuss candidates' views in detail, challenging each other's ideas and receiving feedback from the teacher.

Celebration/Demonstration Phase

Finally, at the sites where students made gains on civic outcomes, opportunities for public demonstration of knowledge were an important part of the final phase of the project. For example, at Anoka High School, students were required to publicly present the results of the research they had gathered during service-learning. One group described their activities in this way:

> Our Psychology II class did a meth prevention project. We talked to the police, the health department, and schools. Then we gave a presentation at City Hall. About 50 people came.

At Quest High School, students gave a formal presentation about their projects to teachers, classmates, and members of the larger community and participated in a question and answer period following a presentation. One student focus group participant described the activity:

> Our project is civil liberties . . . how it is affecting (different groups) and a big part of our research is sort of like a call to action. So we're going to different schools. We start here at Quest teaching each of the families, and then we're going to different middle schools and high schools. We're comparing the current situation now with World War II Japanese internment camps and just how history has a tendency to repeat itself. So we're trying to make them aware of how their rights are being compromised.

For their teachers, the experience of sharing knowledge with an audience beyond the classroom gave students a sense of empowerment and self-esteem. One teacher felt that presentations to adult audiences helped to promote student efficacy:

> I know that I have lots of students who have presented at adult venues, such as the City Council or the school board, who feel very excited, and very proud of themselves for addressing adults about an adult issue

An additional benefit of public demonstration was that listeners accorded students adult status, including critiquing their evidence. A teacher reflected upon this, saying:

One of the things I have appreciated . . . is that they treat them as adult citizens, and ask the tough questions and point out weaknesses in their arguments. . . . And they (the students) go back and realize that maybe the people they are talking to have already thought about their idea, and they need to do some more thinking about it. And that's power and good for a learner to have. It's like a continuum of skills and information, and they realize at the next venue, I have to add information.

In summary, presenting the results of their research, their activities, and their recommendations to people in authority appeared to strengthen students' confidence in their public speaking abilities and their commitment to providing accurate information. In addition, students came to understand that they could influence governmental and public decision making by organizing information and experiential learning into logical arguments.

Conclusions

This chapter reports qualitative findings from three service-learning programs in which participants made greater gains than comparison students in civic knowledge, skills, and/or dispositions. These findings indicate that service-learning can be an effective tool for promoting democratic citizenship within the public high school, even at a time when the curriculum is undergoing increased constriction in response to accountability pressures. However, the findings also suggest that programs that advance civic development are not characterized by the apolitical orientation or emphasis on charity rather than change for which service-learning has been criticized (Morton, 1995; Strand, 2003). Instead, successful programs in this study featured components that required students to learn about political institutions and processes and practice skills for shaping them. These components included

a. Preparation for service that included research, advocacy, and student voice;
b. Action/implementation of service activities that were of sufficient duration, and that offered cognitive challenge, opportunities to affectively connect to the community, and teacher facilitation of student work; and
c. Reflection activities that were continuous and in-depth;

d. Public demonstration of results that included students engaged in a public demonstration of learning with adults who were previously unknown to them.

Although the findings have important implications for service-learning practice and professional development, they should be viewed with some caution. Their basis in case studies limits their generalizability. In addition, because public high school students comprised the sample, the findings may not be applicable to middle or elementary schools or even to private schools since those schools were not part of the sample. The teachers who had the strongest results were outstanding instructors, and their students' performance may have been due to factors external to their service-learning programs. These teachers had extensive experience implementing service-learning and were comfortable in allowing students to have more of a voice and more choice in the activities they conducted. Not all teachers are willing to do this and even when willing, many teachers need years of experience to develop the facilitation skills needed to maximize outcomes. Finally, these teachers were particularly passionate about their work and it may be that teachers' own dispositions towards citizenship education matter.

References

Billig, S. (2000, May). Research on K–12 school-based service-learning: The evidence builds, *Phi Delta Kappan, 81*(9), 658–664.

Billig, S., Root, S., & Jesse, D. (2005, May). *The impact of participation in service-learning on high school students' civic engagement* (CIRCLE Working Paper 33). College Park, MD: University of Maryland, The Center for Information & Research on Civic Learning & Engagement. Retrieved August 23, 2005, from http://www.civicyouth .org/PopUps/WorkingPapers/WP33Billig.pdf

Billig, S., Root, S., & Jesse, D. (2006). *The impact of high school students' participation in service-learning on academic and civic engagement.* Report prepared for the Carnegie Corporation of New York. Denver, CO: RMC Research Corporation.

Gibson, C., & Levine, P. (2003). *The civic mission of schools.* New York and Washington, DC: The Carnegie Corporation of New York and the Center for Information and Research on Civic Learning.

Kahne, J., & Westheimer, J. (2003). Teaching democracy: What schools need to do. *Phi Delta Kappan, 85*(1), 34–40, 57–67.

Kirlin, M. (2003). *The role of civic skills in fostering civic engagement* (CIRCLE Working Paper 06). College Park, MD: University of Maryland, The Center for Information & Research in Civic Learning & Engagement.

Lopez, M. (2002). *Civic engagement among minority youth.* College Park, MD: University of Maryland, Center for Information & Research in Civic Learning & Engagement.

Lutkus, A., & Weiss, A. (2007, May). *The nation's report card: Civics 2006.* (NCES 2007-476). Washington, DC: U.S. Government Printing Office.

Melchior, A. (1999). *Summary report: National evaluation of learn and serve America.* Waltham, MA: Brandeis University, Center for Human Resources.

Metz, E., McLellan, J., & Youniss, J. (2000). *Types of voluntary service and the civic development of adolescents.* Unpublished manuscript, Catholic University, Washington, DC.

Morton, K. (1995). The irony of service: Charity, project, and social change in service-learning. *Michigan Journal of Community Service Learning, 2,* 19-32.

Niemi, R. (2000, June). *Trends in political sciences as they relate to pre-college curriculum and teaching.* Paper presented at the Social Science Education Consortium, Woods Hole, MA.

Patrick, J. (2003, October). *Essential elements of education for democracy: What are they and why should they be at the core of the curriculum in schools?* Paper presented in Sarajevo, Bosnia, and Herzegovina.

Rahm, W., & Transue, J. (1998). Social trust and value change: The decline of social capital in American youth, 1976-1995. *Political Psychology, 19*(3), 545-565.

RMC Research Corporation. (2005). *Evaluation report: Philadelphia partnerships in character education.* Denver, CO: Author.

Scales, P., Blyth, D., Berkas, T., & Kielsmeier, J. (2000, August). The effects of service-learning on middle school students' social responsibility and academic success. *Journal of Early Adolescence, 20*(3), 332-358.

Skinner, R., & Chapman, C. (1999). *Service-learning and community service in K-12 public schools* (NCES Statistical Brief 1999-043). Washington, DC: U.S. Department of Education, National Center for Education Statistics.

Strand, K. (2000). Community-based research as pedagogy. *Michigan Journal of Community Service Learning, 7,* 85-96.

Torney-Purta, J., & Vermeer Lopez, S. (2006). *Developing citizenship competencies from kindergarten through grade 12: A background paper for policymakers and educators.* Denver, CO: Education Commission of the States. National Center for Learning and Citizenship.

Walker, T. (2002). Service as a pathway to political participation: What research tells us. *Applied Developmental Science, 6*(4), 183-188.

Yamauchi, L., Billig, S., Meyer, S., & Hofschire, L. (2006). Student outcomes associated with service-learning in a culturally relevant high school program. *Journal of Prevention and Intervention in the Community, 32*(1/2), 149-164.

Inside Schools At Large

CHAPTER 6

Democracy's Practice Grounds

The Role of School Governance in Citizenship Education

Richard M. Battistoni

> Project 540 is that boost that a lot of students need. The youth, we all
> have ideas and I think the main problem is that we don't know who to
> talk to, we don't have doors to open, I think that Project 540 is that step
> up, it is that door, I believe that the more strength with Project 540, the
> better off our generation is going to be, the better off we all will be when
> we have a group of students who are more open minded, a group of
> students who are not afraid to dig deep and make action.
>
> —*Student Leadership Team member,*
> *urban New England high school*

> I was one of those music and science people last year before, but this
> year I started to speak more and be more confident and we had just two
> leaders and I was one of them who was chosen. I'm still like a math and
> science person but I am more. I like looking through other people's
> eyes, seeing how other people see things and realizing that things are a
> lot different from what they seem.
>
> —*Student Leadership Team member,*
> *suburban Midwestern high school*

Over the past decade, policymakers, researchers, and educators have been
lamenting the decline in political engagement among young people (*The
Civic Mission of Schools,* 2003; National Commission on Civic Renewal, 1998).
Many studies show that this generation of young people pays less attention
to public affairs and participates less in public life than their similar-age
counterparts in previous generations (Galston, 2001; Keeter, Zukin, Andolina, & Jenkins, 2002). In response to the perceived decline in youth

civic engagement, concerned citizen educators have designed programs aimed at increasing political knowledge, skills, and participation, and philanthropists have made funding available to different kinds of educational "interventions." This chapter studies the implications for citizenship education of Project 540,[1] one such program funded by a grant from the Pew Charitable Trusts from 2001–2004.

Project 540 was envisioned as a large-scale initiative aimed at addressing the problem of youth civic disengagement. Its purpose was to empower youth—over 100,000 of them—in high schools across the nation, by allowing students to participate directly in a democratic process of deliberation and action in their high school. The idea was to confront the evidence suggesting that schools were inappropriate platforms for youth civic education and involvement.

Project 540: A "Democratic School Practice" Approach

Traditionally, the dominant approach to educating young people for democratic citizenship has centered on formal civics education in schools. Through the social studies curriculum, teachers transmit vital civic knowledge and skills to their students. Research over the past decade indicates that this approach is not without its merits. A number of recent studies have produced evidence that exposure to civics courses in schools positively affects civic knowledge and skills (Kurtz et al., 2003; Niemi & Junn, 1998; Torney-Purta, 2002). In fact, this evidence is the basis for recommendations that students receive more in the way of formal civics instruction (*Civic Mission of Schools*, 2003). Though the evidence is not conclusive, other approaches to citizenship education—service-learning and simulations of voting, trials, legislative deliberation, and diplomacy—also have garnered support in producing positive civic impact (*Civic Mission of Schools*, 2003).

Project 540 was based upon a different approach to civic education. Rather than using the social studies curriculum to bring civic knowledge to students, or exposing students to experiences such as simulations, mock elections, or community service-learning to develop civic skills, Project 540 sought to empower students to make decisions in their schools and communities. Students in Project 540 engaged in a democratic process that enabled them to discuss issues that mattered to them and then take public actions to address these issues. This "democratic school practice" approach to civic education—as opposed to the "formal civics instruction" approach—allowed students to participate in a process of dialogue, decision making, and action. At the same time, students would gain valuable civic skills through the experience of creating a democratic culture in their schools. Thus, the overarching assumption going into the project was that schools themselves could be the "practice grounds" for democratic civic education, by providing exercises in community governance, voice, and public problem solving (see Dewey, 1916).

More specifically, Project 540 engaged high school students in a series of small-group, peer-facilitated dialogues involving most (or sometimes, all) of the school's population. Students began with their own interests and passions. The process began by creating space for students to identify issues that they really cared about in their school, community, nation, and world. Dialogue facilitators elicited from their peers a list of issues by asking three specific questions: (1) "If you could change one thing about our school, what would it be?" (2) "If you were in charge of your city, town, or neighborhood, what issue would you tackle first?" (3) "What national or global issue would you want to address?"

After a deliberative process, students then made recommendations for action on the issues that mattered most to them, and worked with adults in the school and community to actually implement their action recommendations. Table 6.1 summarizes the top issues addressed in participating schools during the 2002–2003 school year, while Table 6.2 summarizes the issues students chose to tackle in the 2003–2004 school year. As you can see, in many schools, students chose to work on "local issues": changes to school attendance and tardy policies, the conditions of lunchrooms and bathrooms, or additions to the curriculum. One student from Southern California put it this way:

> I think the best kind of issues for Project 540 to solve are school issues because other issues would be harder to tackle. We should start off with the school first to see if it works or not and if it does maybe we can move onto higher things and then maybe we can help out the world.

There are specific examples, however, where students took on larger questions. In one suburban Midwestern community, students succeeded in obtaining a $65,000 budget allocation from the school board to create a unified bell and public address system for the two different sections of the

Table 6.1 2002–2003 Top Issues Reported (184 schools reporting issues)

1. School lunch and lunch policies (52%)
2. School schedule and curriculum concerns (49%)
3. School policies, including homework, tardy, electronics, and dress code (39%)
4. War and Terrorism (34%)
5. School Bathrooms (30%)
6. Parking issues (24%)
6. Concerns with Alcohol and Drugs (24%)
8. Environmental Issues(20%)
8. Activities for youth in the community (20%)
8. School Sports (20%)
11. Poverty, homelessness, and hunger (17%)
11. Racism, Sexism, Homophobia (17%)
13. Standardized Testing (13%)
14. Books (8%)
14. Police Harassment (8%)

high school, thus solving an ongoing problem of tardiness and some students missing out on important opportunities and announcements. Suburban West Coast students attempted to get a skate park built in their community. And at one rural southern school, Project 540 students attempted to reverse a countywide court desegregation order that would require the removal of a number of African American teachers from a predominantly African American school in order to achieve racial balance across the county.

Throughout this process of implementing school change, a small group of students acted as a "Leadership Team" in each school, helping to organize other students, train dialogue facilitators, and coordinate the entire process as it worked its way through to completion. Leadership Team members were selected to represent the entire school—in some schools by student election, in others by teachers—and were oriented to the curriculum and process of Project 540 by national staff in regional training sessions. All students were taught a particular model of dialogue, deliberation, and action planning, and all school wide dialogues were conducted during the school day, but the Leadership Teams in each school chose the particular context and timetable for their democratic process. As director of Project 540, I worked with the other national staff members to establish an organizational structure, recruit schools within regions to participate, develop a simple yet flexible curriculum and training regime, and oversee

Table 6.2 2003–2004 Top Issues Reported (24 new schools reporting issues)

1. School lunch and lunch policies (58%)
2. School policies, including tardy, electronics, and dress code (54%)
3. School schedule and curriculum concerns (38%)
4. Activities for youth in the community (25%)
5. School Bathrooms (21%)
5. Other school facilities (21%)
5. Parking issues (21%)
8. School policies: tardy (17%)
9. Dress Code policies (13%)
10. School Funding (8%)
10. Community Concerns (8%)
12. Environmental Issues(4%)
12. Poverty, homelessness, and hunger (4%)
12. Terrorism and Drugs (4%)
12. School Violence (4%)
12. Student Voice (4%)

the implementation process across the country. Over the course of two years, over 150,000 students in over 270 high schools—urban, rural, and suburban—participated in the project in some way.

The following four descriptions will give the reader a better sense of how Project 540 played out in different schools across the country:

Salem High School, Salem, Massachusetts. The Leadership Team (19 students and two teachers) decided to run the project through the school's social studies classes, which meant that about 75% of the student body—with a total of over 1,400 students—participated in the process (not all students take social studies classes). During a two- or three-day process every month, 80 student facilitators visited all of the school's social studies classes to lead the student dialogues. Out of these discussions came a plan to change the student governance process at the school. Project 540 created a new 9-member School Senate to make policy for the school, comprised of the principal, four students, three faculty, and one secretarial staff member, the latter three categories all elected by their peers. Also created was a new "540 Council," an elected body that serves as a "student caucus" to the student representatives of the School Senate.

Zuni High School, Zuni, New Mexico. At this high school on the Zuni reservation, the dialogue and deliberation process began involving all 350 students in the school, but the Leadership Team found that there was a great deal of silence and nonparticipation on the part of students. The process was changed to invite any students who wanted to participate (which yielded about half of the student body), and students were asked first to write their answers to questions on paper, then participate in a discussion based on what they had written. The Leadership Team found that this was a more effective way to involve quieter students. Eventually, the school's action plan called for an effort to stop mining companies from polluting the nearby salt lake, a sacred place for Zuni people.

Norman North High School, Norman, Oklahoma. The Leadership Team here chose to involve all students (2,200 in the student body) in Project 540, by having one day every three weeks devoted to 540 issues in the all-school student advisory/home room groups. Several of the 117 advisory groups were for students whose primary language was Spanish, so the dialogue process and questions were translated into Spanish for these groups. The student body proposed renovations to the school's interior quad, and attempted to get a bond passed to pay for the renovations.

Bell Gardens High School, Los Angeles County, California. This 3,300 student school posed a major logistical challenge, with about half the population primarily Spanish speaking. The Leadership Team decided to involve the entire student body, and recruited nearly 200 students to facilitate the dialogues in English and Spanish. The issues that emerged from student deliberations included changes in lunchroom choices and access as well as efforts to amend the school's absence and tardy policies.

It is important to note that Project 540 is merely a recent experiment in a long tradition of efforts to democratize school culture and governance. In 1983, the National Council on the Social Studies (NCSS) published a bulletin laying out the research on and practices of democratic schools (Hepburn, 1983), and a number of individual democratic school initiatives date back to the 1940s. Still, there is a growing body of literature that confirms the value of this "democratic school practice" approach to civic education. *The Civic Mission of Schools* report, for example, argues that "the most effective [civic education] programs occur in schools that . . . give students opportunities to contribute opinions about the governance of the school—not just through student governments, but in forums that engage the entire student body or in smaller groups addressing significant problems in the school" (*The Civic Mission of Schools*, 2003). The *Breaking Ranks* report on high school reform initiatives, jointly commissioned by the Education Alliance and the National Association of Secondary School Principals, concurs, recommending in one of its "seven cornerstone strategies" that all high schools "allow for meaningful involvement in decision making by students . . ." (NASSP, 2004). A recent policy brief from the Education Commission of the States similarly endorses involving students in governance, both at the school and district/state levels, to advance students' civic learning outcomes and as a strategy for better educational policy making (Miller, 2004).

At the same time, there also exists a body of research literature endorsing the approach used by Project 540. The NCSS volume mentioned earlier concluded that educational research "supports the conclusion that democratic experiences in the school and the classroom can contribute to the knowledge, skills, and attitudes essential to democratic citizenship" (Hepburn, 1983: 24). At the international level, the most recent 28-country IEA Civic Education Study demonstrated unmistakably the importance of both democratic "classroom climate" and democratic student governance to student civic learning outcomes:

> Schools that model democratic values by . . . inviting students to take part in shaping school life are most effective in promoting civic knowledge and engagement . . . and they are more likely to produce students that expect to vote as adults than other schools. (Torney-Purta et al., 2001)

Additionally, case studies in Finland and Norway, and preliminary data from an English longitudinal study, suggest a strong, positive link between student opportunities to participate in school (both in classroom "lessons" and in governance) and citizenship education outcomes (Kerr et al., 2004; Hannam, 2005). In fact, in these countries (and others) the very definition of citizenship education (or "active citizenship," the term used in England) has come to include a core "democratic practice" orientation, in addition to the development of knowledge, skills, and values (Nelson & Kerr, 2005).

Methodology

The purpose of this study was to examine the impact of Project 540 on students who participated in it. Multiple research questions drove the study. How do high school students think about politics and citizenship? Can an initiative focused on student voice and participation change the way they think? Can civic knowledge, skills, and dispositions be learned through democratic civic experiences outside the formal curriculum? How does an extracurricular student governance project change the relationships between students, teachers, and administrators?

Qualitative data[2] came from two different sources. First, Project 540 staff conducted short interviews and focus group sessions in the course of site visits to 60 Project 540 high schools during the 2002–2003 and 2003–2004 academic years. These 60 schools were representative of the 270 that participated in the project, ranging from West to East coasts, from small to large, from rural to suburban to urban. During these site visits, the five national staff members interviewed at least one administrator, one teacher, and conducted a focus group session with students from the Leadership Team. Project 540 staff also compiled and analyzed "issues lists" submitted by 208 participating schools and Civic Action Plans from 211 participating schools.

In addition, two graduate assistants conducted a dozen in-depth student interviews (60–90 minutes), where interviewers used phenomenological methods to systematically examine the "lived experiences" of students who participated extensively in Project 540 (Hildreth, 2006; van Manen, 1990). A sample of the interview questions is included in Appendix A. All interviews were taped and transcribed, and the transcripts were analyzed by me as principal investigator and my two graduate assistant colleagues to identify the common themes across interviews[3] (Kvale, 1996). Quotations and interview excerpts will be used to illustrate common themes that emerged from the researchers' analysis of transcripts from all the interviews conducted.

This chapter focuses on findings regarding multiple meanings of citizenship developed, the experiential nature of learning guided by teachers as coaches, tensions in democratic school governance, and implications for citizenship education.

Meanings of Citizenship

In our research, students, teachers, and administrators spoke about key aspects of citizenship that were being developed through Project 540. These included civic communication, participation in public policy decisions, and making change. Understandings of citizenship suggest a broadened conception of political participation.

Civic communication was most prevalent in responses from both adults and youth. It involved the development of voice, being heard, taking responsibility, changes in perceptions of others, learning to listen, and respecting diversity. The most frequent and common value attributed to the project by principals was that it provided a "structured" or "responsible" method for students to communicate with administrators. While most admitted that it is always good for students to get involved in "advancing their interests," Project 540 had done this in a uniquely sophisticated way. One suburban Midwestern school principal said that it "gives coherence to student authority," by moving students from complaining or "whining" about an issue to making thoughtful and well-researched positions to address the issue. Several principals claimed that not only was there more open communication between administrators and students as a result of the project, but there was also less animosity ("us–them") between them. One suburban New England principal stated simply, "I have learned from them; I didn't realize what some of the issues are for students."

An urban assistant principal in the Southeast told us that "faculty now have a vision of what student voice looks like in a high school." Several principals talked about how Project 540 helped improve communication and understanding between students and administrators in school. One Southern superintendent said the project had "opened a door between students and the principal." Other principals commented that they had learned from students as a result of Project 540, that it caused them to think differently about issues from the students' perspective. A suburban principal in New England stated, "We need to address these issues as students see them, not as we adults see them." These statements point to greater reciprocity between adults and youth that has the potential to change school culture from hierarchical and closed to being more democratic.

Students emphasized the importance of developing "voice," which specifically referred to the expression of ideas and concerns that were genuinely heard by others. In nearly every site visit we were told that students felt that they had more voice in the school as a result of Project 540. A rural Northeastern student said: "[Administrators and teachers] are within reach—before that, I wouldn't have thought I had a shot at them listening, but now I do." At an urban West Coast school, a Leadership Team member put it this way:

I think we already have the power to change things in school but getting people to listen to us is the first step in this process. I think that the students being heard is the most important part, so that people start conceptualizing and seeing students as more than just bad kids who vandalize or show no respect. Now they are seeing kids taking part in an organization run by adults and this is a better thing.

The development of voice influenced school climate. One of the most important changes in school climate had to do with the different perceptions students, teachers, and administrators had of one another since involvement in Project 540. We received significant reports that faculty and administrators see students differently. Many students said that they felt "listened to" for the first time, like this one from an urban high school on the West Coast:

[In Project 540] you get to see what kids really think. You think all they care about is sex, drugs and music but we think about what adults do. People need to pay more attention to us. They're going to have to turn the world over to us soon. They need to trust us. We know what we're talking about.

We also heard students tell us that they have a different perception of teachers and administrators in their schools. One urban West Coast student claimed:

We thought that teachers could be able to do things really easily and have the power to do whatever they want but we realized in order to do the change that everyone has to work together, students, teachers and administration.

High school students—like this one from a rural Midwestern school—often discussed discovering their individual voices and developing a collective voice:

It's interesting to see students getting involved, because now they know that they do have a voice and that they can speak out if something is bothering them. . . . I learned that everyone has a voice, including my-self. I mean, one person is one person, but that one person can make a difference. And now I'm working on making that true.

Students reported that their participation in the project enhanced their ability to speak up in front of peers and adults, and to listen to and accept everyone's voices and opinions, no matter what they thought of them. The literature confirms the importance of communication as an element of education for democratic citizenship (Battistoni, 2000; Peng, 2000; Torney-Purta & Vermeer, 2004). Students who facilitated small group dialogues, like this one from a suburban school in the Midwest, told us how much the practice transformed them as public speakers:

Usually I'm very shy and I don't like speaking in front of crowds or large crowds, but because of Project 540 and because we have so many get-togethers I speak in larger groups of people and then when I'm going to a ninth grade class they don't know I'm shy, so I don't show that so I can be a good model for them, and that is a challenge for me.

Civic communication is not simply speaking, but also listening, respecting different opinions, and incorporating the voices of others. An urban West Coast student explained it this way:

You have to have good listening. One of the things you don't want to do is just give them your message, and if they tell you something like, no that won't work, we're trying this better but thanks for your opinion. You know that's not really something you want to give to the students. You want to let them know, "Hey we're listening. That's a good idea, we'll write it down.'

Being able to listen to all voices in American high schools requires that students learn about and respect differences that exist among their school's fellow citizens. This was something that students consistently mentioned in interviews, like this one from a student in a suburban Southeastern school:

You need to know how to respect differences in opinion and different perspectives . . . We went to different classes and some things were different and we had to blend that and we had to respect everyone's opinion and everyone is different and they have different ideas.

And, like the larger society, diversity expresses itself in many different forms, including the very way the school is organized academically. A student from a large urban school in the Northeast stated:

I think you have to realize that there is a variety of people in our school because sometimes we have a difference with the students who take AP and those students who take regular classes and being in the leadership team you have to realize that there is a variety of people in our school and sometimes all people do not get that attention and Project 540 wanted to get everybody in our school. We just didn't want the AP students or the students that are in lower classes so that is where we had to realize that there are many differences.

In addition to civic communication, public policy decision making was identified as a key element of citizenship. Students spoke extensively about developing a capacity for organizing and management of diverse people as well as activities. With Project 540, the most frequently mentioned influence on students' citizenship skill building was the practice of developing a common plan of action out of the disparate voices of the entire student body. Students—like this one from rural New England— told us that working together as a team created a sense of mutual responsibility conducive to learning, and to the development of these organizational skills:

[I]t was a nice experience because normally, I used to not be really good in being in groups and having different views from different people and the leadership team we have very different people with different ideas and we had to come to agreement on what was the best thing for everyone and it was a good experience.

A related and critical skill for public policy decision making is to know how to prioritize, strategize and make decisions regarding a problem. Our interview data revealed that for students, working from identification of problems or issues to solutions involved an increased understanding of the complexity of issues, of how systems work, and where the "levers of power" are in schools and communities. This student from an urban school in New England observed:

> I used to not think and just act but with Project 540 I really sit back and think about the situation, see who can help you and can't help you and the resources you already have and think of a way to act . . . Project 540 helps you to sit down and think about the problem, think about who is there to help you, think about who is against you, and think about how to solve the problem and most times you just think that you see the problem and you just want to act, you don't think about it, just act the way you think, so it gives you steps you can take.

In the course of implementing their Civic Action Plans, students became more involved in public policy decisions. Project 540 encouraged students to reach out to school boards, public officials, and other members of the community to present their work, and they did in large numbers. One suburban Midwestern student connected this effort to future political involvement: "We know how things work now, how change happens, and how things are accomplished, so we won't be intimidated if we ever want to do something in the future." A teacher at a rural Midwestern school said that as a result of attempting to make school policy changes her students have a new understanding of democracy and bureaucracy more relevant to their own lives: "Democracy is more than something done by distant adults on a national level," she stated.

An obvious question about the democratic school practice approach to citizenship education is whether lessons learned through student voice and governance add up to increased youth *political* engagement, the primary reason for these projects in the first place. Are there connections between a deliberative democratic school dialogue process and deliberative democratic political participation? We certainly saw connections between student participation in Project 540 and their having a better sense of the political process. Some students, like this one from a rural Southern school, reported that as a result of Project 540 public issue discussions are more prevalent in hallways and classrooms:

We have found our students more open to change, they speak up more, and simply they are more involved with things in our school and our community. My personal experience with this is that I have found myself more interested with what is happening around me. I have noticed myself asking more questions like, how does that work, what is the process it takes, what will be the outcome, and so on. You see this is the process that gets us involved.

But is this really *political* involvement? Is there a direct translation between participation in Project 540 activities and *political* participation? The following students' voices speak to this question:

I will vote definitely, oh definitely. As far as any other things, not really. I was never really that big on politics.

I learned that as a teenager you kind of are flushing out who you are but I think that through Project 540 I discovered that I think I'm growing up to be a real activist in society. I'm really concerned about people and issues that revolve around our daily lives.

I think that students who participate in project 540 are more likely to participate in politics just because of the dialogues. If you go to 12 of them, that's a lot of topics and problems that you weren't aware of before. Even if you don't get involved in politics, you will still vote because you saw how one person's presence could forward the discussions and make a difference. This is too important to let go.

Our interviews with students demonstrated the need to think beyond the traditional categories of political engagement. We heard an initial hesitation about the language and dominant practices of "politics," but then a sense of the possibility for a new kind of politics. One urban West Coast student said:

I see myself helping my community and my school. I don't know if that makes me a political actor . . . With Project 540 we're getting students involved and participating and we're letting faculty members know that we're here. So in a way *it's a new kind of political*, down at the school level.

Our interviews revealed that this understanding of politics is more local, relational, inclusive, and non-partisan. Similar findings are evident in other studies, such as the student-authored report on civic engagement, *The New Student Politics* (Long, 2002).

Students continually expressed ideas about the connection between the political process and being an active member of one's community, as exemplified by this interview excerpt from a student in the urban Southwest:

> I see Project 540 as political, because it is about organizing students for a change. Personally, I definitely feel more a part of the life of my community after being on the Project 540 leadership team, and I have an interest in voting and the political process.

Other students made connections between student voice and motivation for voting. This comment from a student in a suburban Southeastern school is exemplary:

> [The impact of Project 540] is to be heard. That's the greatest part about being a student or being a part of Project 540 is that your voice can be heard. People wonder why there is such a low voting turnout and it is because high school students don't ever have their voices heard.

In our interviews with students it became clear that students' participation in Project 540 created opportunities for students to learn skills of civic communication and public policy decision making. It also encouraged them to struggle productively around the very meaning of concepts like "politics" and "citizenship." In this way, as a democratic school practice initiative, Project 540 gave students the power to voice their concerns and to solve public problems, and in the process, to creatively redefine civic involvement.

Nature of Citizenship Education through Project 540: Experiential Learning and Teachers as Coaches

Project 540 facilitated kinds of learning that were different from what typically happens in classrooms. Learning was experiential, project and performance based, and authentic; it was situated in actual practices of governance. Learning involved deliberative decision making in collaborative, heterogeneous groups.

What about the role of the teacher in this kind of citizenship education? Some readers may come away from this study wondering whether teachers have *any* role in an educational process facilitated and driven by students. This would be a grave mistake. Our interviews revealed how critical teachers were to student civic learning and to the ultimate success of the project. A key element was the teacher's ability to find the appropriate middle ground between total control and a complete hands-off policy, to give students autonomy and yet provide guidance. "My role is to help kids see the possibilities for change over time," proclaimed one teacher from a rural Southern school. Another teacher, from an urban New England school, told us that her objective was to be "*a* resource, not *the* resource, to her students. Sometimes I want to tell [the Leadership Team] no to this or that," she reported, "but it's not my plan, so I need to hold back."

Our interviews also offered a descriptive metaphor appropriate to the aims of democratic civic learning: Teacher as coach. One suburban West Coast teacher responded to a question about the role of adults in student civic engagement by saying, "They should be coaches—stand back as much as possible and let the students do the work." A student from an urban New England school embellished on this "coaching" role:

> [Our teacher] encourages us to go beyond what is expected of us. She fans the flame of our activism. She wants us to learn, so we can't get a word out of her in meetings. But she is totally supportive of us once we decide what we want to do.

Given our findings about the importance of practice to student political education, and the suggestion that we look beyond the traditional classroom as an arena with great potential for civic skill transfer, this metaphor of "teacher as coach" may be appropriate. Or maybe it's "teacher as maestro." The knowledge and skills necessary for political engagement are more akin to what is learned through athletics or music performance than the traditional academic model, so the role of the educator needs to adjust to this reality. As in athletics and music, the main lesson of democratic citizenship is learned through practicing democracy; the "teacher" is one who sets up the practice routine, and is there to guide the student through tasks and in reflecting upon the performance afterwards. This doesn't diminish the role of educators at all; in fact, it enhances their place in setting the ultimate goals and context for practicing politics, and in providing tools and opportunities for reflection on student practice.

Civic skill development is certainly one aspect of learning for political engagement. But perhaps even more important is *skill transfer,* the ability to adapt and apply skills learned in one setting to another, particularly from the academic setting, where most formal citizenship education takes place, to the public arena. Transferable or portable skills have become increasingly important, especially in career development and technical education fields, but one of the earliest arguments about the importance of transferable civic skills can be found in Dewey (1938).

A "democratic school practice" approach to civic education may have the greatest impact here. Formal classroom instruction may be seen by students as "contained," as if in a box. When the course is over, that's it; any content knowledge or skills may be quickly forgotten. But a practice-oriented approach, especially one outside of formal classroom lessons, has the potential to be portable across the different life roles a person assumes (see Hildreth, 2006; Longo, Drury, & Battistoni, 2006).

Students spoke eloquently about how they applied the civic skills they gained in Project 540 to other aspects of their life: leadership in student government, co-curricular activities, even work and family life. One urban Northeastern student talked about transferring skills from Project 540 to student council leadership:

> I'm also the senior class president. I have improved my communication skills and working with others, those two have definitely impacted my role, because I have to talk to students about issues that they don't like and things that they don't agree with and learn to respect their opinions and yet tell them what is what and have them follow what is what. Working with others, I have to work with the second floor school to organize our prom and when it comes to that issue, our school is on one side and their school is on the other side, and a compromise has to be reached and that is very difficult, that if I didn't have my Project 540 background I don't know if could be able to do it.

A suburban West Coast student applied the problem-solving skills learned in 540 to her work as editor of the school newspaper:

What I have realized with Project 540 is if we have a problem we identify the problem and from there we make a step-by-step of what we are
going to do, our resources, and what needs to be done. [T]hat really
helped me because I use it with stuff that I do like journalism, [where]
sometimes we have problems, like should we put this article in and
who should we talk to and that has helped me because I talk to all of
my resources and I get to all of my resources and we come up with the
idea. After Project 540 I realized that that was the best way to solve
problems and I refined the way I do things.

An urban West Coast student talked about how he brought ideas
learned in Project 540 to his workplace:

I work at McDonald's, so most of us just go there, work, and leave. So I
told my manager what if we try doing [a 540 dialogue] and he said
that's not a bad idea. One of the other things I took to work with me
. . . is now we have a box where you can drop suggestions in. Somebody
might not like doing something so now we have a suggestion box.

A student at a rural New England school told interviewers about the
more general impact Project 540 has had in his life:

I think it has made me a stronger person. I feel more comfortable with
myself. I'm learning who I am and what I like. I am just more assertive.
I don't hold back that much anymore. I guess you can say that I respect
myself more. I don't really let people stamp on me. It has made me
more confident . . . It has just made me more aware, more adult, and
more mature.

This evidence of transfer indicates that practicing governance at
school can provide students with the tools and encourage motivation to
further democracy in their lives outside of school as well.

Tensions in Democratic School Governance

Our interviews and interactions with administrators and students revealed a
degree of tension between them in terms of their understanding of what it
means to be a citizen, particularly within the school setting. As an initiative

designed to give students a meaningful voice in school governance, Project 540 often came into conflict with the institutional culture of high schools, where adult educators (teachers and administrators) were used to being in control and making most if not all of the decisions for the school. And this was the case even though schools and their principals or superintendents had agreed to participate in the project! In one rural Southern setting, the principal described the dilemma as he saw it, of moving his high school from a hierarchical and controlled organization to a more democratic one: "It's the fine line between letting the monkeys run the zoo and some structure." His fear—however unfounded—was that giving students voice might move the school from control to chaos.

Our interviews with administrators, teachers, and students exposed this challenge for democratic citizenship education posed by the institutional structure of schools and the culture of adult control. A few principals were reluctant to turn over authority to students, or were concerned about having to respond to unrealistic proposals. One principal from an urban school in the Southeast said: "I appreciate the students' motivation and diligence, but there are many policies that just cannot be changed. In these cases I just had to say no to students' demands." Others were fearful that students would spin their wheels, or get frustrated by the slow pace of school change. Administrators' attitudes played a big role in how students saw their civic roles and authority. One teacher from a large urban high school in the Northeast told us that adults "can make or break the program simply by their attitudes. [I]f the administration and faculty don't convey the value of getting kids engaged in civic life in an active way by responding to their concerns, the message that they send through would be louder than all the words and jingles to push and invite kids to participate."

Students often picked up on adult resistance. At one urban school on the West coast, a student on the Leadership Team told us that students were afraid to "open up their minds" for fear "of getting in trouble with the teachers." During the peer-facilitated dialogues, "if a teacher came in, then students might not say something because they might report them to the principal." "After we told them that the teachers couldn't hold you accountable for what you say, they really responded, opened up and [became] more comfortable."

In addition to tension over authority between adults and youth, tension over authority between the state and the school was another obstacle. We found few high school administrators supporting Project 540 as a way to fulfill the school's civic mission not because they didn't value civic education, but because there were other competing demands, especially coming from federal and state mandates. "This is not what we are judged on," stated one principal from a rural Southern school in response to a question about fulfilling the school's obligation to educate students for democratic citizenship.

Yet, there were some administrators who saw the value in this approach. For example, this urban Northeastern principal was adamant about the civic importance of Project 540:

> If we expect students who are graduating and for the most part can vote and become part of society that they ought to have those practical experiences in their high school, not just talk about them in theory. So this is a perfect environment about what we talk about philosophically that kids should actually be relating to the issues and making a difference in their school and try to change their school and they should be the ones making the rules.

Ultimately, the real tension may lie in the gap between the rhetoric and the reality of citizenship education in most schools today.

Implications for Citizenship Education

> The American learns to know the laws by participating in the act of legislation; and takes a lesson in forms of government by governing.
> —*Alexis de Tocqueville*, Democracy in America

If student voice is an important element of education for democratic citizenship, this raises questions about the appropriate location for its exercise. Most schools have student councils or other forms of student government, a seemingly logical realm for the exercise of student voice and decision making outside the classroom. But in our study, we found that students made clear distinctions between student council and Project 540 in the schools where both operated. In many cases, students detected a clear difference in the goals of the two groups, with student councils being about social planning and Project 540 focusing on planning for change. A Leadership Team in a large New England school put it this way: "Student council plans dances. Project 540 is about action and school change." Student council was often seen as a top-down body, representing the "popular" kids, controlled by the administration; "oligarchical" is how one student characterized the student council in his Southwestern high school. Project 540, by contrast, was seen as the "school improvement group," working on things that students actually care about, and working from the ground up. In addition, Project 540 was seen as more inclusive, an initiative that engaged more types of students, from more cliques in the school, and one that had the ability to take time, deliberate, and reach consensus on issues. In this sense, Project 540 was viewed as being more "democratic."

Of course, the relationship was not always that dichotomous. Some schools had a large membership cross-over between the Project 540 Leadership Team and the student council. We also have evidence of Project 540's impact in reforming or revitalizing student government, with Project 540 students serving as catalysts for the creation of a more democratic structure for school governance. Still, this initiative raises important questions about the role of traditional student government as a vehicle for student empowerment and democratic citizenship education.

If student voice and democratic school practice are to be taken seriously, this raises more general questions about our primary approach to civic education. Citizenship education has tended to focus on content-based civic knowledge and cognitive skills. For example, the recently administered National Assessment of Educational Progress in Civics focuses on measuring students' cognitive knowledge of things like American government and the Constitution, as well as the "intellectual skills . . . that allow individuals to apply civic knowledge to good effect" (National Center for Education Statistics, 2006).

Our interviews suggest that we should look beyond cognitive knowledge and skills to the importance of developing practical civic skills as a key component of civic learning. The findings from this study of one initiative in student voice and governance show that education for democratic citizenship is much more than formal instruction in history and government. The school itself can be the "practice grounds" for democratic civic education, by providing exercises in community governance, voice, and public problem solving. Civic knowledge is an important element in citizenship education, but equally important is developing civic motivation and competencies, which can be instilled through a process that encourages direct participation in the matters that affect students' lives in schools and communities.

Having staked this claim for paying more attention to student participation in school governance, there are real barriers to adopting this approach in the United States. Given the current educational policy climate around standards and accountability, student voice and governance initiatives may be seen as a luxury, especially when we consider that educational assessment regimes have focused exclusively on literacy and mathematics, and most recently, science, not on civics or even social studies more broadly. Democratic civic learning outcomes are rarely mentioned in state educational standards, and when they are, they are not tied to the critical accountability measures afforded other subject matter (Torney-Purta & Vermeer, 2004).

In many participating Project 540 schools, administrators and teachers alike reported that success in civic education was "not what we are judged on," and as a result, time taken away from the areas on which they *were* judged was hard to justify. Teachers specifically cited resistance from their colleagues because of lost instructional time as a major barrier Project 540 faced in their schools. Even students found that time pressures and conflicts with other elements in their busy schedules made it difficult to devote themselves to a lengthy dialogue and democratic action process. One student on the Leadership Team from an urban West Coast school put it this way: "It's really hard to find time. Kids have a lot of really hard classes, we have to do homework, and we need time to sleep."

And yet, the findings from this one example of a "democratic school practice" approach calls us to pay attention to school culture and climate as well as test scores in mathematics and reading. If we want to create citizens who participate in and contribute to the life of their communities, we need to overcome the growing tendency to focus our educational efforts exclusively on narrowly defined academic outcomes and accountability regimes. As one Project 540 teacher from an urban Northeastern high school said:

[High schools] would be an ideal platform [for youth civic engagement] because you're catching students at a stage in their life when they are just starting to formulate opinions. If the seniors' attitudes are any indication, we want to catch them before they get too cynical about the democratic process. I think students certainly want to participate in that process but don't understand what it fully entails. So getting them in a deliberative process like Project 540 in high school is an excellent thing to do.

Appendix A: Sample Interview Questions

Description of Experience/Meaning

1. What types of activities were you involved in as part of Project 540 this past year?

2. What was it like to be you when you were in Project 540?

   Alternates: Can you describe what it was like to take this on?

   How did you experience yourself doing Project 540?

3. Can you tell me a story of when you really felt like this project was working well?

4. How about a story of when it didn't work so well?

   **Possible follow-ups: Why did you tell that story? Why is that story meaningful to you?

Learning

5. What did you learn about yourself from being involved in this project?

6. Can you tell me a story of what this learning looks like?

   **Possible follow-ups: Have you noticed that you have developed any skills over the course of the year? Which do you need improvement on? Is there anything you know now that you didn't know before Project 540?

7. Did you have any good teachers or mentors who helped you? What did they do that helped you out?

Personal Change

8. Project 540 could be seen as a social role; throughout this year you have learned to take on this role and master it to some degree. You take on other roles in life: student, employee, friend, sibling, etc. Have you tried out anything you have learned in Project 540 in other roles or domains of your life since you became involved in Project 540? Can you give a specific example? How have you done them differently? What did you learn by trying this new way of being?

9. Are you in any way different since you began Project 540? How do you see yourself now? Would anybody else see this change? Who? What would they say?

**Possible follow-ups: Are you politically or civically involved in any new or different ways since you began? In what ways? Do you see yourself differently as a civic or political actor? In what ways?

10. Since you began Project 540, what reflections, if any, have you made about your own education or educational biography? Political biography?

11. What other political, community, or service activities or organizations are you involved in? In what ways are they similar or different than Project 540? How does this experience fit in with your other activities and experiences?

Notes

1. The name for this civic engagement initiative was chosen to reflect the dynamic, moving nature of the project in the schools where it operated. In skate- or snowboarding, and in geometry as well, a 540-degree turn is a revolution and a half. In Project 540, students began by identifying issues they really cared about in their school, community, nation and world. They examined the current landscape in their school for civic engagement. Through dialogue involving most, or even all the students in the school, they then made recommendations for action on the issues that matter to them. This brings them "full circle," producing action plans based on an understanding of what their school and community have to offer. Finally, they take an additional turn to actually implement their action recommendations—a 540° turn for civic change.

2. In addition to qualitative data gathered, the Pew Charitable Trusts commissioned a quantitative study of the impact of Project 540 on students. The quantitative study's core results came from a two-wave survey panel involving 1,500 randomly-selected students. A recently published final report to the Trusts contains findings from this quantitative study (Borgida & Farr, 2005).

3. The three researchers independently reviewed all transcripts, made notes, and categorized the major themes represented by interviewee comments. Then, in a series of meetings where we shared notes and charts, we came to intersubjective agreement on common themes.

References

Battistoni, R. (2000). Service learning and civic education. In S. Mann & J. Patrick (Eds.), *Education for civic engagement in democracy.* Bloomington, IN: ERIC Clearinghouse for Social Studies.

Borgida, E. & Farr, J. (2005). *Final report to Pew trusts: University of Minnesota research findings on project 540.* University of Minnesota.

Dewey, J. 1916. *Democracy and education.* New York: Macmillan.

Dewey, J. 1938. *Experience and education.* New York: Macmillan.

Galston, W. (2001). Political knowledge, political engagement, and civic education. *Annual Review of Political Science, 4,* 217–234.

Gibson, C., & Levine, P. (2003). *The civic mission of schools.* New York and Washington, DC: The Carnegie Corporation of New York and the Center for Information and Research on Civic Learning.

Hannam, D. (2001). A pilot study to evaluate the impact of the student participation aspects of the citizenship order on standards of education in secondary schools. London: CSV online at http://www.scv.org.uk/csv/hannamreport.pdf

Hannam, D. (2005). *Education for democracy and education through democracy.* London: Department for Education and Skills.

Hepburn, M., Ed. (1983). *Democratic education in schools and classrooms.* Washington, DC: National Council for the Social Studies.

Hildreth, R.W. (2006). The two sides of democratic education: An analysis of undergraduates' lived experiences of political engagement. *Journal of political science education, 2,* (3).

Keeter, S., Zukin, C., Andolina, M., & Jenkins, K. (2002). *The civic and political health of the nation: A generational portrait.* College Park, MD: Center for Information & Research on Civic Learning & Engagement.

Kerr, D., Ireland, E., Lopes, J., & Craig, R. (2004). *Making citizenship education real: Citizenship education longitudinal study second annual report.* DfES: National Foundation for Educational Research.

Kurtz, K., Rosenthal, A., & Zukin, C. (2003). Citizenship: A challenge for all generations. *National Conference of State Legislatures,* http://www.ncsl.org

Kvale, S. (1996). *Interviews: An introduction to qualitative research interviewing.* London: Sage Publications.

Long, S. (2002). *The new student politics: Wingspread statement on student civic engagement.* Providence, RI: Campus Compact.

Longo, N., Drury, C., & Battistoni, R. (2006). Catalyzing political engagement: lessons for civic educators from the voices of students. *Journal of Political Science Education, 2,* No. 3 (September–December).

Miller, J. (2004). *Involving students in governance.* Denver, CO: Education Commission of the States.

National Association of Secondary School Principals (NASSP). (2004). *Breaking ranks: Strategies for leading high school reform.* Arlington, VA: NASSP.

National Center for Education Statistics. (2006). "What does the NAEP Civics Assessment Measure?" Available: http://nces.ed.gov/nationsreportcard/civics/whatmeasure.asp

National Commission on Civic Renewal. (1998). *A nation of spectators: How civic disengagement weakens America and what we can do about it.* College Park: University of Maryland.

Nelson, J., & Kerr, D. (2005). *Active citizenship: Definitions, goals, and practices.* DfES: National Foundation for Education Research.

Niemi, R., & Junn, J. (1998). *Civic education: What makes students learn.* New Haven, CT: Yale University Press.

Peng, I. (2000). Effects of public deliberation on high school students: Bridging the disconnection between young people and public life. In S. Mann & J. Patrick, (Eds.), *Education for civic engagement in democracy.* Bloomington, IN: ERIC Clearinghouse for Social Studies.

Sizer, T. (1984). *Horace's compromise: The dilemma of the American high school.* Boston: Houghton Mifflin.

Torney-Purta, J. (2002). The school's role in developing civic engagement: A study of adolescents in twenty-eight countries. *Applied Developmental Science, 6*(4), 203–212.

Torney-Purta, J., & Vermeer, S. (2004). *Developing citizenship competencies from kindergarten through grade 12: A background paper for policymakers and educators.* Denver, CO: Education Commission of the States.

Torney-Purta, J., Lehmann, R., Oswald, H., & Shulz, W. (2001). *Citizenship and education in twenty-eight countries: Civic knowledge and engagement at age fourteen.* Amsterdam: International Association for the Evaluation of Educational Achievement (IEA).

van Manen, M. (1990). *Researching lived experience: Human science for an action sensitive pedagogy.* Ontario: Althouse Press.

CHAPTER 7

Civic Development in Context

The Influence of Local Contexts on High School Students' Beliefs about Civic Engagement

Ellen Middaugh and Joseph Kahne

> Those who are white, older, affluent, homeowners, and highly educated
> have a disproportionate say in California politics and representation in
> the civic life of the state.
> —*S. Karthick Ramakrishnan & Mark Baldasarre, p. 81*

Trends toward declining youth political and civic participation observed
throughout the last quarter of the 20th century (Putnam, 2000) have
sparked renewed efforts to increase the presence and quality of civic education in American public schools. At the end of the 90s, social scientists
called attention to what they felt was a "crisis of civic engagement" evidenced by shifts in patterns of social and political participation that suggested the members of the youngest generation were not engaged in public life. These shifts include declining voter turnout among 18–24 year
olds, low self-reported interest in political participation, poor knowledge
of democratic structures and principles, and reported lack of trust in government (Galston, 2001). Recent increases in youth voter turnout in the
2008 primaries have led some to be more optimistic about the future participation of youth. However, when these statistics are examined closely, we
find that the majority of youth are not participating in this level of political
decision-making. Out of 25 states for which the Center for Information &
Research on Civic Learning and Engagement (CIRCLE) reported youth

voter participation rates, only one state—New Hampshire—had more than 1 out of 4 youth aged 18–29 turn out for the primary (CIRCLE, 2008). Seeing youth voter turnout triple in states like Florida from 4% to 14% is encouraging, but does not suggest that youth political participation is the norm.

There is also substantial evidence that some groups of citizens are underrepresented in the political process and have far less voice. As the American Political Science Association Task Force on Inequality and American Democracy (2004) reported,

> The privileged participate more than others and are increasingly well organized to press their demands on government. Public officials, in turn, are much more responsive to the privileged than to average citizens and the least affluent. Citizens with low or moderate incomes speak with a whisper that is lost on the ears of inattentive government, while the advantaged roar with the clarity and consistency that policymakers readily heed. (p. 1)

These inequalities are not only associated with income. As a recent study by the nonpartisan Public Policy Institute of California documents, white Californians participate in electoral politics at a proportionally greater rate than do their African American and Latino counterparts (Ramakrishnan & Baldasarre, 2004). In California, this means that one group has a disproportionate influence over policy decisions, a situation that potentially threatens both the legitimacy and the effectiveness of our democracy.

A healthy democracy is one that adequately represents the interests of the populace as a whole. In a country as large and diverse as the United States, this is no small task. As we saw in the 2004 presidential election, there are considerable differences in the concerns, beliefs, and needs of U.S. citizens. Creating a government that both represents the common interests of these diverse perspectives *and* facilitates dialogue where interests diverge requires the active participation of a large and diverse group of citizens.

In response to these concerns, educators and policymakers have urged schools to provide educational opportunities that extend beyond the standard single semester of instruction on the structure and function of government (Gibson & Levine, 2004). Instead they urge the creation of civic education curricula that discuss not only what the U.S. government is and how it works but also why and how ordinary citizens can be involved and participate. These efforts have taken a variety of forms including the infusion of community service requirements, funding for professional development in U.S. History and civics, teacher training in service-learning and civic education, development of civics curricula that target active engagement and civic skills, and efforts to increase youth voice in high schools. All of these strategies have been seen as a means to reverse general trends toward citizen disengagement as well as to increase youth representation in politics. The assumption is that the health of democracy in the United States will improve if all students are exposed to more knowledge of democratic structures and processes, more opportunities to practice democratic skills (debate, working cooperatively, perspective-taking, analyzing, and acting on social issues), and learn more about their rights and responsibilities as democratic citizens.[1]

We concur that it is desirable for all young people to receive these kinds of educational opportunities, but argue that the equitable provision of civic opportunities is no simple matter. In our recent analysis of our Califonia survey data and the IEA national survey of civic education, we found that race, socioeconomic status, and school achievement were associated with the amount of civic opportunities students experienced (Kahne & Middaugh, 2008). We hypothesize that this is due to both differences in what schools or classrooms may have to offer and student self selection into activities that are relevant to their personal goals and interests. Our focus here is on the ways social context does and does not influence the second factor—personal inclination to seek out opportunities for participation.

This chapter examines and seeks to better understand the common features and social contextual differences of youth civic development. In this paper we define social context by the demographic features of young people's communities—racial and ethnic diversity, socioeconomic status and population density. While conventional wisdom suggests these variables bear some relationship to youth civic development, the relationship has not been fully examined. Does local social context influence youth's views on politics and democracy? Their motivation for civic and political engagement? Their experiences with civic education? And if contextual variation does exist in these areas, what does it mean, if anything, for youth civic development and civic education?

Such questions are of great importance for both practitioners and policymakers as well as for members of the scholarly community. Currently, most advocates for civic education and most visions of "Best Practice" are relatively generic. Practices such as service-learning or the discussion of current events are promoted as good for all students. Will the same approaches and curriculum work in all settings or should policy and practice be tailored to reflect differences that may be tied to the characteristics of students and their contexts? There is widespread recognition that factors such as the ethnic and socioeconomic demographics of the community in which a student lives can shape the ways students experience many civic and political institutions and issues (Conover & Searing, 2000; Torney-Purta, Lehmann, Oswald, Schultz, 2001). The consequences of such dynamics for civic development broadly and civic education, in particular, however, have not received sufficient attention from civic education advocates or educators.

The Study

We address questions about the relationship between social context and youth beliefs and experiences with civic education and civic engagement by drawing on 10 focus groups with high school seniors from a diverse array of five schools in California. The students who participated in the focus groups were selected to represent a range of achievement levels and activity levels within the school and community. It should be noted that because all students who participated in this study were high school seniors, the perspectives represented in these groups exclude those who have dropped out or rarely attend school.

The focus group questions were designed to explore constructs that were part of a survey we administered to 200 seniors at each school (See Educating for Democracy, 2005 for a description). The survey was designed to assess high school students' civic commitments, capacities, activities, and school-based opportunities. The conversations we had with students following the survey administration were intended to allow them to expand on their answers and to discuss the personal experiences relevant to their answers. Students were asked to reflect on their own level of commitment to different forms of citizenship including the importance of personal responsibility, participation in community improvement, working with local government, and working for social change. In particular, we examined the relationship between the social context in which youth live and their views on democracy, their attitudes about politics, their motivations for civic and political engagement, and their experiences with civic and political education.

Clearly, a study such as this should be understood as exploratory in nature. By speaking with roughly 50 students in 10 focus groups it is not possible to fully examine the significance of social context for civic development or civic education. But that is not our goal. What these focus groups permit us to do is to explore and highlight dynamics related to the intersection of varied contexts, civic education, and civic development. Our hope is that such exploration will, first and foremost, help us to recognize and consider the potential significance of contextual factors. In so doing, we hope it will help us to theorize better, to identify hypotheses, and to illustrate dynamics that are worthy of continued attention.

Each school in this study was in the process of planning programs to augment civic education as part of the Educating for Democracy initiative in California.[2] Each of the 12 schools participating in the initiative agreed to implement at least one of six recommendations identified in the *Civic Mission of Schools* (CMS) report (Gibson & Levine, 2004) as particularly promising approaches for increasing civic and political engagement. These include recommendations for schools to provide increased opportunities for:

1. Instruction in Government, Law, History, Economics and other related courses
2. Debate and discussion about current events and issues that matter to students
3. Community service and service-learning
4. Extracurricular activities
5. Student governance and student decision making in school
6. Simulations of political processes (e.g., mock elections, mock trials, lobbying)

Our first phase of data collection served, in part, as a needs assessment process to aid schools in planning and to provide students with an opportunity to reflect on their civic engagement in their schools and community to date. While the participating schools were in the process of designing new programs and new curricula to improve civic outcomes for students, some of the CMS recommended strategies for promoting youth civic engagement were already being used. In the five schools highlighted for this study, there were two practices of which students were particularly aware—community service and opportunities for debate and discussion of current events.

We will use our analysis of students' views on democracy and civic and political engagement along with their interpretations of their current school-based opportunities for civic engagement to consider some possible implications for civic education in our diverse democracy. We will also highlight ways future studies of civic education might help us better account for contextual variation.

Participating Schools

The current study is part of a larger study of youth civic engagement in California. For the purposes of examining contextual variation in youth views on and experiences with civic engagement, we draw on data from 10 focus groups at 5 of the 12 participating schools. At each school, outside consultants who were working with the schools during the assessment phase of the civic education initiative were asked to consult with teachers to select two groups of 4 to 6 students each. They were also instructed to select students who represented a range of academic achievement and engagement in school activities.[3] Students were then interviewed by one or both of the authors in a room or area of school where their answers could not be heard by teachers or school officials. Students were also told that their answers would not be shared with identifying information. The conversations were audiotaped and then transcribed by a professional transcription service and checked for accuracy by research assistants.

Schools were chosen to represent urban, suburban, and rural communities as well as communities with high and low average socioeconomic status. Communities also had three patterns of racial/ethnic composition noted as distinct regional patterns within the state—majority white, no clear majority, and majority Latino. Each school and its surrounding local context is described briefly below.[4]

Sequoia HS is located in a small (population 1,000), rural, middle class town. Residents of the town are mostly White non-Hispanic (>90%), have a minimum of a high school degree (>90%), and a substantial number are college graduates (30%).[5] The median resident age in Sequoia is between 40 and 45, and the median income is a little over $50, 000. The clear majority of students (90%) identify as white, and fewer than 5% identify as Hispanic or Native American. Approximately 15% of students qualify for free or reduced price meals. Sequoia's statewide rank on the Academic Performance Index (API) was 7 out of 10 in the year when the study was conducted.[6]

Sunny Hill HS is located in an upper-middle-class suburb (population >60,000) of a major metropolitan area in Northern California. White non-Hispanic residents make up a clear majority of the residents in the city (>75%), followed by considerably smaller numbers of Hispanic (<10%) and Asian/Pacific Islander (approximately 10%) residents. Residents of the city also have higher incomes (median income > $90K) and higher average education (90% high school graduates and 45% college graduates) than the state in general. The median age of residents in Sunny Hill is between 35 and 40. The school itself is similar with the majority of students (approximately 70%) identifying as white, a substantial minority (approximately 20%) identifying as Asian, and a small number (<5%) identifying as Hispanic. Less than 2% of the students qualify for free or reduced price meals and only 2.5% are English Language Learners. The school is high performing with a statewide rank on the API of 10 out of 10.

Johnson HS is a suburban/urban fringe school on the edge of a major California city (population >400, 000) in a rapidly expanding middle-income neighborhood. Residents of both the city and school are ethnically diverse, a fact of which students in the focus groups were very aware. No single ethnic group accounts for more than 50%. The largest group in the city identified as white, followed in group size by Hispanic and African American. The median resident age is between 30 and 35 and the median income is around $37, 000. At the school, the largest group identified as Asian (>30%), followed by African American (approximately 25%), Hispanic (approximately 20%) and white (<20%). Approximately one-third of the student body qualifies for free/reduced price meals and 13% of students are English language learners. In the year of data collection, Johnson's statewide rank on the API was 6 out of 10.

Hartman HS is located in a city (population >45,000) on the fringe of a major metropolitan area. The town is 93% Hispanic with 50% of the population reporting countries other than the U.S. as their birth country. Residents of the city tend to be young (median resident age between 20 and 25) and to have incomes (median income a little over $30, 000) and levels of education (30% report having completed high school and <5% college) lower than the state as a whole. The poverty rate for the surrounding city is just under 30%. Similarly, nearly all (>95% Hartman students identify as Hispanic with close to 60% of students qualifying for free/reduced price meals. Approximately one-third of students are English Language Learners with Spanish as their first language. At the time of data collection, Hartman HS reported a statewide rank on the API of 1 out of 10.

James HS is located within a major metropolitan area in Southern California (population over 3 million). The school is located in a middle class neighborhood within the city, but students are drawn from a variety of neighborhoods across the city. There is no clear ethnic majority in the city as a whole. The largest group identifies as Hispanic (>45%) with the next largest groups respectively identifying as white (approximately 30%), African American (>10%), Asian or Asian American (<10%). More than 25% of residents in the surrounding city identified as "other." The median age for the city is between 30 and 35, and the median income is just over $36,000. The clear majority of students at James HS report as Hispanic (>65%) with significant representation of students who identify as white (10–15%), Filipino (approximately 10%) and Asian (<10%). Nearly 70% of students qualify for free or reduced price meals and >25% are English Language Learners with the majority of this group reporting Spanish as their first language. James HS reported a statewide ranking on the API of 3 during the data collection year.

Why Focus on Social Context?

California is a well known for its diversity. No single racial group composes a majority of the population. A substantial and increasing percentage (>25%) of the state's residents were born in another country (Ralph and Goldy Lewis Center for Regional Policy Studies, 2001). These trends are more pronounced in California, but are by no means irrelevant to the United States as a whole and are perhaps predictive of the future of the country. Data from the last U.S. Census revealed that 11.1% of the U.S. population in the year 2000 was foreign-born, up from 7.9% in 1990 (Malone, Baluja, Costanzo, & Davis, 2003). Additionally, California is home to communities ranging from those marked by startling wealth to those with pervasive poverty. A recent report by the Public Policy Institute of California suggests that though the increasing diversity in California is a statewide phenomenon noted in 6 out of 9 regions, each region has its own unique demographic profile (Johnson, 2002).

If there were no systematic differences in patterns of civic and political participation among California's diverse citizenry, the motivation to examine the influence of social context would be minimal. Unfortunately, this is not the case. A 2004 study by the Public Policy Institute of California suggests that the voices and interests of some groups are more likely to be expressed and represented than those of others (Ramakrishnan & Baldassarre, 2004). The study found that California citizens as a whole vote and engage in other civic activities at about the same rates as citizens in the rest of the country, but that various groups within California participate at very different rates. For example, white citizens in California vote, sign petitions, write to elected officials, attend rallies, participate in partisan political work, contribute money to political causes, and volunteer at significantly higher levels than other racial and ethnic groups. Only in attending local meetings do whites lag behind Latinos and African Americans. While part of the explanation for lower voting rates may be an artifact of opportunity rather than motivation (e.g., not having citizenship status or disenfranchisement due to incarceration), these factors do not explain the discrepancy in other forms of participation which may influence elected officials or those who can vote. In a state that relies heavily on ballot measures[7] and direct voter participation to make decisions on a number of very important issues such as funding for public education,[8] affirmative action,[9] and access to public services,[10] there is reason to worry that that the lower rates of participation among citizens who are lower income, immigrants, and those from certain racial and ethnic groups reduces the likelihood their interests will be represented in policies that directly affect them. Indeed, in his study of the relationship between income and influence in the country as a whole, Larry Bartels (2004) found that when it comes to the votes of United States senators, the policy preferences of constituents in the 75th percentile of the income distribution were almost three times as influential as the policy preferences of those in the 25th percentile. The policy preferences of those in "the bottom third of the income distribution had no apparent statistical effect on their senators' roll call votes" (p.1).

Given that (1) racial and ethnic minorities, immigrants, and lower income citizens appear to be underrepresented in civic and political life in California, and (2) that many of these groups tend to cluster in different areas of the state, we believe it is important for civic educators to understand whether and how these varying social contexts might influence young people's experience with democracy and civic and political life. While viewed by many as important, researchers are only just beginning to understand these dynamics. This chapter is an effort to support that conversation.

We begin by discussing perspectives on the importance of context in the literature to date. We then describe findings from the qualitative component of our study. We conclude with implications for civic education research and practice.

Broadening the Definition of Civic Maturity: Research on Minority, Urban and Immigrant Civic Participation

While the group differences in civic and political participation presented earlier in this chapter are well documented throughout the U.S., effective ways to interpret and respond to these differences in civic education programs has not received sufficient attention. Indeed, discussions of best practice by educators and advocates often make no mention of the important role context plays in shaping students' experiences of and perspectives on civic and political engagement. Fortunately, some recent scholarship is addressing these issues.

Hart and Atkins (2002) reviewed studies comparing minority and urban youth to their white and suburban counterparts on a number of outcomes believed to be important civic competencies including civic knowledge, participation in civic activities, and civic skills (e.g., letter writing, public speaking). They conclude that urban and minority youth tend to "lag behind" in civic development compared to their white, upper-income, suburban counterparts. This conclusion is drawn from evidence that African American and Hispanic youth score lower on national assessments of civic knowledge,[11] that youth from neighborhoods with higher rates of poverty are less likely to volunteer or engage in community service[12] and that the urban youth they encountered in their own work were less likely to have some basic skills, such as letter-writing, that are useful for communicating with public officials. To explain these gaps in skills, activities and knowledge, Hart and Atkins look to the schools and community contexts. They suggest that failing schools, fewer opportunities for afterschool activities (such as little league) and fewer adult civic role models in urban contexts account for this lag. They conclude that investments at both the school and community level would be necessary to close the gap in civic engagement.

Conover and Searing's (2000) study of the citizen identities of high school students from rural, suburban, urban and immigrant communities focused on outcomes such as students' ideas about the rights and responsibilities of citizenship. They note several contextual differences in students' ideas and behaviors related to citizenship. In particular, the authors interpret urban students' lower rates of endorsement of obeying minor laws as a citizen responsibility compared to suburban students as a "failure of socialization" due to weak norms in their community (p. 291). They also note the tendency of students from the immigrant community (in San Antonio) to hold a conception of citizenship that is more patriotic and civically and politically participatory than their counterparts from other groups. However, based on the limited measures of activity (political discussions and acts of tolerance), they found rural and suburban students more likely to endorse these items. Conover and Searing emphasize the need to support the development of richer citizen identities for *all* students and suggest that contextual differences in the norms and practices of citizenship must be taken into account to provide higher quality civic education.

Other scholars who focus on minority, urban, and immigrant youth civic engagement suggest the need for greater investment in engaging these youth as well, but caution against (1) identifying lower performance on tests of civic knowledge and differences in patterns of political and civic behavior as necessarily a "lag in civic development," not simply a rational difference, and (2) relying on previously established models of civic education to engage urban and minority youth.

Sanchez-Jankowski (1986), for example, examines survey and interview data from his 10-year longitudinal panel study of the political socialization of Chicano youth (conducted from 1976 to 1986) in three different cities. His study documents the influence of the different experiences of the various racial and ethnic groups in American history as well as of the local sociopolitical context on the civic and political priorities of youth (Sanchez-Jankowski, 1986, 1992, 2002). In particular, he suggests that civic socialization for youth who grow up identifying with groups that have historically been excluded from American public life—such as Latinos, African Americans, and Native Americans—is a process of learning knowledge and skills important to the advancement of their specific group as a whole. Thus while civic maturity or adequate civic development is typically measured by "official" political knowledge (e.g., principles of the constitution, structure of the U.S. government) and general ability for and interest in participation in civic and political processes, Sanchez-Jankowski (2002) suggests that that civic maturity for youth in historically excluded groups is more typically marked by knowledge of how their particular group or community works (learned from community elders and local resources) and interest in participation that promotes the welfare of their own community. Thus, the lack of knowledge about the meaning of the 4th of July and the technical skills necessary for communicating with government officials identified as deficits by Hart and Atkins may not be a sign of developmental lag, but a sign of different priorities and models of civic maturity.

Bedolla's (2005) more recent study of 100 1st through 5th generation adolescent and adult Latino residents of Los Angeles also identified historical experiences of ethnic groups as an important component of political socialization. Her comparison of patterns of political engagement among residents of a working class community in East Los Angeles and middle-class Montebello suggested that nearly all participants from both areas, regardless of generation, identified primarily as Latino and viewed this identity as existing in tension with being American. Bedolla attributes this finding to the history of exclusion of Latino and Native American citizens and immigrants from American politics and other aspects of public life. Furthermore, nearly all participants in her study defined "politics" as something that happens at a national (rather than local) level, as the domain of Anglo Americans, and as distant from their own concerns.

However, among her sample, many participants engaged politically in the form of voting and protesting (e.g., against Proposition 187) and civically in the form of community service. In these forms of participation, Bedolla found that the working class residents of East Los Angeles, who were also more likely to be first or second generation immigrants and to live in a more segregated community, were more engaged than middle class Montebello residents. Based on this evidence and participants' discussion of their sense of ethnic identity, Bedolla concludes that among Latino citizens and residents, political engagement is more likely to be motivated by a positive group affiliation than by personal agency or community or national problems alone.

Junn's (1999) analysis of the participation patterns of three generations of Mexican Americans, Asian Americans, African Americans and Anglo-Americans lends further support to Sanchez-Jankowski's (2002) assertion that patterns of participation for groups with more barriers against government access might be different rather than absent altogether. Using two survey data sets selected for their inclusion of greater numbers of minority participants and a greater variety of forms of civic participation than typically included in quantitative studies of civic and political engagement, she found that Latino and Asian American participants were more likely to report engaging in direct forms of political activity (e.g., protests, serving on local councils, and working with others on local problems) than system-directed forms of political activity (voting, contacting public officials, and working on political campaigns). Junn (1999) suggests that there is reason to believe perhaps for more recent immigrants, and to a lesser degree for minorities in general, that participation in the formal structures of the U.S. government is seen as a less productive way of improving their communities. Rather than marking this as a problematic sign of civic disengagement among individuals, she suggests that this may be a more productive form of civic and political activity for groups that do not have the connections, modes of expression, or political cachet that would make their votes or letters to congressmen and -women, yield influence on decisions that affect their lives.

Finally, Cohen, who is currently working to revive the study of civic and political development of African American youth in this post-civil rights movement era, joins the voices urging us to consider the multiple pathways to civic maturity taken by youth who come of age in urban contexts. Drawing on her focus group conversations with young African American men (aged 18 to 21), Cohen (2006) notes that while this group is seen as relatively disengaged from the kinds of participation associated with youth civic engagement (e.g., participation in community and extracurricular activities), they represent a substantial presence in a number of social movements, from the Civil Rights Movement to the anti-apartheid movement to the more recent movement against mass incarceration. Furthermore, she notes that African American youth in urban communities interact on a daily basis with a variety of representatives of the government including public schools, police, and social service agencies. She argues that the extent to which youth try to influence these organizations and control the influence of these representatives on their own lives, they are indeed engaged in a form of political activity unlikely to be captured by most surveys of civic and political engagement (Cohen, 2004, 2006).

These studies of modern-day minority, immigrant, and urban youth civic engagement share some common assumptions and raise interesting issues that shape our research questions here. Specifically, they suggest that youth who grow up in urban environments, as part of a group that has historically been or is currently excluded from public life, or in low-income communities may hold a more skeptical view of participation in the American political system. Furthermore, they raise questions about the effectiveness of civic education programs that stress an obligation to uphold "American ideals," that focus on national issues without strong connections to issues about which these groups care, and that emphasize traditional modes of engagement and knowledge of the structures and functions of institutions. Finally, they encourage an expanded view of what it means to demonstrate mature civic development.

With this literature in mind, we address our broader questions about the role of social context in youth civic development by examining our data with four guiding questions. First, to what extent do youth see our current system of government as being truly democratic? Second, how interested in politics and government are they? How motivated are they to participate in civic and political life and in what ways? And finally, how do students perceive their experiences with civic education?

Findings

Beliefs about Democracy: Ideals vs. Reality

Regardless of social context, students expressed appreciation for a democratic system of government and many of the associated ideals. At the same time, students differed by context in their belief that the current system of government approaches these ideals.

In the two schools with predominantly white middle/upper-middle class student bodies—Sequoia and Sunny Hill—the 20 young people in those focus groups nearly unanimously expressed faith in the basic fairness and utility of the system. Many of these students had critiques about specific policies (e.g., regarding the war in Iraq, gay marriage, funding for education) or current configurations of local and national administrations, but they expressed the belief that more participation by citizens would lead to better solutions for everyone.

The example below was typical of Sequoia students' responses to a question about their definition of democracy and the importance of democracy. They tended to emphasize the importance of rule by majority and expressed faith that the kinds of representatives and resulting policies that come from majority votes would be best for the country as a whole.

Male Student # 1: I'd rather not have my entire life subjected to some maniac's whims. I don't know what one person's thinking. Okay, you've got one person, and one person can be extreme in either way, but if you've got fifty million people, it's going to be balanced toward the center.

Male Student #2: Like what [he] said, the more people involved, the radicals are going to be way at the far edge. The majority's voice is going to be those who are more educated about the whole thing.

At Sunny Hill, where a number of students had taken a course with a social justice theme to fulfill one of their school requirements, the discussion was more nuanced. When responding to questions about the importance of working for social change, the students brought up and engaged in a discussion about a highly controversial issue—gay marriage.

Male Student #1: A lot of people do have problems with homosexuals. You can't just force that upon them. . . . I think sometimes people say it's better for the country. But we're a democracy, right? We should stand up for the views of the majority. I think a lot of time we don't. The minority rules the country.

Female Student #1: I don't agree that the minority rules this country. I get what you're saying, but that's why we have elections. All the big issues, there are elections for.

Male Student #1: There are elections for them, but leading up to them, most people in campaigning don't put their foot down on the hard issues because a large chunk of the country is against them.

Female Student #1: Yeah, but before a bill is ever going to get passed, if gay marriage is ever going to be legal, it'll have to go through the whole process that, if the system is working, we'll have everyone's opinion. Is it working?

Male Student #1: I think so, mostly.

The students in this group articulately discussed a very controversial issue and expressed varied and conflicting personal opinions. There was also some critique of the ways in which the democratic process has currently handled the issue. In conversation, students grappled with the question of whether the majority decision is necessarily the best or most just decision. While they each came to differing conclusions about this, both students had faith that citizens could work through the government and the electoral process to arrive at a just solution in due time.

Students from the two schools representing communities with a clear Latino majority and relatively high rates of poverty viewed our current incarnation of democracy quite differently. When James HS students were asked, as were the Sequoia HS students, to explain the meaning and importance of democracy to them, their responses suggested a belief in the ideal but greater skepticism about the reality. When asked to reflect on their definition of democracy, the responses below were typical of most students' responses:

Male Student #1: I don't know. It's supposed to be the people and stuff, that kind of rule, but not really. I mean to decide who takes care of the country for them, when they vote that's what they're kind of doing. But the decision is not always taken into consideration. I mean it's good that there is such a thing as democracy, but sometimes it's kind of abused. Like, they don't respect it, I think.

Male Student #2: I think about the government. The Democratic Party and the Republican Party, how the Republican Party always wins. And that just shows that—because I think, but I'm not sure, that the Republican Party, they favor the wealthy people, right?

Female Student #1: Democracy is like the [middle] class.

Male Student #2: And so [when] they win, it says the people who have money are always dominant.

Male Student #1: That's why I don't think they take democracy seriously.

Male Student #3: It's not really a country for the people. Like, what do they call it, of the people.

Rather than invoking the construct of the majority, as did the Sequoia students in response to the same question about what democracy means, James students expressed the importance of representation of "the people" and a serious skepticism that, regardless of voter turnout, the government will achieve this representation. While students were not probed on what they mean by the "the people," their comments here and throughout the conversations implied that representation should include people like them. For students who arguably have at least some experiences and community concerns that are not shared or well understood by the majority of

American citizens, having a government "for the people" is unlikely to be a simple matter of listening to the national majority.

Hartman students demonstrated a similar attitude of appreciation for democracy coupled with skepticism about the current system. When asked about the importance of working for social change, as in the example from Sunny Hill, Hartman students reject the system-directed electoral politics in favor of direct action.

> Female Voice: I also agree . . . that the best way is to go to try to make a change through politics, but I think that in this community we kind of see politicians in a negative way. So, sometimes it's hard to do it that way. So, we have to kind of like—I don't know. I think the community itself, not so much through city politicians.

What's striking in this example is the explicit rejection of politicians as representing the community in any way. The student in this example went on to describe the ways in which the community could come together to provide services that are currently the responsibility of the city and a belief that people would more readily support community actions than those of politicians. We will see in the next section that many of these students do not see their own participation in politics, one way that people traditionally assure that government is representative of the community, as a desirable option.

Similarly, when asked to discuss the issues such as how they view democracy and the importance of challenging social inequalities, the Hartman students again raised questions about the utility of system-directed politics. In contrast to Sunny Hill students who debated *how* system-directed politics should be used to achieve more equality (either through majority decision vs. government intervention), Hartman students spent more time discussing why system-directed politics do not achieve these ends.

> Female Voice: I honestly don't think it's, not that we can't reach it, but I don't think we'll ever truly find it in a democracy. It's more like— you like to believe that it's for the people, by the people, from the people. Will it ever be like that? We can get very close to it, but will we reach a perfect democracy, I don't think so. I mean just because we create systems, but the system will always have flaws.

One reason for some of these students' skepticism was the difficulty they noticed in identifying inequalities well enough to challenge them and make democracy work in a more equitable manner.

> Facilitator: "I think it's important to challenge inequalities in society." What did you think when you saw that question?
> Female Voice #1: It is, but it's difficult sometimes. Especially if you don't go out a lot from [this city], you don't realize there's inequalities. You think that's just the way it is. When you start going to other places, you're like, "Wow," there's all of these things that I didn't know about. But you didn't know about them because you don't know they exist. So, it kind of depends.
> Female Voice #2: I don't think you could ever get rid of [inequality]. When I think of that question, I thought of Supreme Court cases. I thought of it as something very, very difficult because Supreme Court cases are very difficult to get up there. Like she said, we live in this little bubble and we think this is how life is and how it works, but it really doesn't. So we don't see that inequality until we step out.

These comments were among many where students expressed the belief that the government in their community was not responsive and that politics did not work well. Yet at the same time they expressed uncertainty as to whether the political system does work better in other contexts and whether those benefits would ever be available to communities such as theirs.

In summary, the young people we spoke with from James and Hartman tended to show a similar appreciation for the idea of democracy but a different experience of the current workings of American democracy than did the students from Sunny Hill and Sequoia. Although they often described the logic of our democratic institutions and, at times, expressed belief in the practices of our current democracy (e.g., community solutions to social problems negotiated through politics, using the judicial system rather than force to challenge injustices, and the importance of citizen participation in shaping the political world), they simultaneously (and to a far greater degree than students from Sunny Hill and Sequoia) expressed skepticism that the system treats all groups of people equally and that participation in the current system would achieve their ends.

These differences appear quite consistent with findings from the literature that low-income youth and youth of color are more likely to be involved in direct forms of civic activity than in system directed forms (see Cohen, 2006; Junn, 1999). Indeed, if experience has led these young people to believe that the system will not be responsive, it is hardly surprising that they are less likely to anticipate engaging in system directed activity.

"It's Not Made for Me"—Views on Politics

Our prior analysis of quantitative survey data on the interests and activities of youth across the state suggests that youth in California are strongly interested in helping others and report doing so through volunteer work, but they are much less interested in working with a group or through government to address community issues and are less likely to engage in activities that relate to formal politics (Kahne & Middaugh, 2005). This finding is consistent with the literature on youth civic engagement. Studies have demonstrated considerable and increasing youth volunteerism over the last 15 years, but very low and in some cases declining interest in system-directed political activities (Gibson & Levine, 2004).

Our focus group conversations with students revealed broad similarities in students' views on civic and political participation regardless of context. In every group, they reported experiences with community service (either voluntary or through a school requirement) and were consistently positive about the importance of helping others and the community in general. A number of students in groups extended their hours after beginning their school-mandated community service.[13] Students' reasons for enjoying community service tended to focus on the interpersonal rewards. As one student put it, it "makes you feel good inside." A number of students made the point that it's good to "think about other people."

There also appeared to be few contextual differences in students' interest in working on community issues through political or community-based organizations. Most students, regardless of context, reported little interest in these kinds of activities, though there were individual exceptions. For the most part, students seemed to agree that political participation is a matter of individual propensity and choice. And most students did not see themselves as the kind of people who would become involved politically. Indeed, the same students who talk about their volunteer activities and how important it is to improve their communities often viewed politics as a completely separate sphere of activity.

This disinterest in politics may be due in part to what appears to be a narrow definition of what it means to be politically engaged. When probed as to why they were not interested in politics, students' answers reflected a stereotypical view of the kinds of people who are involved in politics. For example, as one young man at Johnson HS explained, he didn't see himself having anything in common with the politicians he had seen in the media because of how they present themselves.

> Male Voice: It's not made for me.
> Facilitator: Why not?
> Male Voice: I just don't think I can be a politician. I couldn't do that.
> Facilitator: What about politicians makes you think you couldn't be one? What do you think they're like?
> Male Voice: I don't know. I just, by looking at them, by the way they talk, they're all like preppy and—I can't do that.

In other places, where students did not mention appearance and mannerisms, the image of a politically active person was still quite narrow. For example, the Sequoia student quoted below noted the ambitious or more assertive nature of the kind of person she believes it takes to be politically engaged.

> There are those who are made for being interested in political issues. They're just more driven people. Not necessarily driven, but more opinionated, maybe. And that's other people . . . that's just not my personality.—*Sequoia student*

Finally, at Hartman, a student notes the potential for conflict and ruled out her own participation based on this.

> No. I mean you know I don't like really like it. So I don't want to work with something like that. . . . There's a lot of people you know you have to like please or be fair or whatever. It's too much to think about. So that's like why I don't like it.—*Female Hartman student*

What these students held in common was a belief that being involved with politics takes a very specific type of person. Their various descriptions of that type of person, though focusing on different aspects, call to mind the type of image most immediately available to most of us—the highly polished, articulate, ambitious, and tough talking elected officials we see on television. The many political activists, campaign workers, local advisors among others who work in politics and never make it to television are likely more diverse in appearance, manner, and background, but are often not seen. Imagining that one needs to look, act, and talk in a particular way to participate in democratic decision making is probably much more of a disincentive for participation than many educators would think.

Given this overriding disinterest in the political realm, in the next section we examine in more depth what does or does not motivate youth to be civically and politically engaged.

Influences on Motivation for Civic and Political Engagement

While the last section highlighted a widespread similarity in students' general disinterest in politics and government, some of the factors contributing to their disinterest appear to be highly contextualized.

In the more affluent communities where Sunny Hill and Sequoia are located, students commented on how few problems there were in their community and how little need there was to get involved in organized efforts to improve or change the community. In the following conversation, Sunny Hill students were asked to reflect on whether it was important to work with CBOs or local government to improve the community. The overriding sentiment was that there was little need for that type of activity.

> Interviewer: Are there any particular issues in Sunny Hill and in your community that you think need to be addressed?
> Female Student #2: We're all spoiled.
> Female Student #1: There're not a lot of big problems around here that are big, like homeless people. But there are a lot of other problems that are just like teenagers being stupid, dumb stuff. Vandalism.
> Male Student #1: In Sunny Hill, we expect the community to do the stuff for us. You go to a park and there's going to be everything you need there. It's kind of interesting to see the other side, like in other communities people might have to clean up the garbage themselves.

At Sequoia HS, the conversations were similar.

> Male Student: Maybe if we lived up in [next city over] or something. Like, [the next city over] is one big ghetto, basically. I wouldn't walk the streets there at night. I mean, you said that you're going to go visit schools in [major urban area]. I'm sure there's something there that they could do, because [that city] has a lot of poverty-stricken areas and I think that it's easier to be involved in community service when there's a big problem facing you.
>
> Female Student: We kind of look the other way because it's not hard. You can look anywhere else, you know? There's very little poverty here.

In both schools, the students saw little need to work with local government or community-based organizations absent the kinds of problems people face in lower-income and urban communities. At Sunny Hill, which is situated in a more densely populated part of the state, the students were more aware of the way other communities functioned and of the role their well-funded local government played in keeping the community clean and safe. At Sequoia, a more rural community that conceivably provides fewer opportunities to see how surrounding communities function, students' analyses relied more on vague ideas that their community had fewer problems and therefore less need for citizen involvement in local government. In neither community did students mention the kinds of problems that they might face in their own communities. Eating disorders, drug abuse, depression and anxiety are all significant problems present in affluent communities (Levine, 2006). Clearly, such problems could be the focus of political or community-based initiatives.

In the more urban environments surrounding James and Hartman HS, identifying needs in the community was not a problem. Throughout our conversations, students expressed concerns over a number of issues including gang violence, drugs, immigrant rights, racial tensions, and funding for special education. However, they perceived government as inattentive to or ineffective in responding to these problems.

At James HS, students noted that they would be more interested in following politics if the topics addressed by politicians more obviously related to what was going on in their own communities.

[Following a conversation about not being interested in the presidential debates . . .]

> Male Voice: As long as they say something about trying to help the people out, like actually in the bad communities, that's something I would actually participate in.
> Facilitator: Right, that makes it more interesting?
> Male Voice: That's probably the only thing I would actually pay attention to in the speeches. How they were going to help the people. I would participate and actually see it there, what they were doing. Because most of the time, they say they want to help, but I don't actually see it happening.

This young man's view of politics and politicians as being removed from the concerns that face the local communities echoes Bedolla's (2005) findings that, regardless of generation, her Latino participants defined politics as something that happens at a national level and is largely divorced from community concerns. Unlike Bedolla's participants, our study participants did not raise the issue of Latino identity, race, or ethnicity in their discussion of politics. It is possible that these concepts are implicit in students' statements because the communities in which they live and refer to as being ignored by politicians are primarily Latino. However, students in our study were more likely to spontaneously raise issues of class, referring to the influence of the rich and the neglect of lower income communities. These observations do not refute the importance Bedolla (2005) assigns to ethnic identity in political socialization, but do reassert the importance of the local economic context, which both Bedolla and Sanchez-Jankowski (1986, 1992, 2002) identify as interacting with ethnic identity in the formation of political attitudes and development of broader political identities.

At Hartman, students were similarly skeptical that politicians could or would adequately serve the interests of the community. Here, a local scandal that had happened several years before led several students to doubt the potential effectiveness of political engagement. As one student put it, her family "realized change is not going to happen through politics. So why should I waste my time on it?" This same student, noted in an earlier section, recommended community-based rather than politically based solutions to the communities problems. In this case, the turn to direct action over political action appears rational and to be related to direct experience rather than ignorance of how the system works.

Students' Experiences of Formal Civic Education.

Given the wide-spread student disinterest in politics across local contexts and the differences in student views about government between contexts and differing motivations for political participation, it is important to consider how students view the opportunities for civic and political engagement made available to them at school. Our initial round of qualitative data collection was intended to serve as an exploration of the relationship between social context and students' conceptualizations of civic engagement. However, we did ask students to reflect along the way on such topics as where their attitudes about political and civic engagement came from, how they became involved in their current civic engagement activities, and what kinds of school-based opportunities they believed would increase their interest in civic and political participation. The information we gained, while not a comprehensive examination of what opportunities are available at the school level, had implications for two particular recommended practices in the recent work on civic education—community service and debate and discussion about personally relevant current events.

As noted earlier in this chapter, students in every group reported active participation in community service. At James, Johnson, and Sunny Hill High Schools, community service was either required or offered as an option to meet a graduation requirement. Sequoia and Hartman High Schools also had programs to facilitate community service involvement, though at Sequoia a district-wide community service requirement had recently been revoked. In every group, students reported involvement in some kind of community service. A number of students got involved in these kinds of activities through family, church, or their community and continued these activities as part of a school requirement or on their own. For others, school requirements or school activities were the entry point. In all cases, students viewed messages about civic engagement ("you have to get involved") in a highly personalized way. For example, when asked what they believed it meant to "improve your community," this James HS student drew on her experiences with school-based service activities:

Female Student: Also what's helped me is because I'm in "Leader-ship".... I have to do so much community service because Leader-ship also encourages you. And like, I mean, before, it was just okay, whatever, I didn't even know what's to help your community or stuff like that. But [here], around here, we went to the convalescent home for old people. We always go for Christmas. We go sing. You think singing to them is nothing, but they get so happy. It's like everything. It's like, wow, you know, they come and sing, they get happy, and I don't know. You just have to get involved.

At Sequoia High School, more than 500 miles to the North, students reflected on their service experiences in a similar manner. Students clearly connected these activities to a sense that it was their "civic duty" to be involved and help other people. However, they understood the call to fulfill their "civic duty" as being best met by individual activities or behaviors. Students' visions of fulfilling their civic duty were very much linked to service, but somewhat divorced from politics or organized community involvement. Consistent with findings from other studies, community service and service-learning programs were interpreted by students as encouraging individual helping behavior and personal responsibility rather than participation in or work to change social systems (Barber, 1992; Boyte, 1991; Robinson, 2000; Walker, 2000, Westheimer & Kahne, 2004).

One school-based activity that students said did pique their interest in their civics or government classes were debates and discussions of current events. At Johnson High School, one group of students provided great detail when describing their disinterest in their government class and the fact that they did not talk about anything that mattered. This conversation continued until one student brought up debates that they'd had in class.

Female Student #1: We did have that one debate.
Facilitator: What was the debate?

[Students identify pretending to be candidates and debating several controversial topics that were prominent in the most recent elections.]

Female Student #1 We got a little bit passionate.
Facilitator: Do you guys like having these discussions?

[Several replies of yes.]

> Female Student #2: I like debating. It's fun.
> Facilitator: If you could have more of that in a class, would you want that?

[Several replies of yes.]

> Female Student #2: Yeah, more "now" and less "back then." I don't
> care what the old ten-dollar bill looked like fifty years ago. I don't
> think that's relevant to our [lives].   —*Johnson HS students*

These sentiments were echoed across contexts. These discussions often centered on current prominent political and social justice issues, such as gay marriage and the legal status of abortion as well as such civil rights issues as women's pay and the glass ceiling. Youth repeatedly said things like, "I like debates better than just regular lesson plans." They cited reasons such as getting to "speak your ideas" and "get more involved" in the discussions. However, as routinely positive as students were about the opportunity to be more actively involved in their class discussions, students did not appear to link such discussions to a notion of active citizenship. While they remembered that they liked doing debates, many students were foggy on the details of what it was they had debated.

[Following is a discussion in which students explained that they preferred debates to other lessons and enjoyed having the chance to "speak out."]

> Facilitator: Were there issues that you guys were [discussing] when you
> did debates that people were particularly interested in?
> Male Student #1: Well, when we do a debate, it's basically on some-
> thing that's related to what the teacher was talking about.
> Male Student #2: There was one talking about women's rights, what it
> was back then. Why did men get paid more than women? There was
> a debate about that.
> Facilitator: Okay.
> Male Student #3: Or, um, why women can't get the same position as
> other men. Like the glass ceiling, I think what it was. They'll never
> make it up there. There was a debate about that. There were some
> other debates, too, I just can't really remember.   —*James HS students*

Considering students so strongly recommended these debate opportunities as interesting and engaging, one might ask how a classroom practice that so many students clearly enjoy and prefer can yield such faint memories of the related content. One potential answer is that, at least from the students' point of view, the debates appear to stand as an anomaly or a break from what they normally are learning in the classroom. Students when praising the debates noted that they were more interesting than "regular" lessons and when asked if they have discussions about the causes of social problems, this Sequoia student's answer captures a similar disconnection between curricular content and the kinds of discussions that students' seem to find interesting.

> Well, if we were, it would have to be when the teacher was done with his lesson, because we have to get done with his lessons before we can discuss anything else. —*Male Sequoia student*

Those who prize civic education want students to have opportunities that integrate learning about how government works and about particular issues with opportunities to develop informed opinions and, at times, to act. To the extent that students recalled opportunities to discuss their opinions or to act, they described such opportunities as divorced from the course content. Such discussions were seen more as an engaging diversion than as part of course content. Moreover, the content of their government course was not seen as a means of developing informed opinion or of knowing how to successfully advance those opinions through governmental structures or other institutions.

Furthermore, active learning strategies alone may be insufficient to draw students' attention to course content. Most students, young or old, when presented with required course content will at some point ask (at least to themselves) the question, "Why do we need to know this?" Students in our sample expressed a desire to know and to discuss more about the issues currently facing their schools, communities, and the nation as a whole.

> Yeah, I think that just giving us more information in school about things that are going on, especially in government. I know it's really important, especially for advanced placement classes where we have to take the AP test, that they learn the past information, but I think that

even more would be way better if we actually had discussions about things that were going on, so at least, you know, the people who are now voting age would be informed about things that they're voting on locally and nationally. *—Male Sequoia HS student*

The idea that students with a history of strong academic achievement do not leave their U.S. government class feeling confident about their potential to be informed voters is noteworthy. Few would propose entirely replacing content on the history, structure, and function of the U.S. government with analysis of current political issues. However, curriculum that helps students make connections between the past and the present as well as between government functions and the issues they care about and vote on does seem like a worthy goal.

To summarize, if students had more opportunities to actively engage in conversations about issues currently debated by our politicians as well as school and community issues, they believed they would more interested and engaged in their civics and government classes. However, connections between these kinds of discussions and experiences and the role that government plays in their lives and that they may one day play in the formal political system are not automatically made. Community service, debates about real issues, and opportunities to learn about current local and national political issues were held in students' minds as separate from the core content of the class. Students rarely spoke of these activities as providing meaningful illustrations of a larger curriculum.

Conclusions and Implications

Any person who walks into schools in different communities can see that all educational settings are not the same. The abstract goals of parents and schools are often quite similar in nature—to support the development of young people so that they will be knowledgeable, self-sufficient, employable, and ultimately good parents, workers, friends, and neighbors. However, the experiences people have, challenges they face, and supports and resources available for achieving these ends vary considerably. Knowing that different social contexts exist, however, is not the same as knowing whether and how these differences matter for education. The goal of this study was to explore whether and how social contextual differences matter for youth civic development and civic education. The rest of this section summarizes our initial insights about this relationship. Because this study is an early look at this issue with small groups of students, these conclusions and any resulting recommendations should be treated with caution.

All the students in our study seemed to have an appreciation for democracy, but varied in the extent to which they believed the current system of government truly is democratic. Students from lower-income, high minority environments were more likely to question whether the government represented the priorities of all groups of citizens. This skepticism lends support to both Sanchez-Jankowski (1986) and Bedolla's (2005) assertions that both local context and ethnic group membership play a role in the political socialization of Latino youth. The youth in our study, as in Bedolla's study, did not see the government as representative of them or their needs and did not appear to believe that increased participation would necessarily lead to a more representative government. Furthermore, their motivations to engage were determined by whether or not it would actually help "the people" and seemed to focus on activities done within and by the community, though much of this was hypothetical.

Students in very different contexts shared a relative disinterest in politics and political action. Interestingly, in spite of differences in their view of the government, students across contexts were remarkably similar when it came to their relative disinterest in politics. Sanchez-Jankowski (2002), Bedolla (2005), and Junn (1999) all note that immigrant and minority youth and adults are likely to prefer direct action over system-oriented action, which this study reinforces. However, this phenomenon was not limited to those populations. In spite of considerable interest in issues related to education, senior care, medical care, and environmental causes, students in all contexts viewed politics as something for people who were not like them. Perhaps youth status serves as a temporary equalizer in this respect, but in our focus groups, nearly all students saw politics as an individual choice and one that they would be likely to skip over. They expressed a preference for engaging in service activities and more direct actions to improve their communities.

Beneath a widespread disinterest in politics, however, there appeared to be different kinds of reasoning by youth from different local contexts. In the communities that were affluent, suburban or rural, and majority non-Hispanic white, students were much more likely to note that there were few needs or local problems in their communities that would require an organized effort. In both the demographically diverse and in the lower-income, urban, majority Latino communities, students were more likely to note that they did not see political solutions as a useful or accessible means for addressing the problems that concerned them. Youth from both contexts arrived at the same conclusion that political engagement was a matter of personal inclination rather than citizen responsibility, but these conclusions came from different experiences.

Students experienced civic education in similar ways. Given the widespread implementation of community service, it is not surprising that many youth have experienced this kind of activity as part of their curriculum or extracurricular activities. Students in general were positive about these experiences and the importance of helping others. However, as noted in the service-learning literature, these activities are often perceived as entirely divorced from politics or political engagement (Westheimer & Kahne, 2004). If schools are attempting to motivate students through community service to engage with government curricula in such a way that they understand it and their own potential as political actors, these connections are not being made in the minds of the students with whom we spoke.

Similarly, many students reported positive experiences with debates in their classrooms and expressed a desire to spend more time discussing social issues that face them in their communities and the country at large. These debates are often described as bright spots in class for even relatively disengaged students. However, students did not connect their enjoyment of these activities to any kind of interest in politics.

Promoting an integrated view of politics and society and course content in which students understand how policy decisions can have varying influences on their own lives, communities and the issues that they work on through volunteerism is one reasonable goal of government classes if schools are to play a role in preparing democratic citizens. Active learning strategies can play an important role in helping students connect to what is often seen as abstract or removed material in government classes. However, if the students in our focus groups are typical of (or perhaps more engaged than) many high school students, they need support in making these connections. Furthermore, making the relevant connections may require starting with and directly addressing the differing assumptions youth may currently hold about politics and democracy.

Implications for Civic Education

As explained above, social context does appear to make a difference in youth civic development in some respects and not others. It is not our goal to create a prescription for how civic education should be implemented in one context vs. another. However, we do believe our findings may be worthy of consideration by educators who design and implement civic education curricula. Specifically:

- *Exploring only the virtues of democratic institutions is problematic—for reasons that depend on context.* Approaches to civic education that stress only the virtues of the system appear likely fail to engage students like those at Hartman and James who were skeptical that their participation in the system would increase government responsiveness to the needs of their communities. In addition, exploration of critiques is also clearly central to supporting the intellectual development and the critical insights of students who, like those at Sunny Hill and Sequoia, might benefit from considering critiques of the ways institutions operate in this democracy. As the old saying goes, "Education should comfort the troubled and trouble the comfortable."
- *Forging stronger connections between government curriculum and civic and political engagement appears very important.* Our prior research examining civic education interventions as well as research by many others suggest that use of active learning strategies (such as simulations of civic processes, exposure to civic role models, and community service) and debates and discussions of personally relevant current events, if explicitly connected to politics, is related to increased interest in politics (see Kahne, Chi, & Middaugh, 2006; Kahne & Westheimer, 2003; see Gibson & Levine, 2004 for a review). Our findings regarding students' interpretations of their own community service and of their classroom discussions of social issues as being very separate from their government curricula suggest that considerable support is needed to help students make these connections.
- *Attending to contextual differences may help build commitments to civic engagement.* If youth see politics as irrelevant to the pressing social issues in their communities, it may be useful to start with community issues and draw connections to the many ways in which policy and government relate to

these issues. If youth see government as relatively unimportant because their communities have few pressing issues, it may be necessary to begin with national issues and see how they play out in their communities, or to encourage youth to look more deeply into their own communities where problems (e.g., race, domestic violence, depression) may be less publicized. There is no one best curriculum—but fostering commitments likely requires attention to the ways students in different contexts do and do not connect to particular kinds of issues. That said, educators need not stop with those issues that students already recognize as important. Rather, they can start with where kids are and try to help them broaden to include state, national, and local issues.

Indeed, there is much we have to learn about the influence of local contexts on youth civic development and how to account for differences in civic education. What is clear, at this point, is the need for policy makers, educators, and practitioners to think carefully about context. To assume that a given curriculum will be received similarly in schools like Sunny Hill and Hartman fails to recognize the diversity of experience and priorities that can make democracy so challenging. If our goal is to equitably and effectively educate young citizens to be capable of sustaining and deepening democracy, understanding these dynamics is critical.

Notes

The authors wish to thank the Carnegie Corporation of New York, the Annenberg Foundation, and the W.R. Hearst Foundation for their support of this research and the broader Educating for Democracy Project. The authors are solely responsible for any and all conclusions.

1. What is not accounted for, of course, are the opportunities available for participation, which may differ, of course, non-citizens being the most obvious example of a group with fewer opportunities.
2. For more information about the Educating for Democracy initiative, go to http://www.cms-ca.org/
3. While this method of selection runs the risk that highly engaged students were over-represented in this sample, students' comments throughout the focus group suggested that the groups were not uniformly highly engaged students. Students' comments about their own activities and post-secondary plans suggested a range of interest in school and community engagement.
4. All numbers are rounded to prevent easy identification of schools.
5. All city statistics gathered from www.city-data.com

6. School statistics for the 2004/05 school-year were accessed through the Education Data Partnership web site. http://www.ed-data.k12.ca.us/
7. For example, from March 2000 to November 2005, California voters have been asked to make decisions on 80 state ballot propositions covering a range of important political, fiscal, and social issues. In the year 2000 alone, local voters faced 559 ballot measures including 115 county, 297 city, and 146 community college and school district measures (Educating for Democracy, 2005).
8. For example, Proposition 13, which limited and reduced property taxes in 1978, reduced tax money available for public education (Carroll, Krop, Arkes, & Morrison, 2005).
9. For example, Proposition 209, passed by California voters in 1996, banned affirmative action based on race, sex, or ethnicity in public institutions. http://www.landmarkcases.org/bakke/impact.html (Accessed July 31, 2006).
10. For example, Proposition 187, passed by California voters in 1994, denied pubic services such as public education and health care to undocumented immigrants. The proposition was later overturned by a federal court. http://www.cnn.com/ALLPOLITICS/1998/03/19/prop.187/ (Accessed March 6, 2007).
11. Based on NAEP scores. This finding is also noted in Baldi, et al., 2001.
12. Based on Nolan, Chaney, & Chapman's 1997 national survey of adolescents.
13. The only exception to this trend was in one group of students who were enrolled in a number of AP classes and were assigned a project midway through the year that they perceived as an added time pressure rather than an opportunity to participate.

References

American Political Science Association Task Force on Inequality. (2004). *American democracy in an age of rising inequality*. American Political Science Association.

Baldi. S., Perie, M., Skidmore, D., Greenberg, E., & Hahn, C. (2001). What democracy means to 9th graders: U.S. results from the international IEA civic education study. *Education Statistics Quarterly, 3,* issue 2. Retrieved March 6, 2007, from http://nces.ed.gov/programs/quarterly/Vol_3/3_2/q5-1.asp

Barber, B. (1992). *An aristocracy of everyone: The politics of education and the future of America*. New York: Ballantine Books.

Bedolla, L. (2005). *Fluid borders: Latino power, identity & politics in Los Angeles*. Berkeley & Los Angeles: University of California Press.

Boyte, H. (1991). Community service and civic education. *Phi Delta Kappan. 72*(10), 765-767.

Carroll, S., Krop, C., Arkes, J., Morrison, P. (2005). California's K–12 public schools: How are they doing?" *A RAND Report*. [ISBN 0-8330-3716-1, $24].

CIRCLE (2006). *Press release: Youth voter turnout sharply up in 2006 midterm elections. November 8, 2006*. Retrieved January 5, 2007, from www.civicyouth.org

CIRCLE (2008). Youth Turnout in the Primary Campaign. Retrieved April 20, 2008, from http://www.civicyouth.org/?p=265

Cohen, C. (2004). Deviance as resistance: A new research agenda for the study of black politics. *Du Bois Review, 1*(1), 27-45.

Cohen, C. (2006). African American youth: Broadening our understanding of politics, civic engagement and activism. *Youth activism: A Web forum organized by the Social Sciences Research Council.* Retrieved July 31, 2006, from http://ya.ssrc.org/african/Cohen/

Conover, P., & Searing, D. (2000). The democratic purposes of education: A political socialization perspective. In L. McDonnell, P. Timpane, & R. Benjamin, (Eds.), *Discovering the democratic purposes of education.* Lawrence: University of Kansas Press.

Educating for Democracy. (2005). *The California survey of civic education.* Retrieved June 9, 2006, from http://www.cms-ca.org/civic_survey_final.pdf

Galston, W. (2001). Political knowledge, political engagement, and civic education. *Annual Review of Political Science, 4,* 217–234.

Gibson, C., & Levine, P. (2003). *The civic mission of schools.* New York and Washington, DC: The Carnegie Corporation of New York.

Hart, D., & Atkins, R. (2002). Civic competence in urban youth. *Applied Developmental Science, 6*(4), 227–236.

Johnson, H. (2002, May). "A state of diversity: Demographic trends in California's regions, *California counts: Population trends and profiles, vol. 3*(5). Public Policy Institute of California.

Junn, J. (1999). Participation in liberal democracy: The political assimilation of immigrants. *The American Behavioral Scientist, 42*(9), 1417–1438.

Kahne, J., & Middaugh, E. (2008). Democracy for Some: The Civic Opportunity Gap in High School. CIRCLE Working Paper 59, February 2008.

Kahne, J., Chi, B., & Middaugh, E. (2006). Building Social Capital for Civic and Political Engagement: The Potential of High School Civic Courses. *Canadian Journal of Education, 29*(2),287–296.

Kahne, J., & Middaugh, E. (2005, August). *Preparing citizens for democracy: Strategies and indicators.* Paper presented to Education for the Civic Purposes of Schools Conference. San Jose, Costa Rica.

Kahne, J., & Westheimer, J. (2003). Teaching Democracy: What Schools Need to Do. *Phi Delta Kappan. 85*(1), 34–40, 57–66.

Levine, M. (2006). *The price of privilege: How parental pressure and material advantage are creating a generation of disconnected and unhappy kids.* New York: Harper Collins.

Malone, N., Baluja, K., Costanzo, J., & Davis, C. (2003). The foreign born population: 2000. Census 2000 Brief, U.S. Census Bureau, December 2003. Retrieved October 24, 2005, from http://www.census.gov/prod/2003pubs/c2kbr-34.pdf

Putnam, R. (2000). *Bowling alone.* New York: Simon & Schuster.

Ralph and Goldy Lewis Center for Regional Policy Studies (2001). California is the Most Diverse State in the Nation, Census 2000 Fact Sheet. Retrieved October 24, 2005, from http://lewis.sppsr.ucla.edu/special/metroamerica/factsheets/Census _FACTSHEET6.pdf

Ramakrishnan, S., & Baldasarre, M. (2004). *The ties that bind: Changing demographics and civic engagement in California.* Public Policy Institute of California, 2004.

Robinson, T. (2000). Dare the school build a new social order? *Michigan Journal of Community Service Learning, 7,* 142–157.

Sanchez-Jankowski, M. (1986). *City bound: Urban life and political attitudes among Chicano youth.* Albuquerque: University of New Mexico Press.

Sanchez-Jankowski, M. (1992). Ethnic identity and political consciousness in different social orders. *New Directions for Child Development, 56*(2), 79–93.

Sanchez-Jankowski, M. (2002). Minority youth and civic engagement: The impact of group relations. *Applied Developmental Science, 6*(4), 237–245.

Torney-Purta, J., Lehmann, R., Oswald, H., & Schultz, W. (2001). *Citizenship and education in twenty-eight countries: Civic knowledge and engagement at age fourteen.* Amsterdam: IEA.

Walker, T. (2000). The Service/Politics Split: Rethinking Service to Teach Political Engagement. *PS: Political Science and Politics, 33*(3), 647–649.

Westheimer, J. & Kahne, J. (2004). What kind of citizen? The politics of educating for democracy, *American Educational Research Journal, 41*(2), 237–269.

CHAPTER 8

Examining the Treatment of 9/11 and Terrorism in High School Textbooks

Diana Hess, Jeremy Stoddard, Shannon Murto

The heated conflicts over what should be taught about the September 11, 2001 attacks on the United States and their aftermath illustrate vividly that the school curriculum is an ideological battleground. Some involved in the fray complain that schools' responses to 9/11 have been heavy on multicultural tolerance and light on "patriotism." Chester Finn writes, "We seek to redress the balance between those who would have the schools forge citizens and those who would have the focus on students' own feelings and on doubts about America" (2002, p. 6). On the other hand, rather than focusing on developing traditional feelings of patriotism, educator Alfie Kohn advocates assessing whether schools are taking the right approach by analyzing the "extent to which the next generation comes to understand—and fully embrace—this simple truth: The life of someone who lives in Kabul or Baghdad is worth no less than the life of someone in New York or from our neighborhood" (2001, p. 5).

Ideology and the Curriculum

Clearly, these are radically disparate recommendations about what young people should learn. This is not surprising. Evidence shows that schools in the United States are places rife with conflict about *which* ideologies deserve official recognition (Apple, 1988; Binder, 2004; Zimmerman, 2002). More significantly, schools are places where dominant ideologies are *formed,* which undoubtedly accounts for why so much controversy erupted after 9/11 about what teachers and curricula should impart about what happened on 9/11, why it occurred, and what response from the United States was warranted (Ravitch 2004; Finn, 2002; Rethinking Schools, 2001). Marita Sturken points out that after significant events, such as 9/11, "our various cultures work out the meaning of the events behind them" (quoted in Timmons, 2006, p. 22). The school curriculum is one place where this work occurs (Evans, 2004; Gutmann, 1999; Parker, 2003). But the "working out" in schools also powerfully shapes what people believe about important events and often becomes a form of "official knowledge" (Apple, 1999).

The Significance of 9/11

In the case of 9/11, it is clear that the event is not behind us, but continues to shape decisions about contemporary policy. This situation raises significant challenges because schools are expected to teach "what happened" when so little time has passed that this information is still unclear relative to many events routinely taught as settled stories in history classes. There are also powerful differences of opinion about the wisdom of many of the policies enacted immediately after 9/11 (such as the Patriot Act) and about what policies are necessary now, seven years after the attacks occurred. Still, shortly after 9/11, many organizations and companies developed curricular materials that focus on 9/11 and its aftermath because, according to curriculum writer Chuck Tampio, "the attacks of 9/11 are just too important to ignore, they present the ultimate teachable moment" (quoted in Hess, 2004, p. 2). As Finn argues, "it's right to teach about September 11th because it was one of the defining events of our age, of our nation's history and of these children's lives" (2002, p. 4). Susan Grasack, the executive director of the Choices for the 21st Century Project, agrees that there is no question about whether these events and their aftermath deserve attention in the curriculum. She says, "9/11 was a watershed. . . . before 9/11, the country had two oceans on either side. That was the way we understood ourselves. After 9/11, oceans didn't matter" (quoted in Hess, 2004, p. 4). In addition, interviews with students demonstrate that they "want—and urgently need—to know more about the history (causes, development, changes) and politics of terrorism" (Lévesque, 2003, p. 192). And yet, agreeing on the importance of 9/11 provides scant guidance to curriculum writers and teachers.

It is virtually impossible to construct sound histories of 9/11 given how recently it occurred, but deliberating contemporary issues stemming from 9/11 requires at least some modicum of historical understanding. This deliberation also opens up all manner of controversy about which policy responses make the most sense. Consequently, curriculum writers are wading into difficult terrain when they embark on the mission to bring 9/11 and its aftermath into the curriculum. Given that it is unclear and contested what 9/11 curriculum should say and ask students to do, it is logical that analyzing how curriculum writers negotiate this terrain will illuminate how 9/11 is presented in schools. In other words, if schools not only reflect "official knowledge" but also shape it, then what can we learn from curriculum written since 9/11 about what young people are being taught to believe about what happened on 9/11, why it happened, how the United States and other nations responded, and what kinds of policies make the most sense now?

To address these challenging questions, in 2003 we began studying the content of 9/11 text and video curriculum materials from six major U.S. nonprofit curricular organizations along with materials developed by the State Department (Hess, 2004).[1] In the summer of 2005, we broadened the study to include top-selling U.S. history, world history, and government textbooks published between 2004 and 2006 that included the events of 9/11 and the war on terrorism. The study has two primary aims. The first is to examine critically what curricula are communicating about 9/11, its aftermath, and terrorism more generally. Our second aim relates more broadly to the disputes about what kind of democratic participation schools should promote. In particular, we are interested in how frequently topics or questions related to 9/11 and its aftermath and terrorism are presented to students as genuinely controversial, requiring higher order thinking to wade through, and which either explicitly or implicitly present a "correct" answer that the curriculum writers expect students to believe.

Selecting and Analyzing the Texts

In selecting the textbooks for this study, we questioned whether there would be an ideological range amongst the textbooks and whether the subject area focus of textbooks would treat the events of 9/11 and their aftermath differently. Specifically, we examined the texts to determine how much attention they devote to the events of 9/11 and their aftermath, their purposes for including the events, how they define major concepts such as terrorism, what "truths" students are implicitly or explicitly encouraged to believe, and the nature of the thinking that students are asked to do with that information.

We selected nine high school textbooks intended for use in different social studies courses—world and U.S. history, civics or government, and law—because we are interested in whether the primary content of the course would influence the 9/11 content (see table 8.1). For example, from our experience working with high school textbooks in the past, we found that history textbooks tend to focus on telling a narrative of events that typically does not involve competing interpretations. By contrast, government and law textbooks tend to focus more on content that explicates the form and structure of government in the United States, explains the meaning of core concepts (e.g., such as due process and separation of powers), and sometimes presents competing views about what kinds of policy decisions should be made and their ramifications. We felt that this general difference also might affect the specific coverage of 9/11 in each of the textbooks. All of the textbooks selected are high school level texts published by large media companies that market research shows are the most widely selected by schools (Education Market Research, 2005). While impossible to pinpoint precisely, our analysis suggests that these textbooks are used by almost eight million high school students in the United States. Put more dramatically, it is likely that one out of every two students enrolled in a U.S. history, world history, government or law course will be in a class that uses one of the textbooks.[2]

After selecting the texts, we analyzed the table of contents, index, and glossary to identify narrative and images that related to terrorism, the events of 9/11 and its aftermath, such as the invasions of Afghanistan and Iraq. All pages that include references to, or examples of, terrorism and September 11th were photocopied and then coded. We used a specific list of terms to search in the index (e.g., September 11th, terrorism, Osama bin Laden, Iraq) and searched the glossary for definitions of related words, such as terrorism. Finally, we scanned each book for further inclusion of September 11th or terror related events or topics, especially pages before and after those identified in the glossary, seeking further examples

Table 8.1 Selected Social Studies Textbooks: Texts and Information Listed by Subject Area

Textbook title	Year of publication	Publisher
American History		
American Odyssey	2004	Glencoe/McGraw Hill
America: Pathways to the Present	2005	Pearson/Prentice Hall
The Americans	2005	Houghton Mifflin /McDougall Littell
World History		
World History: Connections to Today	2005	Pearson/Prentice Hall
World History: Patterns of Interaction	2005	Houghton Mifflin /McDougall Littell
World History	2005	Glencoe/McGraw Hill
Government/Law		
U.S. Government: Democracy in Action	2006	Glencoe/McGraw Hill
MacGruder's American Government	2005	Pearson/Prentice Hall
Street Law: A Practical Course in Law	2005	Glencoe/McGraw Hill

of terrorism concepts and examples. We did not thoroughly analyze other sections of the textbooks, although we did compare coverage of 9/11 to Pearl Harbor because we are interested in what similarities and differences exist between how the textbooks treat these two significant events in U.S. history that each occurred on a single day.

The relevant portions of the texts were first cluster coded deductively and inductively using the research questions (e.g., What was 9/11? What is terrorism?). We induced new codes as needed. These clusters were then entered into NVIVO for further analysis; line-by-line, organized by code, and then analyzed for themes within and across the texts in relation to our research questions. In addition to the text narrative and images, we also analyzed all of the questions present in the text for students to answer, as well as other assessment items that relate to the events of 9/11, terrorism, the war on terror, and the war in Iraq (if the text includes Iraq as part of the war on terror), and whether the items are laced throughout the narrative or at the end of a section. In some cases, especially in the government textbooks, we noted that questions and assessment items use 9/11 as an example of a larger concept (for example, separation of powers), and we included these in our analysis as well. We analyzed each question on its face to determine if it required lower or higher order thinking (Newmann & Wehlage, 1993), and whether it was presented as a closed question for which there was one correct answer or an open question that could have multiple and competing answers. Then we analyzed each question as applied to the narrative in the book to determine whether it was a genuine higher order question or whether it really only required lower order thinking, and whether there was sufficient information in the text (what we are calling scaffolding) to enable students to do the type of thinking the question appears to require of them.

9/11 as a Critical Event

What is immediately apparent in high school history and government textbooks is the ubiquity of 9/11. Each of the nine textbooks mentions the 9/11 attacks in multiple places in the text. However, while all of the texts utilize the events of 9/11, the frequency with which the events of that day are mentioned and the length of coverage varies depending on the type of textbook.

The U.S. history books average the fewest number of sections that include 9/11, just under three times per book (two each in *The Americans* and *American Odyssey*, and four times in *Pathways to the Present*). Though fewer, these sections tend to be longer and specifically dedicated to 9/11 and the war on terror; *American Odyssey* devotes 72 sentences specifically to the 9/11 attacks, while *Pathways to the Present* and *The Americans* devote 38 sentences and 44 sentences, respectively. The world history books have a slightly higher frequency of inclusion, averaging just over four times per book (three each in *Patterns of Interaction* and Glencoe *World History* and seven times in *Connections to Today*). However, these sections tend to be shorter than those found in the U.S. history textbooks, with Glencoe *World History* containing 37 sentences on the attacks and *Patterns of Interaction* and *Connections to Today* containing only 22 and 13 sentences on the events of 9/11, respectively.

Finally, the most frequent coverage of 9/11 comes from the government and law textbooks, which include some aspect of 9/11 an average of ten times per book (16 times in *Democracy in Action*, nine times in *MacGruder's*, and seven times in *Street Law*). In spite of the higher frequency of coverage in government and law textbooks, the amount of 9/11 coverage in each of these sections varies widely, from only nine sentences in

MacGruder's to 24 sentences in *Street Law* and 38 sentences in *Democracy in Action.* The fact that all of the books emphasize 9/11 is notable, and the number of times that 9/11 is mentioned in some of the books is quite remarkable.

One of the dominant messages in the texts is that the attacks on 9/11 are extraordinarily important and severe, especially as compared to other terrorist acts in history. The great importance of 9/11 is communicated both by the type and number of words used. The textbooks utilize powerful words such as "horrendous plot" and "unprecedented attack" to describe the attacks. Eight of the nine books describe the attacks of September 11, 2001 as historically significant for the United States and the world. For people in the United States, 9/11 is now a "day imprinted on the minds of many Americans," and something that people in the United States reacted to "in horror." In other books, the emphasis is on how important 9/11 was for the world. For example, one of the world history texts describes 9/11 as a "turning point" in world history and a "crime against humanity" writ large (not just a crime against people in the United States). Clearly, the textbook developers seek not only to include 9/11, but also to emphasize its importance as the *defining* event of the recent past.

In spite of these commonalities in descriptive language, the manner in which 9/11 is utilized in these three categories of textbooks differs. In each type of textbook, the events of 9/11 and their aftermath are emplotted in different larger contexts. The emplotment of an event can affect the overall message students receive from its coverage, as Simone Schweber (2004) illustrates in her study of the teaching of the Holocaust in secondary classrooms. In the case of the 9/11 material in these nine textbooks, the U.S. history textbooks tend to discuss 9/11 as a specific event related to the subsequent war on terror. On the other hand, in the world history textbooks, 9/11 is typically emplotted within coverage of global issues, the aftermath of the Cold War, or issues in the Middle East. Finally, the government and law textbooks tend to utilize 9/11 as an example of a larger concept that students should understand, such as the expansion of executive power or the right to writs of habeas corpus and the detention of enemy combatants. Each of these types of textbooks illustrates how the events of 9/11 and their aftermath can be marshaled to serve as an example of various different topics, themes, or concepts, depending on the overall goal of the textbook.

Narrative Perspective

In addition to examining what is said about 9/11 in the textbooks, it is also important to discuss who provides these perspectives, that is, who is telling the story of 9/11. Textbooks are traditionally written with third-person narrative voice, and the authors of the textbooks examined in this study follow this pattern while also embedding a few quotes in the text of the 9/11 coverage, which serve to reinforce the overall perspectives of the narratives (Paxton, 1999). For example, *American Odyssey* includes an excerpt from a New York Times article about a heroic man who helped others escape from their offices in the World Trade Center. This story provides a snapshot of the kind of heroism that occurred after the attacks, which represents one powerful cultural narrative of the events that is also starting to emerge in films about 9/11 (Timmons, 2006). The majority of first person quotes used in the texts' coverage of 9/11 come from President George W. Bush. Seven of the nine texts include a direct quote from President Bush, some of which are meant to provide justification for the wars in Afghanistan and Iraq. For example, Glencoe *World History* includes an excerpt from President Bush's address to the nation, in which he states, "Freedom and fear are at war. The advance of human freedom, the great achievement of our time and the great hope of every time, now depends on us . . . We will not falter and we will not fail" (p. 968). Also, although the war in Iraq is included in four of the books (*Pathways to the Present, The Americans, Mac-Gruder's*) with the justifications of Iraq's looming weapons of mass destruction and/or links to terrorist organizations, only one text, *The Americans*, also includes the fact that many of these justifications proved to be unsubstantiated. As that text explains, "No trace of chemical or biological weaponry were found" (p. 1073).

Each of these examples reveals that the overall narrative of 9/11 and war on terrorism is one of nationalistic determination to fight against terrorism and for freedom, supported not only through a narrative style in this vein but also through the inclusion of specific direct quotations reinforcing this perspective. This ideological viewpoint is rarely challenged or even complicated. What is revealing here is not just the content of the viewpoint that the textbooks present, but that most of the textbooks typically present only one unchallenged portrayal as the accepted interpretation of 9/11 and its aftermath, when clearly such an interpretation does not exist at this point in time. As William L. Griffen and John Marciano

(1979) argue in their study of textbook coverage of the Vietnam War, "Within history texts, for example, the omission of crucial facts and viewpoints limits profoundly the ways in which students come to view historical events" (p. 163). The unchallenged viewpoint on 9/11 found in many of these textbooks carries throughout the accounts on 9/11 and its aftermath, supported not only by the selection of quotes but also through the inclusion of specific iconic images.

Creating an Iconic Image

All nine texts contain images that show debris resulting from the destructive attacks of 9/11. Two show rubble from the Pentagon, while the other seven show rubble at the World Trade Center site in New York City. The images of New York City are especially striking, as the images all include New York City firefighters. Of the seven, six also include the American flag raised at Ground Zero. Three of the texts have the exact same picture of three firefighters raising the American flag, while two others have a different image of the same event, probably taken soon after the flag was raised,[3] and one other includes both firefighters and an American flag.

Although these same images have been utilized in publications and other forms quite often, it is interesting to note that pictures of the World Trade Center hit by the planes—another image typically shown to represent 9/11—are found in only two of these texts. By selecting the firefighters raising the U.S. flag as the main image to represent 9/11, the text developers are choosing to emphasize patriotism, nationalism, and heroism. This image reinforces the view that the when the United States faces significant challenges, its people rise to the occasion, rally around the flag (literally and symbolically), and put their own personal needs aside to engage in individual acts that will further national interests. Conversely, if the texts emphasized pictures of the destruction caused by 9/11, or people grieving those who were killed that day, the message would be quite different—the United States as harmed and as weakened.

However, in the midst of the relative abundance of coverage, the usage of powerful language, and the creation of certain iconic images for 9/11 and its aftermath, we find it striking that more than half of the texts do not specifically explain what happened on 9/11, who was involved, or why it happened—there seems to be an assumption that students know the details (see table 8.2). With the exception of the Glencoe *World History* text,

Table 8.2 Descriptions of 9/11 Attacks: 9/11 Descriptions by Text

Text	Number of people killed	Number of planes	Who did it	WTC	Reason for Attack	Pentagon	PA	Comm. plane
American Odyssey	thousands	4	Osama bin Laden, al Qaeda, 19 Saudis	X	Attack on capitalism, U.S. support for Israel, oil rich	X	X	
America: Pathways to the Present				X	Racial, cultural and religious strife	X	X	X
The Americans				X	Result of conflicts and Cold War	X	X	
World History: Connections to Today	thousands		Terrorists opposed to U.S. policies in Mid-East	X	U.S. policies in Middle East/fundamentalism	X		
World History: Patterns of Interaction	3000	4			Not provided	X	X	X
Glencoe World History	thousands	4	al Qaeda	X	Fundamentalism/drive U.S. from Middle East	X	X	X
U.S. Government: Democracy in Action				X	U.S. support for Israel, connections to oil industry			
MacGruder's American Government					Not provided			
Street Law: A Practical Course in Law			al Qaeda		Not provided			

the assumption of many of the texts appears to be that student readers re-member the precise details of 9/11, as many of the texts use 9/11 fre-quently but never explain what actually happened on that day. Note, for example, that two of the U.S. History textbooks do not explain basic de-tails about 9/11, such as who did it, the number of people killed, or the number of planes involved. Moreover, the three government and law texts contain virtually no details about what happened on that day, even though 9/11 is frequently mentioned throughout the texts, which may result from the emplotment of 9/11 in these types of texts as an example of larger is-sues or governmental processes.

Still, we doubt that many students who will read these books actually know the details of 9/11. Keep in mind that a 15-year-old sitting in a high school class in 2007 was only 9 when 9/11 occurred. Second, there is evi-dence that even adults who were old enough to pay careful attention to the details of 9/11 believe many things that are simply not true. To support this claim, consider what a 2005 report issued by the nonprofit organization, Public Agenda, said: "The Gallup poll found 44 percent believe Hussein was 'personally involved' in the Sept. 11 attacks, down from 53 percent in December 2003" (para. 7). When the questions are phrased more broadly, the number who say there is a link also rises. The June 2004 ABC/Washing-ton Post poll found 62 percent of those surveyed believe Iraq provided "di-rect support" to al Qaeda, and Gallup showed 67 percent who said Hussein had "long-established ties to Osama bin Laden's terrorist organization."

Given that five of the books we analyzed do not say who "did it" with re-spect to 9/11, and one has the fairly generic "terrorists opposed to U.S. policies in the Mideast" as the explanation, it is likely that students reading these books will not know the answer to this critical (and in some quarters, highly controversial) question. In sum, the books use 9/11 quite a bit, but many of them fail to provide even rudimentary background information about the event.

Pearl Harbor as a Comparison

On the other hand, coverage of the attack on Pearl Harbor in these same textbooks provides an interesting contrast. Like 9/11, the Japanese attack on Pearl Harbor occurred on only a single day and involved a surprise at-tack on the United States. Unlike 9/11, the coverage on Pearl Harbor in these textbooks explains events that occurred not in the recent past but well over 60 years ago. However, based on the basic similarities between the events, the way in which the two events are described in each of the textbooks provides an interesting comparison. As in the coverage of 9/11, the coverage of attack on Pearl Harbor varies depending on the type of textbook. Two of the U.S. Government and Law textbooks omit any reference to Pearl Harbor, and the third focuses mainly on the domestic effects of the attack, such as suspension of the writ of habeas corpus in Hawaii. This contrasts with the obvious presence of 9/11 and its aftermath in each of the nine textbooks included in this study. In addition, although the coverage of both events in U.S. History textbooks varies widely, the coverage of Pearl Harbor in the World History textbooks is more consistent than the coverage of the terrorist attacks of 9/11 in those same books. The number of sentences devoted to Pearl Harbor in the three world history textbooks ranges from 14 sentences in Glencoe *World History* to 20 sentences in *Connections to Today*, while the 9/11 coverage in those same three books ranges from a low of 13 sentences in *Connections to Today* to a high of 37 sentences in Glencoe *World History*.

Among these six World and U.S. History books, five include detailed narrative coverage of the events of December 7, 1941 (see table 8.3). These events follow a general style that begins with the reasons why Japan decided to attack the United States naval base at Pearl Harbor. Three of the books include information on Hideki Tojo's rise to power, while two attribute the attack to Admiral Isoruko Yamamoto. Four of the textbooks mention U.S. government knowledge of a looming attack on an unknown target. All five of these books also include casualty reports and estimates of material damage to the U.S. Pacific Fleet. Finally, each of these accounts concludes with President Roosevelt's speech to Congress declaring December 7, 1941 "a date which will live in infamy" and asking for a declaration of war.

This detailed narrative for the attack on Pearl Harbor provides a stark contrast with the textbook coverage of 9/11, which is surprisingly thin on details. Unlike the coverage of 9/11, the textbooks that cover Pearl Harbor do not assume that students already know the details of the attack. Even though the specific coverage of the attacks varies by nearly one thousand words among these five textbooks, each of the five features a narrative with similar main points. The apparent assumption that 9/11 is so recent and so important that its details are emblazoned in the minds of students is problematic. Moreover, with respect to 9/11, the fact that

Table 8.3 Descriptions of Attack on Pearl Harbor: Descriptions by Textbook*

Reasons	Who	Attack expected	Casualties	Material damage	Result	Day of infamy	Ger. & It. declare war
American Odyssey							
U.S. restricted trade, cut off oil; Destroy Pac Fleet	Plan of Adm. Yamamoto	Didn't know where	>2,300–2,400	19 ships; 188 planes	Roosevelt asked Congress to declare war; Congress declared	X	X
America: Pathways to the Present							
U.S. limited trade, froze assets; Need for raw materials (esp. oil); Plan to cripple Pacific Fleet	Japan; General Tojo Hideki, "militant army officer"	As of November 27; Didn't know where	2,400/1,200	200 warplanes; 18 warships; 29 Japanese planes	Roosevelt asked to declare war; Congress declared; Only "pacifist Jeannette Rankin . . . voted against"; America First Committee supported	X	X
The Americans							
U.S. cut off trade; Need for oil	Hideki Tojo ordered attack	Didn't know where; "war warning" sent out	2,403/1,178	21 ships; >300 aircraft; >WWI Navy losses	3 carriers at sea missed damage; Roosevelt asked to declare war; Congress declared; Isolationists supported war (ex: Burton Wheeler); Americans "trembling with . . . rage" united to "prove Japan wrong"	X	X

Reasons	Who	Attack expected	Casualties	Material damage	Result	Day of infamy	Ger. & It. declare war
World History: Connections to Today							
U.S. restricted trade	General Tojo & "extreme militarists"		2,400	19 ships; planes	Roosevelt asked to declare war; Euro and Amer colonies fell to Japanese	X	X
World History: Patterns of Interaction							
U.S. cut off oil	Adm. Yamamoto called for attack	Didn't know where or when	>2,300, >1,100	19 ships	Roosevelt asked to declare war; Congress declared; Japan also attacked Hong Kong, Guam, Wake Island, Thailand	X	X (Germany)
Glencoe World History							
Destroy Pac Fleet					American opinion unified, U.S. joins		
U.S. Government: Democracy in Action							
Relationship b/w U.S., Japan worsened after Open Door Policy	Japanese				"Direct" U.S. involvement in WWII; Forced "evacuation" of Japanese Americans along Pacific Coast; Writ of habeas corpus suspended (later overturned)		

*Neither *MacGruder's* or *Street Law* included Pearl Harbor there are significant differences in how the books describe the answers to key questions, such as why the attacks occurred, represents the reality that there are many things about 9/11 and its aftermath that are highly contested. Yet, the texts do not acknowledge or hint to these disagreements or ambiguities.

Terrorism Is . . .

In our study of 9/11 curricula from the nonprofit organizations, we noticed that the definitions of terrorism in use have many similarities but also include stark differences, particularly in terms of what a terrorist attack includes, who terrorists are, and who the targets could be. The same holds true for the textbooks in this study. Only two books do not include a definition of terrorism in either text or glossary, *Street Law* and *Pathways to the Present*. The seven books that define terrorism, either in the text or in their glossary, describe or imply that terrorist acts include violence (see table 8.4). Six of the books use the term violence in the explicit definition, and the seventh implies violence through examples of terrorist acts (e.g., terrorists kill civilians, take hostages, hijack planes). While most terrorist attacks include violence or a threat of violence, this type of definition does not include non-violent but still destructive acts, such as cyber terrorism.

There are other interesting consistencies in the definitions, especially in books from the same publisher. The two texts in the study from Houghton Mifflin/McDougall Littell, *The Americans* and *Patterns of Interaction,* use an identical basic definition of terrorism, that it is "the use of violence against people or property to try to force changes in societies or governments." These definitions are both included in sections at the end of the text dedicated solely to terrorism, the events of 9/11, and the war on terror. The fact that the textbook companies appear to have an "official" definition of terrorism that cuts across their books is stunning—especially given that terrorism is a contested concept (Holt, 2002) and that there are many inconsistencies between their own definitions and the examples of terrorism that they include.

While the shared language and themes among textbooks from the same publishing house could be the result of mergers, shared resources, or the downsizing of authorial teams, it puts in bold relief the fact that many authors whose names are attached to texts clearly are not doing the writing. According to Gilbert Sewall, the director of the American Textbook Council, "you have well-established authorities who put their names on the spine, but really have nothing to do with the actual writing process, which is all done in-house or by hired writers" (quoted in Schemo, 2006). Even so, some of the commonalities across texts are also a reflection of the nature of contemporary textbooks in general, which have been shaped to meet state adoption standards and thus have lost some of their independence (Sewall, 2005).

The Ubiquity of 9/11

The standard way that textbooks deal with concepts is to provide a definition and examples. It is not surprising that 9/11 is frequently given as an example of terrorism, but it is important to note that it is the only example of terrorism that appears in all nine of the textbooks. The next most frequently included terrorist attacks are the 1998 attacks on the U.S. embassies in Tanzania and Kenya, and the ongoing battle with insurgencies in Afghanistan and Iraq, used in six books each. Following these attacks are the post 9/11 anthrax mail attack, the Israeli-Palestinian conflict, and the attacks on the U.S.S. Cole, each of which is included in five books. The table below lists the attacks that are included in the texts and the number of books in which they appear. Moreover, given the number of examples of terrorism that involve the United States, the resulting message that many of the books send is that terrorism is a more significant problem for the United States than for other nations. While the terrorist attacks that have occurred against U.S. targets are significant, the United States is by no means the most frequent target for terrorist attacks, even in recent years. According to the U.S. Department of State, North America as a region has the lowest number of terrorist attacks for the period 1997 through 2003, with only 17 attacks. In contrast, the Department of State identifies 274 attacks in Western Europe during that same time period and a staggering 820 attacks in Latin America (including South America) (cited in U.S. Army Training and Doctrine Command, 2005).

Not only is 9/11 used as an example in each book, but it is also used as an example in multiple places in the text of many of the books. The attacks of 9/11 are included most frequently in the government and law textbooks, with *Democracy in Action* using it 16 times, *MacGruder's* nine, and *Street Law* seven. September 11 is included within the context of the events, its aftermath, and implementation of the Patriot Act and other organizational (e.g., creation of the Department of Homeland Security)

Table 8.4 Textbooks' Definitions of Terrorism

Publisher/Textbook/Definitions of terrorism	Includes violence	Politically motivated	By non-governmental groups	Civilian target	To influence or intimidate an audience
Glencoe/McGraw Hill					
American Odyssey					
Terrorism occurs when nongovernmental groups use violence against civilians to frighten governments into changing their policies (p. 930).	yes	yes	yes	yes	yes
World History					
Acts of terror have become a regular aspect of modern Western society. Terrorists kill civilians, they take hostages, and hijack planes to draw attention to their demands or to achieve their political goals (p. 890).	implied	yes	doesn't say	yes	yes
U.S. Government: Democracy in Action					
Terrorism: the use of violence by nongovernmental groups against civilians to achieve a political goal (in glossary, p. 855)	yes	yes	yes	yes	yes
Street Law					
No definition					

Publisher/Textbook/Definitions of terrorism	Includes violence	Politically motivated	By non-governmen-tal groups	Civilian target	To influence or intimidate an audience
Pearson/Prentice					
America: Pathways to the Present					
No definition					
World: Connections to Today	yes	yes	doesn't say	yes	yes
Terrorism: deliberate use of random violence, especially against civilians, to achieve political goals (in glossary, 1021)					
Macgruder's American Government	yes	yes	doesn't say	doesn't say	yes
Terrorism is the use of violence to intimidate a government or a society, usually for political or ideological reasons (p. 478)					
Houghton Mifflin					
The Americans	yes	yes	doesn't say	doesn't say	yes
Terrorism is the use of violence against people or property to try to force changes in societies or governments (p. 1100).					
World: Patterns of Interaction	yes	yes	doesn't say	doesn't say	yes
Terrorism, the use of violence against people or property to force changes in societies or governments, strikes fear in the hearts of people everywhere (p. 1087).					

Table 8.5 Examples of Terrorist Attacks in each Text (X=included in text, U=U.S. related attack included in text)

Examples of terrorism included in specific textbooks	Houghton Mifflin		Pearson/Prentice Hall				Glencoe/McGraw Hill			Total Number of Books with Example
	The Americans	World: Patterns of Interaction	America: Pathways to the Present	World: Connections to Today	MacGruder's	American Odyssey	Glencoe World History	U.S. Government: Democracy in Action	Street Law	
Assassination of Archduke Ferdinand 1914			X							1
Munich Olympics 1972	X			X			X			3
Iranian Hostage crisis 1979						U				1
Beirut, Lebanon, bombing of U.S. Marines barracks 1983			U	U		U				3
Bombing of Berlin night club 1986			X			X				2
Pan Am 103—Lockerbie 1990	X					X				2
Unabomber—Kaczynski 1970s–1990s	X									1
Aum Shinri Kyo—Tokyo subway attack 1995	X	X					X			3
Oklahoma City bombing 1993	U		U			U				3
WTC bombing 1993	U		U			U				3
IRA/Protestants attack in Northern Ireland	X	X		X			X			4

	Houghton Mifflin		Pearson/Prentice Hall			Glencoe/McGraw Hill				Total Number of Books with Example
Examples of terrorism included in specific textbooks	*The Americans*	*World: Patterns of Interaction*	*America: Pathways to the Present*	*World: Connections to Today*	*MacGruder's*	*American Odyssey*	*Glencoe World History*	*U.S. Government: Democracy in Action*	*Street Law*	
FARC Columbia—Latin America	X		X							2
U.S.S. Cole 2000	U		U			U	U	U		5
Israeli–Palestinian/Hezbollah	X	X	X	X			X			5
U.S. embassies in Tanzania and Kenya 1998	U	U	U			U	U	U		6
September 11, 2001 attacks on New York and Washington, DC	U	U	U	U	U	U	U	U	U	9
U.S. anthrax attacks 2001	U		U			U	U	U		5
Attempted millennium Seattle bombing 2000								U		1
Afghanistan–Iraqi insurgencies 2001–present	U	U	U	U	U	U				6
U.S. related/Total number of terrorism examples	7/13	4/7	7/10	3/7	2/2	8/11	5/9	5/5	1/1	65

and foreign policy decisions (e.g., policy of preemption), and within the ensuing war on terror. September 11 is used most frequently as an example related to the policies and reactions of the Bush Administration (22 times), including the Patriot Act, presidential powers, the Department of Homeland Security, and foreign policy initiatives. The next most prevalent usage relates to the war on terror that followed the events of 9/11 (16 times) and includes actions in Afghanistan and Iraq, issues with enemy combatants, and cooperation with NATO. The final three categories of use include terrorism and the world (nine times), the events of 9/11 per se (six times), and issues related to effects on the economy and increased defense spending (six times). In short, the texts communicate clearly that 9/11 is an exceedingly important event that has far-reaching and numerous effects. It is certainly not presented simply as a tragedy that occurred on one day.

Terrorist Attacks Beyond 9/11

In addition to the attacks on 9/11, the texts also include a large number of other examples of terrorism. The U.S. History texts include more examples of terrorism than the World History texts, and terrorist attacks where Americans or U.S. property or territory are present are featured more frequently and prominently than non-American attacks in all of the texts, even in the World History textbooks. The three U.S. History texts include an average of just over 11 examples of terrorist attacks (11.13) compared to just under eight for the World History texts (7.67) and just under three for the Government texts (2.67). The three U.S. History texts also include more examples that involve Americans or American property. On average, just over seven (7.33) or 65% of the examples in the U.S. History texts involve the U.S. While not using as many examples, the World History texts also include a high percentage of attacks that involve Americans. On average, the world texts include four examples (52%) of terrorist attacks that involve Americans. The U.S. Government texts, as one might expect, use only American examples, and average just fewer than three examples per text (2.67). As we identify earlier in how these texts described the events of 9/11, the focus of the overall number of examples is on the United States as the most common victim, despite the relatively few terrorist attacks that have occurred on American soil or against Americans over the past several decades. The inclusion of a high number of attacks on Americans reflects the anxiety of American society post-9/11 and the desire of the texts to reflect nationalistic or patriotic support for the country and its efforts in the war on terrorism.

Conceptual Confusion

However, in focusing on terrorist attacks on Americans, and in attempting to construct an account of 9/11 and the war on terror as a neutral telling of what happened, discrepancies and inconsistencies appear. As noted earlier, while there are many similarities in the definitions of terrorism contained in the books, we are struck by how many of them give definitions of terrorism written in an authoritative manner, as if it were an uncontested concept, and then use examples that do not support the definition.

As an illustration, only one of the texts, *Patterns of Interactions,* includes domestic terrorism in its definition, but all three American History textbooks include the Oklahoma City Federal Building bombing as an example of terrorism. In a similar fashion, one World History text, *Connections to Today,* identifies terrorism as "the deliberate use of random violence" (p. 1021), but then uses examples of terrorism such as the taking of Israeli hostages by Palestinian terrorists during the 1972 Olympics in Munich, hardly the best possible example of a random event. Further, while four of the texts (*American Odyssey, Democracy in Action,* Glencoe *World History,* and *Connections to Today*) claim that terrorism is conducted against civilians, they include examples that were directed at military targets, not civilians. For example, *American Odyssey,* and Glencoe's *Democracy in Action* and *World History, all* include attacks on the U.S.S. Cole, a U.S. naval destroyer; *American Odyssey* and *Connections to Today* both include the bombing of the U.S. Marine and French army barracks in Beirut in the 1980's; and *American Odyssey,* Glencoe *World History,* and *Connections to Today* include the insurgencies in Afghanistan and Iraq as terrorist acts, even though when these textbooks were published the attacks were directed primarily at U.S., Afghani, and Iraqi military and police forces.

Finally, two texts from Glencoe/McGraw Hill, *American Odyssey* and *Democracy in Action,* are the only books that state that terrorism is conducted by "non-governmental groups," which would eliminate or limit the presence of state-sponsored terrorism. Both of these texts also emphasize that terrorist attacks are done "against civilians" for political purposes. At least two of the examples in *American Odyssey,* however—the bombing of a Beirut night club in 1986 and the bombing of Pan Am flight 103 over Lockerbie, Scotland—have been attributed to intelligence agents from Libya, and led to U.S. military retaliation against Libya and U.N. sanctions, respectively.

It would be one thing to state that the definition of terrorism is contested and explain the nature of the disputes about its meaning; then these disparate examples could be used to help students understand the disputes and perhaps even determine which definition makes the most sense to them. But it is quite misleading to say that terrorism has a clear definition and then give examples that do not meet the definition. What we know from research on concept understanding is that there needs to be a connection between how a concept is defined (its critical attributes) and the examples (Parker, 1988; Taba, 1967). While we recognize how difficult that is to do with a concept like terrorism, it seems like the books should go one way or another. They should either present the concept as contested and engage students in the dispute by having them work with examples that may or may not be terrorism, which is done in a very sophisticated and meaningful way in some of the nonprofit curricula, *or* they should give a clear definition and find examples that back it up.

As the above analysis reveals, these texts generally identify 9/11 as an iconic and tragic event with no equal among terrorist attacks, provide examples of terrorism that emphasize attacks on the U.S. over attacks on other countries or peoples, and present definitions of terrorism and examples as universally accepted truths when they are contested concepts, inconsistently defined within the texts themselves.

What Students Are Asked to Think About

Given the controversies that exist about what students should be taught to believe about 9/11 and its aftermath that we summarize at the beginning of the chapter, we are quite interested in the types of thinking that the books promote. Here we are not suggesting that the 9/11 sections of the texts require thinking that is different from that required throughout the rest of the texts. Instead, this analysis explores 9/11 as a "case of" a larger phenomenon—which is the extent to which textbooks reinforce the notion that history is settled, and therefore what is most important for students to do is find and explain the right answers, or whether the textbooks support the notion that it is legitimate to have multiple and competing explanations of what

Table 8.6 9/11 & Terrorism Related Assessment Items by Assessment Category and Placement

Assessment categories	Pathways to the Present	American Odyssey	The Americans	MacGruder's	Democracy in Action	Street Law	Connections to Today	Patterns of Interaction	Glencoe World History	Totals
Total items	8	4	6	10	7	21	10	20	9	95
HOT-LOT	3–5	1–3	6–0	6–4	4–3	19–2	6–4	11–9	4–5	60–35
HOT	3	1	6	6	4	19	6	11	4	66
In text	1	1	5	1	2	5	3	3	3	24
End assessments	2	0	1	5	2	14	3	8	1	36
LOT	5	3	0	4	3	2	4	9	5	35
In text	4	3	0	0	1	2	0	4	1	15
End assessment	1	0	0	4	2	0	4	5	4	20

happened and why it matters. Similarly, with respect to the government and law texts, we think there is a connection between what kinds of thinking questions promote and require, and whether students are taught that it is honorable and necessary to engage in meaning-making—particularly about issues that are controversial. In short, questions posed to students are imbued with powerful messages about what thinking is and what it is important to think about.

We first analyze just the questions (not the accompanying text) because we assume that textbook adoption committees perusing many texts will quickly scan the types of questions to get a sense of what kinds of thinking students would be required to do if the teacher assigned the questions and other assessment prompts. We categorize each of these questions using Newmann and Wehlage's (1993) definitions of higher (HOT) and lower order thinking (LOT). Higher order thinking takes place when an assessment item "requires students to manipulate information and ideas in ways that transform their meaning and implications, such as when students combine facts and ideas in order to synthesize, generalize, explain, hypothesize, or arrive at some conclusion or interpretation" (Newmann & Wehlage, 1993, p. 8). As an example, we code the following question from

Street Law as HOT: "Is the war on terrorism similar to other wars where rights have been restricted? How is it the same? How is it different?" (p. 206). Lower order thinking (LOT), then, "occurs when students are asked to receive or recite factual information or to employ rules and algorithms through repetitive routines" (Newmann & Wehlage, 1993, p. 8). This question from *American Odyssey* is coded as LOT: "Who directed the terrorist attacks on the World Trade Center and the Pentagon in Washington, DC?" (p. 910).

We notice immediately the wide range of the number of questions in each book. One book has only 4 questions related to 9/11, while another has 21. In total, we find 95 questions. Significantly, we initially code 70 of these questions as HOT, while only 25 are LOT, which challenges our assumption that most textbooks are asking students LOT questions. Next, we examine the text narrative to determine what students would have to do in order to answer the questions, thus distinguishing between facial and applied analyses. Here we seek to determine whether the "on the face" HOT questions actually require this type of thinking (labeled HOT in table 8.6), or whether the question "as applied" is an *unintended LOT* because an explicit answer is given in the text (labeled LOT Unintended in Table 8.7). An example of a question that appears to be a HOT, but is really a LOT unintended comes from *Street Law:* "Why did the US. Government create a new agency after the September 11, 2001, terrorist attacks?" (p. 25). Although the question asks students "why" it provides them with a declaratively stated and "correct" answer within the text section, "In response to the attacks of September 11, 2001, the federal government created new agencies, and reorganized existing ones, to protect homeland security" (p. 24). We find that ten items initially coded as HOT are really unintended LOT items, as there is a verbatim "correct" answer that can be identified from the text and therefore the question does not require HOT. In total we find that there are 60 HOT items compared to 35 LOT items after this applied analysis.

Next, we look at the placement of the questions to determine which occur in the narrative and which are at the end of a section. As teachers, we often assigned the end of section questions as homework and viewed the questions embedded in the narrative as helpful prompts that may assist students' reading. Of the 60 HOT questions, only 24 are in the narrative, while 36 are at the end of the section. The placement of the LOT questions is more evenly divided between the narrative and the end of the sections, with 15 items located within the text and 20 in the end assessment sections. This initial analysis suggests that the majority of the questions students might actually have to write out answers for are HOT. This initial finding surprises us because textbooks often have been criticized for emphasizing questions that do not require students to think very hard (e.g., Giannangelo & Kaplan, 1992).

As part of the second round of analysis, we differentiate not only HOT vs. LOT and unintended LOT items, but we also categorize the HOT items as being Open or Closed. A HOT Open item is one that has multiple and competing "correct" answers while HOT Closed items require students to do HOT but have only one logical correct answer based on the information provided to students in the text. For example, we categorize the question from *MacGruder's,* "Do you think the United States could ever return to isolationism? Why or why not?" (p. 489) as a HOT Open. The narrative in the text explores the history of American isolationism and then includes various events in recent history that have provided challenges to the policy of isolationism in the face of globalization and terrorism. No correct answer is given in the text, which makes it more likely students would use HOT when constructing an answer. Conversely, we categorize the item from *Patterns of Interaction,* "How were the September 11 terrorist attacks unique? How were they similar to other terrorist incidents?" (p. 1092) as HOT Closed. The narrative of the text in this case provides information about the 9/11 attacks and other examples of terrorism, thus requiring synthesis and comparison, but would provide for one logical "correct" answer based on the information provided. Of the 60 questions that appear to require HOT on their face, 40 are categorized as HOT Open while 20 are categorized as HOT Closed.

Finally, we move to one additional step of analysis to determine whether the questions are properly scaffolded. In particular, we are interested in whether the text narrative provides enough information to support students so they can answer the questions. Not surprisingly, all of the LOT items are scaffolded. The HOT Open items ask students to share an opinion or take a position on an event or topic, nearly always asking for supporting evidence, rationale or explanation. However, only 14 of the 40 HOT Open items are sufficiently scaffolded. For example, a question in *The Americans* that we categorize as HOT Open and scaffolded asks students "Do you think the U.S.-led strike against Iraq will result in similar wars against other dangerous regimes?" (p. 1105). This item asks students

Table 8.7 9/11 & Terrorism Related Assessment Items by Type of Thinking and Scaffolding

Assessment Categories	Pathways to the Present	American Odyssey	The Americans	MacGruder's	Democracy in Action	Street Law	Connections to Today	Patterns of Interaction	Glencoe World History	Totals
HOT	3	1	6	6	4	19	6	11	4	60
HOT-Open	2	1	6	3	4	9	5	7	3	40
HOT-Open-scaffolded	0	0	0	3	1	5	2	2	1	14
HOT-Open with limited scaffolding	1	1	5	0	3	3	3	2	0	18
HOT-Open nonscaffolded	1	0	1	0	0	1	0	3	2	8
HOT-Closed	1	0	0	3	0	10	1	4	1	20
HOT-Closed-scaffolded	1	0	0	3	0	10	1	4	1	20
HOT-Closed-nonscaffolded	0	0	0	0	0	0	0	0	0	0
LOT (All closed and scaffolded)	5	3	0	4	3	2	4	9	5	35
LOT-Intended	4	2	0	2	3	0	4	7	3	25
LOT-Unintended	1	1	0	2	0	2	0	2	2	10
Total items	8	4	6	10	7	21	10	20	9	95

to apply the text's information on the Bush administration, foreign policy, and the circumstances under which the United States and its coalition invaded Iraq to the circumstances in other nations, such as Iran and North Korea. The student needs to do a considerable amount of intellectual work in order to come to a conclusion, and then needs to ground his or her answer in the information provided in the chapter. Of course, it is crucial to point out that students are not being asked to question the assumptions on which the question is based. The question makes clear that the issue of whether Iraq, Iran, and North Korea are dangerous regimes is off the table.

However, unlike the LOT and HOT Closed items (all of which contain the "right" answer in the text), many of the HOT Open items do *not* have the necessary scaffolding to successfully complete the task. Eighteen of the 40 HOT Open items have limited scaffolding, meaning there is some information available but not enough to fully complete the task, and eight have no scaffolding available. Most of the questions in this last category deal with local, personal, or family issues for which the text does not and could not provide support. It may be that students would have to engage in HOT to answer these questions, but the text has nothing to do with the content of the question.

An example of a question that is HOT Open but has limited scaffolding is found in the *American Odyssey*, "Do you agree with the assumption that terrorism affected the 2002 midterm elections? Why or why not?" (p. 912). While this question is a solid HOT question, the text does not provide enough evidence for the students to make a reasoned judgment. It includes information about President Bush's campaigning efforts on behalf of Republicans and that "Voters also seemed to feel that the nation should solidly support the commander in chief during the crisis over terrorism" (p. 912), but does not provide enough information on the election itself or the multiple reasons why the election turned out the way it did.

This leaves only 14 questions of the 95 questions present in the textbook sections on 9/11 that are not only asking students to do difficult thinking, but also providing the informational scaffolds for them to be successful in constructing an informed, independent response. Comparing the books against one another, three of them contain no HOT Open questions that are scaffolded and two have only one such question. Remarkably, only four of the nine textbooks we analyzed have more than one question that requires students to do challenging thinking *and* provides the sufficient information for them to use in doing so. Virtually all of the questions—81 of the 95—either engage students in low-level intellectual work, have a "correct" answer embedded in the text, or ask students to do challenging thinking without providing the necessary in-text support. This is obviously a far different picture than the one initially painted when we noted that 70 of the 95 looked—at first glance—to require HOT. Moreover, the fact that so many of the HOT Open questions are not properly supported by the text points out that even when students are asked to do challenging thinking, they are not given sufficient help in the text to do so.

Our analysis of the kinds of questions about 9/11 and its aftermath in these textbooks suggests that the most important task for students is to locate facts and copy them down or work toward answers that are either already set or unanswerable based on the information provided. This clearly reinforces the notion that history is "settled"—that there are single right answers to questions—even though many of the books fail to provide even rudimentary information about what actually happened on 9/11. Not surprisingly, none of them wade into the thick of whether what the government said about what happened on 9/11 is actually true. Even when questions appear to ask students to engage in more challenging thinking about 9/11 and its aftermath, these are often *closed* questions or, on the other hand, strong HOT questions that students probably could not develop answers to because there is not enough information in the text. Recall, only 14 of the 95 questions in the books ask students to engage in HOT and provide enough scaffolding, even though the vast majority of questions appear—at first glance—to ask students to engage in challenging thinking.

This thinking sleight of hand, so to speak, is particularly problematic because it has the potential to mislead teachers (and curriculum adoption committees) into believing that the traditional critique of textbooks—that they reinforce the false idea that the most important questions have single right answers—does not apply to these more recent texts. More significantly, we are concerned not just that teachers may think the questions demand HOT when they are really focused on LOT, but that the actual thinking students would need to engage in to answer most of these questions is so low level. We are not suggesting that all of the thinking that students should be asked to do should be higher order, but it would be nice if at least some of it is. With the notable exception of *Street Law,* the texts simply do not ask students to engage in important thinking about significant ideas related to 9/11 and its aftermath. Unfortunately, the rest of these textbooks fail to help students do what is most needed from all of us in these difficult times, which is to think deeply about important questions.

Conclusion

Thus, we end up with the following. These texts present 9/11 as exceedingly important, so much so that students must already know about what happened, and as representative of a broader trend that the United States is the nation most often victimized by terrorists, which is simply untrue. This narrow and nationalistic perspective on the events is evident across the texts, even those written for world history courses. Also, 9/11 and terrorism are presented as uncontested, even though the definitions of terrorism in the text and the examples used do not support one another—which is clearly evidence of the very opposite, that the meaning of terrorism is fluid and contested. We think part of what makes 9/11 so important is that it has sparked enormous controversy in the United States and throughout the world about what should happen in its wake. But the texts do not present this controversy, and thus we should not be surprised that the questions posed to students do not require them to think hard about such issues either.

Additionally, even though most historians would scoff at the very notion that sound histories can be constructed about an event that just occurred, these texts present an historical tale—what we would call "first draft" history—as settled truth. In her stunning book on historical thinking and collective memory, Marita Sturken writes that "the way a nation remembers a war and constructs its history is directly related to how that nation further propagates war" (1997, p. 122). The way that people in the United States remember 9/11 and construct its history, then, is no small matter. While we recognize the challenges of writing curriculum generally, and know that it is even more difficult to write about something so recent that continues to have such an enormous impact, much of what is in these texts about 9/11 is both highly misleading and confusing.

Finally, while this study looked specifically at how 9/11, terrorism, and the war on terror have been encapsulated in these popular texts, this study also illustrates the importance of analyzing text and images that form the "content" of the book, *and* what students are being asked to know and be able to do as a result of interacting with this content. As textbook development is currently being driven by the movement for standards and standardized testing, it becomes ever more important to understand what events, issues, and concepts these texts present as controversial versus those with a predetermined correct answer. As our analysis suggests, these texts fail to treat events deemed controversial in society as being such, and fail to provide students with the tools to successfully analyze and deliberate the few issues about which they ask students to think intensely. Consequently, in the main, the textbooks fail to help young people do what is most needed during extremely troubling times—which is to think deeply and hard.

Notes

The authors would like to thank Walter Parker, William Muthig, Eric Freedman, and the editors of this volume for providing feedback on previous drafts of this chapter.

1. Professor Hess worked with a team of graduate students on the first stage of the study analyzing the nonprofit and U.S. State Department curricula: Kristen Buras, Ross Collin, Hilary Conklin, Eric Freedman, Jeremy Stoddard, and Keita Takayama, and with Jeremy Stoddard and Shannon Murto on the second stage focusing on the textbooks.
2. Our estimated figures are based on enrollment statistics for grades 9–12 from the National Center for Education Statistics (U.S. Department of Education) and the combined 63.8% share that these texts hold in the Social Studies textbook market for grades 9–12. As textbooks are often purchased once every five to six years, it will be several years before schools will have these most recent editions.
3. The image referenced in this section can be viewed at http://www.groundzero spirit.org/

References

Apple, M. (1988). *Teachers and texts.* New York: Routledge.

Apple, M. (1999). *Official knowledge: Democratic education in a conservative age.* New York: Routledge.

Binder, A. (2004). *Contentious curricula: Afrocentrism and Creationism in American public schools.* Princeton, NJ: Princeton University Press.

Education Market Research. (2005). *The complete K–12 report: Market facts & segment analyses.* Rockaway Park, NY: Education Market Research & Open Book Publishing.

Evans, R. (2004). *The social studies wars: What should we teach the children?* New York: Teachers College Press.

Finn, C. (2002). *September 11: What our children need to know.* Retrieved January 12, 2003, from http://www.edexcellence.net/Sept11/September11.html

Giannangelo, D., & Kaplan, M. (1992). *An analysis and critique of selected social studies textbooks.* Retrieved July 31, 2006, from EDRS database.

Griffen, W., & Marciano, J. (1979). *Lessons of the Vietnam War: A critical examination of school texts and an interpretive comparative history utilizing the Pentagon Papers and other documents.* Totowa, NJ: Rowman & Allanheld.

Gutmann, A. (1999). *Democratic education.* Princeton, NJ: Princeton University Press.

Hess, D. (2004, April). *Examining the nature and range of ideologies embedded in curricula about 9/11.* Paper presented at the meeting of the American Educational Research Association, San Diego, CA.

Holt, P. (2002, March 7). The tricky art of defining "terrorism." *Christian Science Monitor.* Retrieved April 6, 2002, from http://www.csmonitor.com/2002/0307/p11s01-coop.html

Kohn, A. (2001). Teaching about Sept. 11. In *War, terrorism, and our classrooms: Teaching in the aftermath of the September 11 tragedy,* p. 5. Retrieved January 13, 2002, from http://www.rethinkingschools.org/special_reports/sept11/pdf/911insrt.pdf

Lévesque, S. (2003). "Bin Laden is responsible; it was shown on tape": Canadian high school students' historical understanding of terrorism. *Theory and Research in Social Education, 31*(2), 174–202.

Newmann, F., & Wehlage, G. (1993). Five standards of authentic instruction. *Educational Leadership, 50(7)*, 8–12.

Parker, W. (1988). Thinking to learn concepts. *Social Studies, 79(2)*, 70–73.

Parker, W. (2003). *Teaching democracy: Unity and diversity in public life.* New York: Teachers College Press.

Paxton, R.(1999). A deafening silence: History textbooks and the students who read them. *Review of Educational Research, 69(3)*, 315–339.

Public Agenda. (2005). Special report on terrorism. Available at http://www.public agenda.org/specials/terrorism/terror_pubopinion10.htm

Ravitch, D. (2004). *A consumer's guide to high-school history textbooks.* Retrieved July 31, 2006, from http://www.edexcellence.net/institute/publication/publication.cfm?id =329&pubsubid=1018

Rethinking Schools. (2001). *War, terrorism, and our classrooms: Teaching in the aftermath of the September 11 tragedy.* Retrieved January 13, 2002, from http://www.rethinking schools.org/special_reports/sept11/pdf/911insrt.pdf

Schemo, D. (2006, July 13). Schoolbooks are given F's in originality. *The New York Times,* 1.

Schweber, S. (2004). *Making sense of the Holocaust: Lessons from classroom practice.* New York: Teachers College Press.

Sewall, G. (2005). Textbook publishing. *Phi Delta Kappan, 86(7)*, 498–502.

Sturken, M. (1997). *Tangled memories: The Vietnam War, the AIDS epidemic, and the politics of remembering.* Berkeley: University of California Press.

Taba, H. (1967). *Teacher's handbook for elementary social studies. Introductory edition.* Reading, MA: Addison-Wesley.

Timmons, H. (2006, January 1). Four years on, a cabin's-eye view of 9/11. *The New York Times,* 7, 22.

U.S. Army Training and Doctrine Command. (2005). *A military guide to terrorism in the twenty-first century.* Retrieved July 29, 2006, from http://www.terrorism.com/modules .php?op=modload&name=Documents&file=get&download=276

Zimmerman, J. (2002) *Whose America: Culture wars in the public schools.* Cambridge, MA: Harvard University Press.

In the Community

CHAPTER 9

Engaging Urban Youth in Civic Practice

Community-Based Youth Organizations as
Alternative Sites for Democratic Education[1]

Jennifer L. O'Donoghue and Ben Kirshner

Recent years have witnessed the increased marginalization of youth from participation in the public realm. In urban communities, in particular, rising poverty and inequality, increased isolation, and decreasing support from communities, families, and schools limit youth's opportunities to influence policies that shape their lives (Blanc, 1994; Hart & Atkins, 2002; Hart, Daiute, & Iltus, 1997; Torney-Purta, 1999). Broader societal trends of citizen disengagement and disempowerment (National Commission on Civic Renewal, 1998; Putnam, 2000) are complicated for urban youth along racial, ethnic, and socioeconomic lines. Young people of color are frequently marginalized by "powerful signals . . . about their value, social legitimacy, and future" and many respond to these signals by "distrusting the possibility or desirability of ever becoming part of broader society" (McLaughlin, 1993, p. 43). Research has identified lower levels of trust and a greater sense of political powerlessness among youth of color than among their white counterparts (Flanagan & Faison, 2001; Mo, 2000). These trends have been coupled with low and decreasing civic participation among youth of color (Flanagan & Faison, 2001; Pittman, Ferber, & Irby, 2000).

Despite, or perhaps reflective of, these declining levels of participation, urban settings offer few spaces where youth can learn needed democratic skills. As McLaughlin (2000) writes, youth in distressed urban neighborhoods face an "institutional discontinuity"—a lack of access to spaces to engage in sustained, active learning, especially around democratic education and participation. Researchers have found, for example, that urban schools often present limited opportunities for youth to experience participatory democracy or engage in public change efforts (Berman, 1997; Carter, 1988; Conover & Searing, 2000; Costello, Toles, Spielberger, & Wynn, 2000; Flanagan & Faison, 2001; Hart & Atkins, 2002; Seigel & Rockwood, 1993).

Urban schools seldom provide meaningful opportunities for young people to develop the identity, skills, and knowledge necessary to be active democratic citizens. To find examples where urban youth engage in experiential, youth-driven projects that seek to address deep-seated public problems, it may be necessary to look to "alternative spaces" for civic development (Espinosa & Schwab, 1997). Community-based youth organizations (CBYOs) represent one such space worthy of investigation. While CBYOs often sit in the same sociopolitical context as urban schools, they rarely face the same sets of constraints or accountability demands. Many CBYOs, for example, have more egalitarian structures that allow for greater youth autonomy and participation (Costello et al., 2000). The flexibility of these CBYOs could allow them to present broader and more youth-centered conceptions of citizenship, such as building on the diverse talents, skills, and interests of young people or featuring youth leadership and voice in the organization (McLaughlin, 2000).

While certainly not all CBYOs share these features, some do seek to facilitate civic engagement for urban youth through direct forms of civic action, in which youth participate as leaders and decision-makers in projects designed to address pressing social problems through research, advocacy, education, and action. Although practitioners have begun to promote this emerging field, there is little empirical research describing learning processes in these settings or their significance for youth's development as citizens (Rajani, 2001). The purpose of this chapter is to shed light on urban youth's civic development by reporting key "civic practices" in which youth in CBYOs engaged. In doing so, we address the broader issue of civic education and demographic diversity, focusing in particular on the experiences of young people of color and low-income youth. Attention to civic practice is a critical step in an effort to understand CBYOs as learning environments that may foster particular democratic outcomes for urban youth.

Methods

Data Collection

Given the early stage of research in this area, we designed our studies with exploration and discovery in mind. We sought an understanding of youth civic development that was grounded in youth's interpretations of their experiences as well as our own observations of those experiences. Toward that end, we each conducted qualitative research in five community-based youth organizations in working class and poor urban neighborhoods on the West Coast: Student Power, Teens Restoring the Urban Environment ("TRUE"), Youth as Effective Citizens ("Effective Citizens"), Youth Engaged in Leadership and Learning ("YELL"), and Youth Supporting Youth Change ("Youth Change") (see table 9.1). Although these organizations varied in specific mission and goals, all five organizations had as a stated purpose involving urban youth in civic action or community change. Youth's civic work ranged from efforts to redress negative media portrayals of youth by producing news stories based on their own research to governing and sustaining a youth-initiated charter high school. Effective Citizens and YELL served as "primary sites" and were studied for more than two years each. The additional three CBYOs were "satellite sites," with the researchers spending a minimum of six months in each. None of the groups had academic prerequisites for involvement; to the best of our knowledge CBYO participants were not significantly different academically from their school-going peers. All of the sites, except for Effective Citizens, offered paid stipends as incentives for participation. During the school year groups mostly met after school.

Data collection at each site involved weekly or bi-weekly observation of program activities, meetings, events, and performances as well as formal and informal interviews. Formal interview data was collected from a sample of 55 youth participants: 24 African American, 18 Asian/Pacific Islander, 4 Latino, 4 Caucasian, and 5 multiracial youth. This sample was divided almost evenly between female (28) and male (27) youth. Youth ranged in age from 14 through 19. Each sample participant was interviewed at least once, with more than half interviewed at least twice, for a total of 115 interviews. Formal interviews with adult staff members were also conducted at most of the sites (n=18).[2]

Table 9.1 Background of Focal Community-Based Youth Organizations

CBYO	Student Power	TRUE	Effective Citizens	YELL	Youth Change
No. of Youth	12	6	68	24	7
No. of Adults	3	4	26	5	3
Ages of Youth	15 to 18	15 to 18	14 to 18	14 to 18	14 to 19
Racial/Ethnic Background of youth	Asian American, African American	Asian American, African American, Latino, European American	Asian American, African American, Latino, European American	Asian American, African American, Latino	Asian American, African American, Latino, European American
Meetings	Twice weekly, September to June	Weekly, year round	Daily, year round	Twice weekly, September to June	Weekly; September to June
Organizational context	Program of grassroots nonprofit advocacy organization	Program of environmental justice nonprofit organization	Charter high school	Program of university research center focused on youth development	Program of youth leadership development nonprofit organization
Mission/Goals	Organize students to lead a youth social justice movement	Teach young people about environmental justice and urban sustainability	Develop a strong, just community and a diverse generation of daring leaders	Promote youth voice by training students in research and leadership skills	Empower young people and engage them in community change
Recruitment method	Outreach in high schools; peer-to-peer recruitment	Outreach in high schools; peer-to-peer recruitment	Referred from school counselors, teachers, parents, friends	Recruited from one high school through presentations; peer-to-peer recruitment.	Recruited from schools, community organizations, youth groups; participants selected through youth-led interviews

Data Analysis

The claims presented in this paper were derived from a three step process. First, we each worked independently to identify themes from our research sites. Guided by egalitarian democratic and social learning theory, Jennifer explored how environmental and design features of CBYOs influenced urban youth's learning and experience as they worked to change their communities (O'Donoghue, 2006). Ben developed a framework rooted in the learning sciences to examine patterns of adult guidance strategies and how these strategies influenced youth development in each group (Kirshner, 2005). Despite our different foci, we shared a similar inductive approach to analysis, in which the researcher develops thematic codes based on recurring patterns observed in field notes and interviews (Creswell, 1998; Miles & Huberman, 1994). With regard to civic education practices, one starting point for both of us was to analyze how participants talked about what they had learned or how they had changed while part of these groups. But we did not rely solely on these self-report data: we also made judgments and inferences about youth civic development based on observations of growth in the young people or experiences they undertook.

The second step in our data analysis for this chapter took place while we were still in the early stages of our independent projects. During this time we realized that there were enough similarities in the goals and participants at our research sites that it would be generative to discuss themes that held true across our two studies. In so doing, we were able to identify commonalities across sites as well as variations. This collaborative interpretive process was a crucial step for each of us in refining our claims and checking our biases; in conversation with each other we explained the warrants for our claims, compared our interpretations of similar phenomena, and gained new ideas about what to look for in our data.

Finally, we endeavored to bring an emic perspective to our analysis through a process of member checking. This took varied forms across sites and occurred both during and after fieldwork. At Youth Change, for example, young people asked for a presentation of the "results" of interviews; adult staff made time for this, which led to a discussion of the themes that had emerged and youth's reaction to and interpretation of them. At other sites, such as Effective Citizens and YELL, member checking was both formal and informal, with each of us sharing our observations with adult staff and youth throughout our time in this program. Once our projects were complete we shared preliminary reports with adults and some youth participants in each setting to get their feedback about the accuracy and credibility of our findings (Becker, 1996).

Civic Practices of CBYOs

The CBYOs we studied shared a common interest in engaging young people in public action. Although the specific curricula and activities that these groups developed varied from group to group, we identified five shared practices across organizations: (1) working with others; (2) decision making; (3) interpreting public problems; (4) taking action; and (5) promoting youth public efficacy. Some of these practices reflected implicit goals. For example, "interpreting public problems" was something that young people in all of the groups did when discussing the community issues on which they worked, but only some groups included interpretation as an explicit part of the curriculum. Other practices reflected explicit goals in all groups; promoting youth's public efficacy, for instance, was a purpose stated by all five groups in mission statements and program materials. To make these civic practices real, we provide two vignettes drawn from our field notes. The first illustrates the internal workings of Effective Citizens; the second highlights a public action event facilitated by the young people of TRUE. We then draw on these vignettes to discuss each of the five practices, and the tensions that emerged within them, in greater depth.

Vignette #1: Preparing for Action at Effective Citizens

8:30 a.m. A group of 16 youth came together, seated in a circle. Nicole, their adult coach, turned to Brianna, a youth in her second year with the organization, and asked, "What are we doing today?" Brianna stood and began going over the "To Do" list hanging on the wall, writing down who was doing what for that night's event, a meeting to gather community input on a charter school project the group was working on.

8:50 a.m. The youth broke into pairs and headed off to work on their agendas for the small-group activities they would facilitate that night. Katherine, a senior in her third year, worked with Antonio, a junior new to the organization. When Nicole came over to check in with them and answer questions, Antonio voiced his concerns about taking notes from the brainstorming session on flip chart paper. Nicole asked him, "Ok, but if you were on the other side, how would having your ideas written on the board make you feel?" Antonio replied, "It would draw you into the community." Katherine added, "They could see that they're heard." Antonio worried the group would see his spelling mistakes, so Katherine suggested that maybe he should facilitate instead. Antonio said he was not sure he was ready for that, so they decided to take turns facilitating and notetaking.

9:20 a.m. Nicole and Brianna called the youth together to do a full run-through of the event. Youth moved to different areas—some by the front door to welcome people, others at a petition table, others standing up waiting to bring parents into the semi-circle or their children to childcare, and others taking on the role of "new parents" coming in for the event. Brianna then asked everyone to have a seat in the semi-circle for the opening presentation. At the end, youth gave each other feedback about content, energy, body language, and eye contact.

10:00 a.m. Nicole headed toward the white board, but then stopped herself and gave the pen to Brianna, saying "I forgot you were facilitating today." Brianna led the group in brainstorming what they had left to do: come up with a clean-up plan, prepare visuals for the presentation, get all the materials ready for that night, set up the greeting table, and practice the presentation. The youth headed off to work on these different activities.

Vignette #2: Taking Public Action: An Accountability Session with Local Politicians

In May 2003, soon after the U.S. invasion of Iraq, members of TRUE organized a youth conference designed to educate their peers about the effects of the U.S. military on their neighborhood, such as environmental hazards posed by a former naval shipyard and military recruitment in their schools. The day began with workshops led by local community groups and concluded with an "accountability session" with congressional representatives, city supervisors, and school board members. Political officials sat on chairs on the school auditorium stage, facing the roughly two hundred middle and high school students and their teachers in the audience. Charles, a youth participant in TRUE, served as emcee. TRUE staff members stood on the side, making sure that the sound system was working and that the event moved along without interruptions.

After the panelists had been introduced, youth organizers approached the microphone to ask questions. Patrice, one of the youth who had organized the conference, challenged his congressional representative about her positions towards the war. After noting that the congressperson had said she was pro-environment, but also supported the war, he asked, "If you could, could you please explain how these views do not contradict each other?" Another youth asked about the dearth of healthy food options in her neighborhood: "I'm Viviana, and I'm in TRUE. We advocate for food security in our community. I want to know are you aware that Hillside does not have an adequate supermarket?" The political official responded by saying she was making efforts to increase healthy food options in the neighborhood.

Later more youth got involved, including students from the audience who were not part of TRUE. A variety of issues were discussed— the prospect of a light rail, school testing policies, school funding, and requests for a cleanup of the naval shipyard. Adults were not afraid to disagree with or challenge youth. Several panelists called on youth to get "more involved" by using the phone or e-mailing them. And some youth did not hesitate to disagree with adults. One TRUE member pointed out that not all youth have access to e-mail at home, making it hard to get involved in that way. TRUE members concluded by asking for support for their resolution against military recruitment in high schools, based on their concerns that minority and low-income communities were being targeted. The panelists expressed support for it.

These vignettes illustrate some of the goals of the five CBYOs we studied. As suggested by the event preparation at Effective Citizens, youth routinely worked collaboratively to complete projects and make decisions. As depicted by the accountability session, youth grappled with public problems and found ways to take action to address them. In both examples, the primary emphasis of these groups was on putting youth in a position to take leadership and develop a sense of public efficacy. In the following sections, we discuss these practices in greater depth.

Working with Others

The Effective Citizens vignette illustrates the central place of teamwork and collaboration in CBYOs. Participants first worked in pairs to prepare for the event, then did a run-through of the agenda as a large group. They evaluated one another's performance, providing support and critique. Indeed, this CBYO saw giving and accepting feedback as a central feature of working effectively with others. The vignette ended with the group deciding together how to best use their remaining time.

Across all of the CBYOs, working with others was the skill pointed to most often by youth when asked about their learning experiences. Although they sometimes expressed frustration over the challenges of working with others, nearly all youth interviewed felt they had learned valuable skills related to teamwork. For example, youth talked about the importance of not always dominating conversations, working in a team, listening to others, seeing beyond first impressions of people, mediating conflicts between others, having patience with novices, sharing personal feelings with peers, tolerating contrary opinions, becoming like family with people, being more respectful to others, trusting peers not to divulge secrets, and overcoming racial differences. Rather than offer pat phrases about "teamwork," they offered specific examples of what it took to accomplish goals with others.

Youth's reports about collaboration and teamwork corresponded to our own observations of activities in the CBYOs. Youth participants worked together in small groups. They made decisions through democratic processes. They relied on each other for help by taking advantage of each other's skills: if one person was a good artist, and another good with technology, they found ways to distribute expertise across the group in order for projects to get completed. Unlike typical school classrooms, accountability for work was never reduced to an individual level in the form of grades and test scores. Instead accountability was distributed across small groups. In essence, the basic "work unit" was, almost without exception, greater than one. It is perhaps not surprising, then, that when asked to describe what they had learned, youth's responses cohered around this theme.

Collaboration led to a number of sub-skills, including learning to trust others, make and stick to commitments, hold others accountable, ask for help, have an open mind, and work with and through diversity. While these lessons came both from positive and less positive experiences, they were grounded in the public work of the CBYOs. At Effective Citizens, for example, youth described becoming more responsible because they knew others were depending on them to get things done; if they did not write their speech for the city council hearing, the whole project could fail. A participant in YELL made a similar point, after being asked to clarify what he meant when he said he had learned "teamwork."

> *Can you tell me what you mean by that? Or can you give me an example?*
> Just like working with others to get the job done. But I used to be the type of person who is just like, like, really independent. Like, "I can get this done on my own." And at YELL, I just realized that it's not always the best thing to do—it's not always the easiest . . . to want to do it on your own.

This participant described his transition from being the type of person who got things done on his own to realizing that it can be easier to get the job done if you "work with others."

Through working together on public projects, youth came to see the importance of taking others' opinions into account and of trying to understand others' points of view, even when they were different from one's own. Indeed, diversity within groups—of background or opinion—was something youth valued and learned from.

> Youth Change participant: When there's not a big diversity within the group, it's hard to see different perspectives; like for [name of youth in Youth Change], she's a lesbian, and we had some groups [applying for grants] that were about being gay or lesbian or transsexual, and hearing what she had to say about those groups is something that I didn't even think about because I don't know that perspective.

> Effective Citizens participant: I used to not listen to as much people. Like before, I would listen to only one person, and everyone else's point of view, I didn't really care for it. But then now, it's like it does matter now, and they have, even if their point of view is different from mine, I can still respect that.

The result of collaboration among diverse youth, they felt, was improved quality in the work.

Learning to work with others also extended to the relationship between youth and adults. Youth-adult relationships are complicated, particularly in settings that strive for non-hierarchical "partnerships" between young people and adults (Camino, 2005; O'Donoghue & Strobel, in press; Zeldin, Larson, Camino, & O'Connor, 2005). In the CBYOs we studied, youth had extensive opportunities to collaborate with adults on their civic projects. This partnership took different forms within different organizations from one-on-one pairings to one adult working with a team of youth. These types of relationships allowed youth to experience new ways of interacting with adults that led them to have a changed understanding of youth-adult relationships and a new sense of responsibility. As one youth from Effective Citizens explained:

> My relationship with [adult staff member] has changed me, like made me kind of understand more the theory of, like, adults and youth being equal . . . Just by having relationships with [adult staff], you develop better relationships with . . . all other adults.

Collaboration between adults and youth was not problem-free. For example, partnerships sometimes broke down when adults assumed too much authority or acted in a manner that was controlling. As the vignette above showed, Nicole, the adult coach, unintentionally started to play the role of facilitator even though one of the youth had been assigned that role. Across sites, youth expressed frustration when adults made decisions about project ideas or took on responsibilities that had previously been delegated to youth. These tensions between adults and youth reflected challenges that exist in a democracy when people try to shift from hierarchical to more egalitarian or collaborative forms of interaction. Rather than simply swallow their frustration, however, many youth put their new collaboration skills to work, speaking up to hold adults accountable for the commitments they had made to support youth voice and initiative. At Youth Change, for example, youth were extremely upset when adults made phone calls to notify youth groups that they had been funded. Young people had always been the point of contact with the youth groups, and they were appalled that adults would step into this sphere of responsibility. Youth asked to have a meeting with the adults in which they voiced their concerns and reminded adults of the importance of keeping youth at the center of the work. In the resulting interaction, youth learned how to assert themselves in disagreements with adults.

Decision Making

Youth across these CBYOs made both large and small decisions about their work, deciding together how they would spend their time, as in Vignette #1, what public issues they would take on, and what approaches they would use to do so. Decision making processes involving youth varied both across and within organizations. As one youth from Effective Citizens described it, decision making was "different at every time," ranging from "majority rules" style voting to consensus-building to less inclusive forms. Sometimes, these processes would be combined. At Effective Citizens, for example, youth engaged in a "Decision Day" to determine organizational structure for the remainder of the year. Young people first used consensus-building techniques in small groups to develop proposals and then later used "majority rules" voting in the large group to select one of the presented proposals. What characterized all organizations was that youth learned decision-making skills while engaged in a real-world process that would have public impact, as a member of Youth Change explained:

> I never really had to make any decisions like this before this kind of experience . . . whereas, in school you work with a group to finish a project and do it the best you can, [here] you work in a group to make a good decision that will benefit other people and go farther and constantly expand.

This opportunity to shape something meaningful increased motivation for young people to engage in processes that were sometimes lengthy and frustrating.

Although not used at all sites, consensus-building processes stood out in youth's minds when discussing their civic learning. Youth often came to the CBYOs with an understanding of voting, but were less familiar with the process used to arrive at consensus. Indeed, almost all youth who were asked reported that they had *no* prior experience of consensus decision making, either in school or in other community organizations. Several youth, however, pointed to the role of consensus in allowing youth voices to be heard, as did one member of Youth Change.

> Majority sort of makes people feel like they don't have a voice. Because, like, when you're saying, "Oh, because we like it and there's

more of us than you, our voices are more important because there's more; so your ideas are not good. Don't share them."

The specific processes used to reach consensus varied across organizations. No matter what the method used, youth reported that respect, for people and for their ideas, and learning to take others' opinions into account were the keys to good decision making.

Tensions often arose in decision making. Although youth talked about the value of consensus-style decision making and the techniques they had learned, they also expressed frustration with the lengthy process it often entailed. In one example, youth at YELL spent several weeks revisiting a decision they had made to work on the problem of "stereotypes" because of the complaints of some members. However, several youth felt that this was "wasted" time that ultimately took away from working on their campaign. Similarly, some youth at Effective Citizens questioned whether every decision, down to "what color to paint the walls" required an extended, drawn-out process, and other youth pointed out that sometimes there just is not enough time to "be democratic." Youth across sites confronted the tensions between the time-consuming realities and the ideals democratic decision making.

Adults also struggled over when to use different decision-making techniques. Some occasions when adults bypassed longer, more inclusive decision-making processes resulted in anger and rebellion from youth. At Youth Change, for example, adult staff members made the decision to cancel an event because they felt that youth were "burnt out." Youth were extremely upset about this. As one young person from this CBYO reported, "When you have a decision like that made, it's really hard on people in the group when you don't include them or at least let them know that this might happen." A second participant echoed this concern:

They made a decision without discussing it with us to cancel it. So, [that made me upset]—the not making it a priority of letting the youth say something is important to them, and also not really asking and just making decisions for the group.

Youth's sophistication in decision making, both in terms of participation and of discernment of the subtleties of different processes, varied based on experience levels. Veteran youth were often most involved in and most critical of decision making processes, whereas novice youth were often pleased just to be part of the group and get to vote on decisions. The distinction between new and experienced youth was further highlighted by the fact that decision making in these CBYOs was primarily a verbal process that assumed that youth would speak up if they did not agree. In interviews several young people, particularly those with less experience in community work, described being too shy to speak up, demonstrating a limit to truly inclusive decision making. There was also variation in the opportunities youth had to participate in decision making within the organization, particularly in larger CBYOs that struggled to create inclusive and democratic processes with greater numbers of youth. Amid the diversity of youth background knowledge and skill, those with the most experience tended to be more involved in decision making opportunities. Across all sites, we noted that not all youth became expert in or wholeheartedly embraced one style of decision making, but rather were practicing democratic processes and learning about the tensions and tradeoffs inherent within them through real work around things that mattered to them.

Interpreting Public Problems

Because each of the CBYOs we studied sought to achieve some kind of public impact, youth participants had multiple opportunities to think and talk about the origins of problems facing their communities. This was evident in the resolution put forth by TRUE about military recruitment mentioned in Vignette 2. Rather than view enlistment solely as a personal choice, members of TRUE were concerned about contextual factors pushing low-income youth of color in inner city schools towards the military, such as the disproportionate presence of JROTC programs in their schools and the lack of college prep classes. They viewed limiting military access to students' personal records as one solution. Each of the CBYOs we studied developed a campaign that rested on a specific analysis of a problem or issue (see table 9.2).

Youth participants discussed the causes of social problems as they worked on their campaigns together. These discussions sometimes brought out tensions between individualistic and systemic interpretations of public problems endemic to U.S. democracy. While some people emphasize individual behavior as the primary cause of social problems, others attribute responsibility to contextual factors, such as lack of equal opportunity or disinvestment from cities (Watts & Flanagan, 2007). These broader tensions emerged in youth's work with each other.

Table 9.2 Problem Frames and Public Actions at Each Site

CBYO	Problem frame(s)	Public/Community actions
Student Power	Drop-out rate & lack of student voice in schools	Change student leadership classes to include governance
TRUE	Toxic consequences of war and military on local neighborhood	Educate other youth about war and the environment
Effective Citizens	Lack of quality educational options and meaningful public opportunities for youth	Create charter school to serve as basis for collaborative social change work
YELL	Negative media images of neighborhood youth	Pressure media outlets to produce more positive stories
Youth Change	Multiple: violence, racism, poverty, homophobia, food security, technological access, education	Build capacity of city youth to instigate change by giving grants and technical-assistance to grassroots youth-led initiatives

For example, when discussing problems at their school, some members of YELL alleged that the cause had to do with misbehavior or laziness among fellow students, which reflected a more individualist explanation. Others attributed poor achievement at the school to lack of resources and lack of job opportunities for graduates, which reflected a more systemic or structural interpretation. The difference between these views was not always so stark—many young people took positions that reconciled their own sense of personal responsibility and agency with their awareness of the influence of social context on people's behavior.

Adults in some of the groups made it an explicit goal to help young people see the systemic or institutional causes of problems in their neighborhoods. Student Power, for example, designed an intentional curriculum to teach youth about multiple factors influencing the high school drop out rate. Staff members at Student Power led activities—from discussions to an original board game—that challenged youth to identify social or policy factors that might have an impact on students' behavior. Rather than fault students as lazy, unmotivated, or irresponsible, youth were invited to reflect on other factors that might influence the drop-out rate. After a process taking several months, which included reflection, discussion, and surveys of other young people, youth identified factors such as poor retention of quality teachers, limited student voice, and lack of counseling services. Discussions among adults and youth also linked school district problems to even more distal factors, such as state and federal budget priorities.

At other sites, such as YELL or Effective Citizens, adults were more likely to adopt a neutral position as facilitators without espousing a particular explanation for the causes of social problems. Even in these cases, however, adults played a central role in helping youth participants turn problems they had identified into campaigns that could have clear policy implications. At Effective Citizens, a group of youth was asked to choose a public project based on the criteria that it "impact the community." The adult coach then left to "remove adult influence" from the decision. Observation of the youth's discussion, however, showed that they struggled with understanding these terms; it was not clear to them who the "community" was, what public problems were most pressing, and what "impact" meant. In this case, the youth needed to have a stronger adult presence to help them think through public issues before jumping into a project. Adults at YELL, for example, asked critical questions and guided youth through a lengthy process of reflection and voting that helped them identify their chosen issue of media representations of youth.

Some youth related in interviews that participating in CBYOs exposed them to ways of thinking about the world that they did not get at school. As one youth in TRUE summarized, "I'm looking at the world at a completely different angle now." Another young person, from Student Power, compared the CBYO to school by saying: "The school is going to teach you the good side of everything, but up in here, they going to show you the good side, the bad side. They going to show you all four corners of everything." This comment underscores a theme that was true across groups—they sought to give opportunities for youth to reflect on the causes of problems that mattered to young people. And, as discussed in the next section, they also worked with youth to find ways to take action to solve them.

Taking Action

TRUE's "Toxic Consequences of War" conference illustrated the range of ways that groups took action to address problems. On one level their action focused on sharing information: The conference workshops offered a way for neighborhood youth to learn about the history of military involvements in the area. It also promoted communication with adult policymakers: By organizing the accountability session, TRUE set up an authentic, open-ended interaction between youth and local political officials. Finally, by submitting a formal resolution to end military recruitment, TRUE took action through conventional political channels to change a local policy that affected young people.

These different aspects of TRUE's work were reflected in the other CBYOs. Youth across sites learned strategies for making their voices heard by a broader public or influencing policymakers. The social change strategies were locally based and linked to the specific campaign goals being sought. Groups built grassroots coalitions made up of "allies" from other youth organizations. For example, members of Student Power and Effective Citizens often discussed how to build "power in numbers," that is, attract nonaffiliated youth to show their support at public events and meetings. All of the groups invited local journalists and television reporters to cover their events. YELL organized several meetings with editors and reporters as part of its campaign to change media representations of young people. At Effective Citizens, TRUE, and Student Power, participants learned how to influence political officials by writing formal resolutions that were submitted to government agencies or deliberative bodies. Because of their status as grant makers for multiple youth initiatives, members of Youth Change spent much of their time discussing whether projects would actually have an impact on the problems they were trying to solve. In debating whether the youth and the community would gain skills or knowledge from the proposed projects, these young people came to believe that strategies that lacked follow-up or educational components were less effective at producing lasting change.

In addition to learning about campaign strategies, youth also gained important knowledge about local civic leaders and powerbrokers. Their interactions with civic leaders—school board members, city council members, mayors—gave them insight into the personalities and political stances of these figures. Youth at Effective Citizens, and to a lesser extent Student Power, TRUE, and YELL, referred to the names of local political leaders in conversations with each other and adults, indicating the specificity of their knowledge about local government.

Youth were sometimes surprised by the positive response they received from civic leaders. One participant in Student Power recounted her excitement about feeling that the school board was listening to her when she spoke:

I was like, "Oh, are they listening to me? . . .I'm not even going to shut up." You know? That's how I was. I was like, "I'm finally being listened to. I might as well say everything I've got to say and not hide no words."

But there were also occasions when adult power-brokers took actions that angered youth. For example, members of Effective Citizens learned a great deal about their place in the local power structure after hearing that school board members had sought to reward a contractor for *not* working with the CBYO. These face-to-face interactions gave youth valuable experiences with the realities of local politics, as one young member of Effective Citizens explained:

When I got involved with Effective Citizens, I got more into politics . . . and when I joined the CBYO board of directors, we discussed about the situation between us and the school board. And then I got more angry, so I got more involved. . . . So, that's how, I guess it just built up during coming here, because I knew if I didn't come here, I know I wouldn't be interested at all or wouldn't know what was going on.

Both through positive and more frustrating encounters with local government, youth in these CBYOs became more aware of and interested in the processes involved in taking public action.

Promoting Public Efficacy

One practice that was common across all sites was for adults to position young people as powerful public actors and for youth to articulate their own sense of agency and power. These were settings that emphasized and encouraged "public efficacy," which refers to the extent to which young people see themselves as capable of affecting or influencing both the CBYO and the broader community (based on Perkins & Miller, n.d., in Tolman & Pittman, 2001).[3]

Public efficacy was treated in these organizations as a developmental, dynamic belief rather than as a linearly developed trait that youth either had or did not have. The adult co-founder of Effective Citizens described public efficacy as a pendulum, saying that youth would swing back and forth between feeling powerful and not. As they began to see their impact through their community projects, she described, they would begin to swing to an even higher level of efficacy, but there would also be swings in

Engaging Urban Youth in Civic Practice

the other direction as youth "geared up" for their next move forward. Indeed, for many youth, having the experience of trying to make an impact on an organization, a policy, or a community often provided a keener sense of the challenges involved in such tasks. Rather than simply increasing their own sense of agency, these experiences provided them with a greater understanding of what it takes to make change. At Student Power adults offered a framework that identified eight variations on the theme of efficacy, ranging from "passive" to "eyes open" to "organizing others." Youth were encouraged to think of this as a process of self-growth that people would move through at their own pace.

Youth voiced a variety of ideas about what "making an impact" meant to them, ranging from a greater sense of their ability to make change in the community to increased awareness of the complexity of the problems they were trying to change, to efficacy in less conventional political activity, such as being able to serve as a positive example to others. One young person from Effective Citizens described the growth in her own sense of influence:

> They would always, constantly tell me, "people follow you, whether you do bad stuff or good stuff," and I didn't know that. It was like it took me to this year to really look back and see that if I do this, then people will follow; if I do this, then people will follow; what decisions do I need to make for people to follow in the right direction or lead them in the right direction?

Members of YELL, who worked on the problem of stereotypes about youth in their neighborhood, often talked about two different ways of making an impact. While the program's campaign encouraged media outlets to offer more balanced coverage, several youth also talked about their ability to make an impact by defying stereotypes through personal conduct.

These varied understandings grew from experiences across multiple levels—from interpersonal relationships, to organizational decision making, to public action. At Effective Citizens, for example, the organization maintained that youth's efficacy developed from seeing their impact first on the organization and others within it and then out into the broader community. In addition, youth's development of and understanding of public efficacy was influenced by having a space not only to work to create public impact, but also to reflect upon their own experiences and abilities, as described by one youth from Effective Citizens:

I feel like I am able to see what I'm capable of doing, what I can accomplish. And I feel like they taught me how to look, self-reflect, how to look inside myself and see that I, "oh, I have this skill, this skill, this skill, let me use it in different ways."

Creating this reflective space provided young people with opportunities to become more aware not only of the power they had, but also of the public impact that they sought to achieve.

Finally, perhaps not surprisingly given the collective orientation of these CBYOs, many youth saw efficacy not as an individual trait, but rather as a group quality. When asked if they felt they could impact their communities, many youth responded "No, not alone." While at first glance this seemed to reflect a lack of efficacy, further probing showed that youth had developed a more nuanced understanding of what was necessary to effect change in the public realm. Indeed, for some youth, the idea that they *alone* should be the one to decide what was best for their community was anathema. As one young person from Youth Change explained:

Ideally, [having a say in my community] would mean that I would have a say and everyone has a say; because if I'm just the only one having a say, how is that any better than what we have right now?

Her words reflect a focus on working toward the common good rather than individual power. Many youth felt that they would only be able to make an impact if there were others willing to support them or an existing group that they could join. This was particularly true as the scale of the problem—and the desired effect—grew, as in the following excerpt, from an interview with a young person in TRUE.

When something bothers you about the community or school, what do you usually do?
It depends on what the problem is. If it's a little problem that I can just talk to someone directly, I would usually do it. Say there wasn't enough toilet paper in the school bathroom: I would just go to the principal and tell him. . . . But if it's a really big problem, a really big injustice—like more pollution in the air at Hillside—I would try to work with other people to solve that problem. It depends on what the problem would have to be and if it's fixable and if it can be changed or not.

Why would you want to work with other people?

Let's say there was like a really big problem. I would say that the Hillside power plant is a really big problem in this community. That's why I worked with TRUE to try and shut it down. . . . And I think that you just have a bigger influence if you're . . . like, you have strength in numbers. That's basically my philosophy.

This young person articulated two common themes voiced by youth: they had the power to make change, but it was often only through collective action that intractable problems could be solved.

Variation Across CBYOs: From Purpose to Practice

The five civic practices discussed here were common across research sites. Variations in how these practices were enacted at each site were often linked to CBYO mission or purpose. All sites maintained a goal of engaging young people in collaborative public work and developing youth leadership. Not surprisingly then, we saw little variation in these organizations' emphasis on teamwork and youth agency. Organizational purpose did, however, influence youth's involvement in decision making, their interpretation of public problems, and their engagement in public action. Youth Change, for example, had developed a particular empowerment and change strategy, providing grants to community youth groups, which resulted in a heavy emphasis on consensus-based grant decision making. Student Power and TRUE were part of organizations that promoted particular styles of organizing around specific issues, which led to more guidance from adults around public problem interpretation and influenced the types of public actions youth performed. The university-sponsored YELL program highlighted research-based problem analysis and action. Finally, Effective Citizens' emphasis on community building resulted in a special focus on relationship development throughout their work, in everything from collaborative project teams to public work partnerships with community members.

Conclusion: CBYOs and Education for Democratic Citizenship

In this chapter we identified civic practices that youth experienced through their participation in public work-oriented community-based youth organizations. By engaging in these civic practices, young people developed important competencies for democratic participation, ranging from collaborative work and decision making to practical knowledge about local issues and how to make an impact on them. These competencies shared a common experiential, applied quality, which meant that youth experienced the ups and downs, the successes and failures, which only come from authentic encounters with complex public problems. While youth at times experienced frustration, this was part of a learning trajectory that prepared them to continue their democratic work in other venues with greater wisdom.

The challenges youth encountered were linked to some of the core tensions in U.S. democracy. Youth and adults struggled to create new relationships based on democratic ideals, but grounded in the realities of age segregation and power inequalities. Diversity of background, and of knowledge and experience in particular, challenged the ability of these CBYOs to promote inclusive decision making. In working to understand and take action on public issues, young people confronted broader questions about individualism, systems, and the common good and gained first-hand experience in the realities of U.S. democracy and politics. Finally, promoting youth efficacy led to learning about individual as well as collective power, rights, and obligations.

In communicating the potential benefits of CBYOs for youth civic education, it is also important to recognize potential trade-offs that stem from their approach. For example, by focusing their attention on local issues, groups rarely encouraged youth to become engaged in national or international issues. Similarly, there was little attention paid to traditional civic content knowledge such as the relations between the three branches of government or electoral processes. Even on the occasions when lessons about legislative processes were shared, the point was rarely to achieve individual mastery of content knowledge, but instead a "good enough," provisional mastery needed to complete a task.

Nevertheless, our research suggests that CBYOs offer a valuable set of opportunities for urban youth to learn about and practice active democratic citizenship. As new programs develop and researchers seek to build knowledge about civic engagement, we see several important implications of our study. First, this research demonstrates that CBYOs can be effective at reaching urban youth, by providing them opportunities to learn and practice needed civic skills and habits, develop a changed sense of power and agency as democratic actors, and make meaningful public change. Our findings support the conclusions of the recent Congressional Conference on Civic Education, which called for the "development of programs that provide students opportunities to do real work on community or public problems and issues . . . aimed at civic outcomes rather than personal development . . . using explicit political and public dimensions" (COPE, 2003).

Second, our research suggests that this kind of civic education requires skilled adults to work with youth. In order to offer environments that are flexible enough for youth to engage in this work, adult educators need to design compelling, intentional, but still open-ended, structures to support youth initiative (O'Donoghue & Strobel, in press). As the public projects come to drive much of the skills and knowledge that will be learned, how they are framed becomes all the more important. Adult support, oftentimes, can make the difference between projects that are relatively ineffectual and projects that accomplish ambitious goals. Such an approach puts essentialist definitions of *youth* and *adult* aside in favor of broader concerns about social justice and urban youth's participation in meaningful civic practice and democratic education.

Notes

1. Research for this paper was supported by The Center for Information & Research on Civic Learning & Engagement (CIRCLE) and the John W. Gardner Center for Youth and Their Communities.
2. Sampling for interviews varied across sites. At Youth Change and YELL all participants were included in the interview sample. At TRUE and Student Power some of the more peripheral participants—those who did not show up every week—were not interviewed because of difficulties obtaining consent forms or scheduling. At Effective Citizens, which had a much larger number of youth, sampling was purposeful, aiming to garner information-rich cases along dimensions of interest, including demographic background, time in the organization, level of involvement, and leadership, as defined by adults and youth in the CBYO.
3. We intentionally use the term "public efficacy" rather than political efficacy. Political efficacy has been defined as the "sense of one's ability to participate effectively in the political process" (Kahne & Westheimer, 2006, p. 289). By using the idea of public efficacy we hope to expand this understanding and capture the extent to which youth feel able to have an impact on the public realm broadly rather than the political process in particular.

References

Becker, H. (1996). The epistemology of qualitative research. In R. Jessor, A. Colby, & R. Shweder (Eds.), *Ethnography and human development: Context and meaning in social inquiry* (pp. 53–72). Chicago: University of Chicago Press.

Berman, S. (1997). *Children's social consciousness and the development of social responsibility.* Albany: State University of New York Press.

Blanc, C. (1994). *Urban children in distress: Global predicaments and innovative strategies.* Florence, Italy: UNICEF International Child Development Centre.

Camino, L. (2005). Pitfalls and promising practices of youth-adult partnerships: An evaluator's reflections. *Journal of Community Psychology, 33*(1), 75–85.

Carter, T. (1988). *Application of organization development theory and practice to improve citizenship education.* Unpublished dissertation, Seattle University, Seattle, WA.

Conover, P., & Searing, D. (2000). A political socialization perspective. In L. McDonnell, P. Timpane, & R. Benjamin (Eds.), *Rediscovering the democratic purposes of education* (pp. 91–124). Lawrence: University Press of Kansas.

Costello, J., Toles, M., Spielberger, J., & Wynn, J. (2000). *History, ideology and structure shape the organizations that shape youth, youth development: issues, challenges and directions* (pp. 185–231). Philadelphia: Public/Private Ventures.

COPE: Council on Public Engagement. (2003 October). Ideas for action. *Civic Engagement News, 11.*

Creswell, J. (1998). *Qualitative inquiry and research design: Choosing among five traditions.* Thousand Oaks, CA: Sage Publications.

Espinosa, M., & Schwab, M. (1997). Working children in Ecuador mobilize for change. *Social Justice, 24*(3), 64–70.

Flanagan, C., & Faison, N. (2001). Youth civic development: Implications of research for social policy and programs. *Social Policy Report: Giving Child and Youth Development Knowledge Away, 15*(1), 1–15.

Hart, D., & Atkins, R. (2002). Civic competence in urban youth. *Applied Developmental Science, 6*(4), 227–236.

Hart, R., Daiute, C., & Iltus, S. (1997). Developmental theory and children's participation in community organizations. *Social Justice, 24*(3), 33–63.

Kahne, J. & Westheimer, J. (2006). The limits of efficacy: Educating citizens for a democratic society. *PS: Political Science and Politics, 39*(2), pp. 289–296.

Kirshner, B. (2005). *Democracy now: Activism and learning in urban youth organizations.* Unpublished doctoral dissertation, Stanford University.

McLaughlin, M. (1993). Embedded identities: Enabling balance in urban contexts. In S. Heath & M. McLaughlin (Eds.), *Identity & inner-city youth: Beyond ethnicity and gender* (pp. 36–68). New York: Teachers College Press.

McLaughlin, M. (2000). Community counts: How youth organizations matter for youth development. Washington, DC: Public Education Network.

Miles, M., & Huberman, A. (1994). *Qualitative data analysis.* Thousand Oaks, CA: Sage Publications.

Mo, K-H. (2000). *Citizenship education for Korean-American youth.* Unpublished dissertation, University of California, Berkeley.

National Commission on Civic Renewal (1998). A nation of spectators: How civic disengagement weakens America and what we can do about it. Washington, DC: National Commission on Civic Renewal.

O'Donoghue, J. (2006). *Powerful spaces: Urban youth, community-based youth organizations and democratic action.* Unpublished doctoral dissertation, Stanford University.

O'Donoghue, J., and Strobel, K. (2007). Directivity and freedom: Adult support of urban youth activism. *American Behavioral Scientist, 51*(3), pp. 465–85.

Perkins, D., & Miller, J. (n.d.) *Why community service and service-learning? Providing rationale and research.* Baltimore: Quest International. Retrieved November 11, 2000 from www.quest.edu/slarticle2.htm

Pittman, K., Ferber, T., & Irby, M. (2000). Youth as effective citizens. Takoma Park, MD: International Youth Foundation—U.S.

Putnam, R. (2000). *Bowling alone: The collapse and revival of American community.* New York: Simon & Schuster.

Rajani, R. (2001). The participation rights of adolescents: A strategic approach. New York: United Nations Children's Fund.

Seigel, S., & Rockwood, V. (1993). *Democratic education, student empowerment, and community service: Theory and practice. Equity & Excellence in Education, 26*(2), 65–70.

Tolman, J., & Pittman, K. (2001). *Youth acts, community impacts: Stories of youth engagement with real results. (7).* Takoma Park, MD: The Forum for Youth Investment, International Youth Foundation.

Torney-Purta, J. (1999). *Background convening paper.* Paper presented at the Creating Citizenship: Youth Development for Free and Democratic Society, Stanford University, Center on Adolescence.

Watts, R., & Flanagan, C. (2007). Pushing the envelope on civic engagement: A developmental and liberation psychology perspective. *The Journal of Community Psychology, 35,* 779–792.

Zeldin, S., Larson, R., Camino, L., & O'Connor, C. (2005). Intergenerational relationships and partnerships in community programs: Purpose, practice, and directions for research. *Journal of Community Psychology, 33*(1), 1–10.

CHAPTER 10

To Think, Live, and Breathe Politics

Experiencing Democratic Citizenship in Chicago

Janet S. Bixby

> "In terms of the future . . . the whole stigma about youth, that needs to change . . . [that] youth don't care, youth don't know anything, youth don't vote . . ."
> —*Akeem*

Akeem,[1] an African American/Latino youth from Chicago, believes that the common perceptions that youth lack knowledge of and don't care about or engage in the political system are wrong. While he hopes that society will come to see these views as misperceptions, much research suggests that he is overly optimistic. Findings about the civic knowledge and civic engagement of U.S. youth in general are somewhat mixed, as discussed in chapter 1. However, low-income youth demonstrate less civic knowledge and engagement than their middle class peers do, and youth of color demonstrate less civic knowledge and engagement than their White peers do (Baldi, Perie, Skidmore, & Greenberg 2001; Gibson & Levine 2003; Hahn 2002; Johanek & Puckett 2005; Niemi 1998; Putnam 2000). Many structural factors that disempower low-income people contribute to these inequities by creating impoverished civic environments within which youth in urban communities mature. Furthermore, as Lipman (2004) points out, recent shifts in educational policy including "the emphasis on standards and testing are eroding the concept of education for participation in democracy." Specifically, Lipman says:

Accountability and the centralized regulation of schools and teachers sharpen disparities in curriculum and teaching, widening the gap between schools serving low-income students of color and schools serving mixed- and high-income populations. I also suggest that current policies undermine efforts to help students develop tools of social critique and culturally centered identities that can help them survive and challenge the new inequalities. (p. 3)

Within this standards-based reform context, when schools are meant to be the primary institution educating youth to become thoughtful citizens, it is not surprising that low-income youth and youth of color from urban schools are demonstrating low levels of civic knowledge and skills.

From Akeem's perspective, though, these measures are misleading. His perspective springs not from naiveté, but rather from a depth of personally transformative experiences with a community youth organization that seeks to engage and mentor youth in the day-to-day working world of politics and governance. Through his involvement with this organization he has worked for years with his peers, youth from across Chicago where he lives, who, like him, are politically knowledgeable, committed, and engaged.

As Akeem's experience shows, community organizations can play vital roles for youth in difficult urban environments. They can "give young people the opportunity to engage in positive activities, to develop close and caring relationships, and to find value in themselves—even in the face of personal disruption, poor schools, and neighborhoods generally devoid of supports" (McLaughlin 2000). While these organizations may help youth develop into healthy adults, less is known about what role they might play in helping youth develop into vigorous and effective citizens.

The study upon which this chapter was based was developed as an exploration of what can be learned from urban youth's narratives about the changing nature of their civic identities from their deep involvement with a community-based organization focused on education for democratic citizenship. The organization that these youth participated in is called the Mikva Challenge.[2] This private, nonprofit foundation was established in Chicago in 1996 with a goal of engaging Chicago youth directly in politics and governance. It currently runs a wide variety of programs that work with high school-aged students. The youth that I interviewed were all alumni of the programs at the time of the interviews, which took place between

December, 2004 and June, 2005. One of them had done a summer internship in the Chicago office of U.S. Senator Barack Obama.

The research questions were

- What do young adults say about their understandings of and experiences with civic engagement prior to their work with Mikva?
- What do young adults say about how involvement with Mikva impacted their understandings of and experiences with civic engagement?

This chapter focuses on two factors that participants reported led to the transformative impact their participation in the Mikva programs had on their sense of themselves as civic actors: (1) the intensely social nature of their experiences, both with high status adults and with youth peers from across the city, and (2) the highly active, engaging, and authentic (Newmann & Associates 1996) work that they did within the programs. I examine these factors in light of Lave and Wenger's (1991) framework for understanding learning as apprenticeship in which learners increase participation in communities of practice. Thus as these youth worked directly with presidential campaigns on a trip to New Hampshire in the days leading up to the 2004 primary, interned with their city aldermen, or sponsored debates for Illinois gubernatorial candidates, both the nature of the work that they did and the social context in which they did it transformed, often dramatically, their sense of themselves and their political efficacy. This study shows the importance of examining efforts to promote education for democratic citizenship among urban youth that take place in community organizations. Furthermore it underscores the value of examining such civic learning as apprenticeship rather than as narrowly defined knowledge acquisition.

Site, Sample, and Methodology

Mikva Challenge is a community-based organization where:

> Democracy is a VERB. We challenge high school students throughout Chicago to be active participants in the political process through election and issue campaigns. Mikva Challenge works to develop the next generation of civic leaders, activists and policymakers by providing young people with opportunities to act, think, live and breathe politics. (www.mikvachallenge.org; retrieved 9/20/06)

It works with Chicago high school–aged youth and teachers, the vast majority of whom attend or teach in Chicago Public Schools. In the 2005–2006 school year, Mikva worked intensively with approximately 1000 students and touched over 2,500 more students through their programs. At the time of the study, the staff had a list of approximately 450 alumni. Of these alumni, the staff estimated that 61% were female and 39% male; 42% African American, 38% Latino, 10% White, and 5% Asian, and 5% were other or unknown. Many of these students were either first or second generation immigrants and many were low socioeconomic status, though the Mikva staff did not have an estimate for how many alumni were in either of these categories. Of the twenty alumni who were interviewed, twelve were female (60%) and eight were male (40%); seven were African American (35%), four were Latino (20%), four identified themselves with both African American and Latino identities (20%); three were White Eastern European immigrants (15%); one was White non-immigrant (0.5%), and one (0.5%) was not identified. Nine (45%) came from low socioeconomic status families and eleven (55%) came from middle socioeconomic status families.

In order to address the question of what kinds of students joined Mikva programs in the first place, I asked staff members, teachers, and alumni that question in various ways. The data suggest that youth who joined Mikva programs were more likely to be involved in extracurricular activities than other students in their schools, but that they were not much more likely to have an initial interest in politics than other students. Many students joined, as I discuss below, out of a simple interest in fulfilling the Chicago Public Schools Service Learning requirement, as a way to meet students from other schools, or because a favorite teacher talked them into it.

Though a staff member and teachers reported that they believed that students who joined Mikva programs ranged fairly evenly from being modest to high academic achievers, eighteen of the twenty alumni in the study were relatively highly academically successful as evidenced by the fact that they either attended a college-oriented private school (five or 25%); a public college-oriented magnet school (four or 20%); or took many AP or IB courses in their neighborhood school (eight or 40%). It is not clear whether the alumni in the study were somewhat more academically successful than the alumni at large, but the contradiction between the staff and teacher perceptions as well as my own participant observations suggest that this may be the case.

Data for this study were collected from a number of sources over the course of eighteen months. A Mikva alumnus and employee worked as a research assistant for me. He and I recruited twenty alumni whom we interviewed one on one. In order to recruit alumni for participation in this part of the study, I used the most updated alumni contact list that the Mikva staff had to attempt to make an initial e-mail connection with individual alumni,[3] and my research assistant recruited and interviewed alumni as they made contact with the Mikva office. We tried to recruit an interview pool that was similar demographically to the total alumni group in terms of race, ethnicity, and gender. I also tried to ensure that our individual interview group included alumni who had attended a wide range of high schools and, since I wanted to interview youth who could speak more knowledgeably about the programs, I recruited those who had been more deeply involved with the programs. I did not interview anyone who, for example, had taken only one high school class in which Mikva curricula was used or youth whose only connection to Mikva was that they had been trained as election judges in their senior year of high school. The Mikva staff and I also recruited another nineteen alumni to participate in focus groups, one of which consisted, intentionally, entirely of first or second generation alumni. For these events we asked all of the alumni who attended alumni events to come to one of the scheduled focus groups. Clearly the alumni in the study were likely to have been more deeply impacted by their participation with Mikva than the total alumni group. However, it is not clear that they were impacted in fundamentally different ways from those alumni who had also been more deeply involved in the programs but were not in the study. In fact, judging from the responses of the nineteen other alumni who participated in the focus groups, their experiences were similar to the larger pool of alumni who had been more deeply involved in Mikva programs.

My research assistant and I conducted phone and face-to-face interviews of the alumni. Each of the twenty alumni was interviewed by one of us once for 45 minutes to an hour. I interviewed each of three teachers whom I had met at Mikva events over the phone as well as four staff members face-to-face once for approximately one hour. I conducted four focus groups with alumni in Chicago following alumni events. I was also a participant observer for a number of Mikva alumni events including an organized trip of high school–aged Mikva participants to Wisconsin in the days leading up to the 2004 presidential election, a workshop for Mikva teachers in Chicago, and numerous hours hanging out in the Mikva office and at restaurants eating pizza with Mikva students and alumni. I reviewed videos as well as print and digital documents provided by Mikva including newspaper clippings, cable access issue discussion shows put on by Mikva youth, promotional materials, and written reports.

The Development of Civic Identity

A significant body of research has examined the development of civic identity in youth. Conover and Searing (2000), working within the tradition of political socialization, examine the extent to which students identify as citizens, how they understand the meaning of citizenship and the nature of their practice as citizens, and the extent to which contextual factors influence these outcomes. They conclude that context matters, and that "local understandings of the practice of citizenship . . . necessarily must inform any attempts at reforming civic education" (p. 119). Overall they find that:

> Although most students have strong citizen identities, these identities are experienced as free-floating abstractions that are not tied to the students' understanding of what it means to be a citizen or to their behaviors. Similarly, most students have thin understandings of what it means to be a citizen, understandings dominated by a focus on rights and deficient in a sense of obligation. For most, being a good citizen requires only that one obey the law, vote, and act patriotically (p. 117).

Rubin (2007) also examines the impact of context—in the form of lived experiences and schooling—on youths' civic identity. Using a sociocultural approach to conceptualize civic identity, she suggests that "students' daily experiences in a society marked by racial and socioeconomic inequalities become part of their evolving understandings as citizens" and that civic identity "is constructed or developed amid particular structures and practices" (pp. 7–8). She examined the relationship between students' reflections on their lived experiences in relation to ideals of the United States and their stances, from active to passive, towards civic participation. She found that both the students' lived experiences and their school settings contributed to the degree to which they felt U.S. society needed to change and their own relative power to impact such change.

Youniss, Bales, et. al, (2002) seek to understand what leads to positive examples of political socialization, or what they call "civic competence." They argue that:

> Political socialization is not something that adults do to adolescents, it is something youth do for themselves (Yates & Youniss, 1999). Families, schools, service activities, and involvement in political events provide raw material—knowledge, models, and reflective matter—and various forms of feedback, but it is ultimately youth themselves who synthesize this material, individually and collaboratively, in ways that make sense to them. (p. 133)

Much of the research on the development of civic identity examines the role of community organizations. Flanagan and Van Horn (2003) see a generalized sense of social trust as critical to the health of a democracy, and youth involvement in youth organizations as important avenues for promoting such social trust. They argue that: "In the activities of nonformal youth organizations, young people come to understand the reciprocal relationship between trust and trustworthiness. Trust among peers is earned by working together toward goals defined in common, by working through differences that could otherwise divide them" (p. 284).

This study of alumni of the Mikva programs is designed to examine the dynamic nature of youth's civic identity. That is, to the extent that youth's understandings of their own identity in relation to civic action has the potential to change over time, and given that this civic identity develops in relation to larger sociocultural factors around them, how and why might it change? Specifically, this study seeks to address the interaction between youth's understandings of their civic identities and their involvement with a particular community-based organization focused on education for democratic citizenship.

In order to analyze the alumni's civic identities in relation to their involvement with the Mikva programs, I utilized Lave and Wenger's (1991) conception of legitimate peripheral participation.[4] Rooted in the concept of apprenticeship, this learning theory foregrounds the sociorelational aspects of learning and argues that "persons, activities, knowing, and world" (p. 121) cannot be neatly divided from each other conceptually. That is, in order to understand participants' experiences in an apprenticeship learning environment, their movement within the community from newcomers toward full membership as well as their learning and their shifting identities must be analyzed in relationship to each other. This analytic perspective rejects notions that knowledge and learning can be measured or isolated from the sociorelational worlds within which participants work, learn, and make meaning. Rather it offers strategies for understanding how and why the youth in this study reflect on their shifting civic identities in the ways that they do. This approach also helps illuminate the role of a community-based organization focused on education for democratic citizenship in this process.[5]

Civic Identity and Involvement in Mikva Programs

The youth that I interviewed typically describe having experienced a significant increase in their interest in and knowledge about politics and governance since they first became involved in the Mikva programs. Most of the alumni, who were 10th, 11th, or 12th graders when they started participating in Mikva programs, report having been completely inactive relative to politics and governance prior to their involvement with the Mikva programs, though a few of them reported that they had always followed the news. At the time of the study, all of the Mikva alumni were between the ages of 18 and 23, all of them were attending postsecondary programs part or full time, and all of them discussed being actively involved in multiple civic or community organizations outside of and beyond the Mikva programs. The Mikva Alumni Program at the time of the study organized a few social events with political themes—for example, to watch televised debates—each year and did its best to keep an up to date contact list of the alumni. As such it provided an opportunity for the alumni to maintain contact with each other, but was not an organized and active program on par with the rest of the Mikva programs.

In order to give a sense of youth in this study, I provide brief sketches of two of the alumni.

From Apathetic to Engaged: Two Examples

Jelena, a white woman, had been born in Eastern Europe where her father was a professional. Due to warfare and dislocation, the family moved to Chicago where she attended public neighborhood schools from middle school on. Though she had always followed the news, her initial participation in a Mikva program her junior year in high school had a profound impact on her. She explained: "The minute that I got involved in Mikva I saw that there was a passion that was just hidden inside me, and it was just a matter of finding it and discovering it. And once I got involved in the Campaign Program, I just saw that that's what I want to do in life." Her parents had serious reservations, based upon their life in their country of origin, about her becoming involved in electoral politics and governance. They feared for her basic safety, for her personal happiness as a woman in politics, and later disagreed fervently with her views on social issues. However, they stayed steadfastly supportive of her and came to be very supportive of her involvement in the Mikva programs when they saw how passionate she was about it as well as the networking opportunities it offered her.

Jelena was thrilled with the connections she made with other youth from across the city in the Mikva programs as well as the opportunities to work with or meet high profile politicians and policymakers. She came to participate in many different Mikva programs. During one event, a guest speaker said something to her that made her think. She explained:

> She told me that um, if you get an opportunity to be somewhere and be part of a group, make your voice heard and give your ideas to the group, even though they're not the best ideas, but make yourself heard ... make your presence known. That kind of touched me, because very often I would sit in groups and I would be the quietest person there ... and that was because I was very shy before. . . . She made me think about those past times that I was quiet, and she made me realize that I was dead. I was dead during those times. I wasn't alive in the group. And if I wasn't alive, I wasn't sharing anything with the world. Through Mikva Challenge and that particular experience, she taught me that whenever you're given an opportunity to be a part of a group, be a part of it and speak up, and give your ideas and share your thoughts ... And Mikva Challenge, through the campaign opportunities and the leadership opportunities also told me that uh, you can always contribute, and always whenever given a chance, speak up. That's what I got out of it.

When I interviewed her, Jelena was eighteen years old, looking forward to summer Mikva programs that included work in Senator Barack Obama's office and going to college. She also hoped to run for office one day and play a role in international relations.

William, a young African American man, had lived most of his life in Chicago though he had lived in his parents' country of origin for a time in his childhood. A teacher that he liked convinced him to participate in a Mikva program to help him meet youth from other schools and to become more outgoing. He explained how his teacher encouraged his initial involvement with the Mikva programs:

I was kind of hesitant at first because she said it's very political, and at the time I knew nothing about politics. I just knew that all um, like politics was kind of like um, like shady practice and things of that nature. So I was kind of hesitant at first, and so she kind of forced my hand into it. And so you know, I don't, I kind of thanked her for it because I kind, I've been here at the Mikva Challenge ever since.

William participated in numerous Mikva programs and began to feel that "politics didn't seem as dry because everything is politics." He spoke about the value, as he saw it, of the Mikva programs:

This is teaching me how to use power, you know. How, how we as young people have all this power, and no one even bothered to tell us this, you know. They say that . . . all the suburban kids who like, who have parents who are like just into politics know all this stuff. But no one, all the inner city kids, which is what this is about, getting inner city youth involved in politics and getting them to know the power.

We as inner city kids . . . most of our parents are not even involved in politics, let alone like, teach—will want to teach us how to use certain tools or who to talk to because . . . most of them just go out and vote . . . and don't know what's out there besides what's advertised on TV or the newspapers.

You know, and they taught us how to teach our parents how to do proper research about a candidate if you're going to vote for them. How to look between the lines of what they're saying, you know and, you know, Mikva started like the first generation, our generation is like the generation of all, like we're all independent voters. We're not all just Republican, or we're not all just Democrat or Republican, we're like, most of us are just kind of just, we'll vote for who will do the job right. Be it Democrat or Republican.

As he became more politically knowledgeable and engaged, his mother began asking him questions about the news. He said that that was "weird" because it was "kind of like a reality check that wow, adults don't know everything." He said that he would analyze campaign speeches made by candidates for and with his mother. When I interviewed William he was attending college part time, working nearly full time, and volunteering to help out with Mikva events whenever he could.

Across these and the rest of the youths' stories there is a trajectory, from inactive in civic life to highly, passionately engaged. The youth in the study describe experiencing a fundamental shift in their civic identities, whether they were interested in politics prior to their involvement in the Mikva programs or not (most were not). In this shift they went from viewing themselves as detached from any kind of power or responsibility to impact the civic worlds around them to feeling very empowered to work through political, governmental, and community channels to effect needed changes locally and, to a lesser extent, nationally. Their families were affected by their involvement with the Mikva programs and their roles within their families changed as well.

All of the youth that I interviewed were thrilled with their experiences in the Mikva programs. In particular, they responded positively to two central features: (1) the intensely social nature of their experiences, both with youth peers from across the city and with high status adults, and (2) the consistently highly active, engaging, and authentic (Newmann & Associates, 1996) work that they did within the programs. The remainder of this chapter examines how these features in the Mikva programs led to transformations in civic identity and involvement among these youth.

Entering a Community of Practice by Working with Peers

Few of the youth who joined Mikva Challenge programs did so out of an intrinsic interest in politics. Their friends, supportive teachers, or a simple desire to complete service learning requirements typically got them to attend their first event. But once they walked in the door, it was the charge that they got from interacting with youth from across the city as much as anything that initially got them coming back. Nearly every youth interviewed talked with enthusiasm about working in Mikva programs with their peers from other schools. As they became more involved in the programs, they became equally impressed with the opportunities they had to work closely with adults who worked in the field of politics, such as elected officials, campaign organizers, and community organizers. Looking back over their years of involvement, the participants often spoke about these opportunities to interact directly with these adults campaigning in the New Hampshire primary or interning with an elected official over the summer as highlights of their Mikva experiences. These youth thrived on the authentic opportunities that Mikva programs gave them to become full members of the community of politically engaged people as they transformed themselves from tentative newcomers first attending a Mikva event to politically experienced activists.

Jelena came to the Mikva programs as a newcomer to the community of civically engaged people. She had always followed the news. However, prior to her involvement with Mikva she had identified herself, perhaps without realizing it at the time, as an outsider on the world of politics and governance. Reflecting on her perspective before she had done door to door campaign work in Wisconsin through Mikva, she explained:

Before, you hear you know you see on the news, you see the campaign trail, you see students or the people going along, and you never knew what it was actually like to be involved. And once you get involved, and you realize how much hard work goes into working on the campaign, and you were just there for one day, and people go through this every day. So it was fascinating, very interesting.

Jelena describes a transformation here, where she begins as an outside observer, detached from the world of politics, "You never knew what it was actually like to be involved." After campaigning for a day, as well as the workshops and bus travel time with Mikva before and after, she sees herself as involved in a peripheral way, "and you were there for just one day, and people go through this every day." After this event then, she is beginning to see herself as a member of the community of civically engaged people.

Jelena's initial steps toward inclusion though, even in just the Mikva programs, were difficult for her. She had had little opportunity to work closely with the wide array of students that she encountered in the Mikva programs, like most of the youth in this study. She found her first encounters with Mikva students from other schools nearly overwhelming:

When I first met some of the students, honestly I was very disappointed and intimidated because they were so intelligent and so bright. And I looked at myself, and having come from another country I was inexperienced. I didn't grow up here. I wasn't informed about not just the political system, but the social life. And I would often feel like an outcast because I didn't know what to say in a conversation.

This sense of being an outcast did not last. When I asked her what she learned on the trip to Wisconsin, she replied:

Well the best part about it was the socializing, because I wasn't a social person before that, before Mikva Challenge. And when I got involved, I realized the importance of building relationships with people. And when I was on that trip, even the ride to Wisconsin and back, it was just fascinating to know that so many young people around me are involved in the same thing, and to understand that we're all in it for the same reasons. And to see the passions in those young people, and to know you are not alone in it and there are people in your generation who are um, willing to do the same thing you are, have the same passion. I loved that part of the trip, that part of getting to know the people I was getting to work with.

The social and relational aspects of her involvement with Mikva programs are central to Jelena's thinking. She describes moving relationally from being alone to being a part of a larger community, at least of youth, active in politics. In the process of going from someone who is interested in yet outside of politics to someone who is part of a community of youth active in politics, she also implies a shift in her own identity. She goes from being someone who "wasn't a social person before" to someone who realizes the "importance of building relationships." This theme, of youth going from someone who is shy or quiet to someone who is outgoing and outspoken came up repeatedly during the interviews and focus groups. Jelena's explicit reference to building relationships indicates that while her work with Mikva was social in nature, it was not "just social." It was also fundamentally political in nature. That is to say through their social interactions with each other in the Mikva programs the youth learned, from each other as well as from adults, how to become active and effective in the world of politics and governance.

Lave and Wenger (1991) discuss the significance of the learning that can go on among learners in apprenticeship settings:

In apprenticeship opportunities for learning are, more often than not, given structure by work practices instead of by strongly asymmetrical master-apprentice relations. Under these circumstances learners may have a space of "benign community neglect" in which to configure their own learning relations with other apprentices. There may be a looser coupling between relations among learner on the one hand and the often hierarchical relations between learners and old-timers on the other hand, than where directive pedagogy is the central motive of institutional organization. It seems typical of apprenticeship that apprentices learn mostly in relation with other apprentices. (p. 93)

One staple of the Mikva programs that best illustrates this kind of interaction and that came up consistently in the interviews and focus groups was Saturday morning workshops. During these events staff threw youth who arrived, often for their very first Mikva event, immediately into ice-breaker activities and group work with youth from across the city. The activities typically mirrored the kinds of tasks that campaign workers, elected officials, and community activists might engage in, such as developing campaign speeches or developing a proposal to address a community problem. The fact that these were authentic tasks, where the work involved in doing them was like the work done in the real world of politics and governance, was highly engaging for students. Their open enededness—there was no "right" way to respond to the challenges—and the fact that the groups were always intentionally mixed so youth would work with people they did not know forced the youth to find ways to work collaboratively and with little direct adult intervention.

While group work within school classrooms is typically fraught with issues of varied levels of student skills, motivations, and status (Cohen & Lotan, 1997), these youth from widely divergent academic backgrounds were remarkably positive about the degree to which they felt they learned from each other during these workshops. One student, Lupe, had grown up with her single mother who worked in a factory, had gone to a prestigious college preparatory school in Chicago during her involvement with Mikva and was attending a private, elite, eastern college when I interviewed her. She discussed the Saturday morning workshops:

Going back to the group projects that we did . . . I think some students just knew more about books as well, whereas other students actually had a lot more experience with actually dealing with people . . . I think one of the main things that we did discuss was the inequalities that existed um, within the voice . . . the students that had experience with inequality because of where they came from, because of their background. And other students knew more things more like the political theories and stuff like that. Um, but working within the group we got to hear what each of us thought, what our opinions were, what our experience had been. So it's like just learning from each other.

Within schools, knowledge and skills are often narrowly defined by the adult world of educators, curricula, textbooks, standards, and tests. The processes of schooling, including tracking, serve to sort students into categories of those who have attained the defined knowledge and skills and those who have not (Oakes, Wells, et al., 1997). Students in classrooms typically perceive their classmates as higher or lower status depending on their academic achievement, while these status dynamics impede the extent to which students are willing and able to learn from each other (Cohen & Lotan, 1997).

In contrast to these common dynamics within schools, the data suggests that the Mikva programs engendered more egalitarian working relationships among youth participants. Indeed youth as well as staff were often explicit, during Mikva events, about their belief that in addition to the knowledge and skills that they gained from each other, the relationships themselves might be vital to their futures, as Jelena's quote above about "the importance of building relationships" implies. Randal is a young African American man with ambitions of becoming a lawyer and later running for elected office. Speaking of his peers in the Mikva programs he said:

I think all of them are smart and savvy, like they know how things work. And the more knowledge you have about the way things work, the better you have a chance at changing them. And so the person who knows how to play the game always most of the time wins. I think that's smart and in the future it's good to know them, because aldermen and senators and probably a president or something, they're all going to be passing through here.

The Mikva staff actively encouraged the youth to look to each other in this way as future actors and collaborators in the world of politics and governance and many of the youth did talk about valuing their relationships with each other in part for this very reason. At the end of a workshop for alumni and a pizza dinner at a local restaurant, a Mikva staff member had all of the youth present stand in a circle and reflect on what they had seen and learned that day. He closed the discussion with this very same sentiment that Randal expressed above.

Youth involved in Mikva programs then learned with and from each other, and through that learning process came to feel that they were a part of a community of civically engaged people that included, but reached beyond, the Mikva programs themselves. Indeed they began to identify with civically engaged people. But beyond the positive social relations that the youth experienced in the Mikva programs, what facilitated this significant identity transformation that nearly all of the youth mentioned? Certainly the passage of time and the natural adolescent development that corresponds with that was one factor in this process. As the youth grew older, they became more aware of, curious about, and engaged with the world around them. However, research suggests that for most youth, especially low-income youth and youth of color, maturation does not necessarily lead to higher rates of civic engagement (Gibson & Levine, 2003). The Mikva programs addressed this concern about the low civic engagement of urban youth by structuring opportunities for them to become directly involved in political and governmental processes. By creating these opportunities for youth to work directly with elected and appointed officials, policy makers, community organizers, and other civic leaders, the Mikva programs created apprenticeship opportunities in the world of politics and governance that these urban youth generally did not have otherwise. In the process, the Mikva programs facilitated the youth's participation into a culture of practice characterized by civic engagement and action.

Participation in a Culture of Practice

Mikva's work with youth is guided by the perspective that youth should have the opportunity to engage in and reflect upon the political world directly. Thus there is a wide range of Mikva programs that include opportunities for youth to develop and promote policy positions on local issues of concern to them, to hold debates for candidates running for a range of offices, to intern with elected officials, to volunteer on political campaigns, and to work as official election judges in Chicago. The teachers and staff consistently referred to the experiential nature of the youth's participation in Mikva. One staff member explained the rationale behind this approach:

> You can't really learn politics in a classroom totally because so much of it is very, what's the right word, it's very hidden. It's very grey area, very subtle, it's about human interaction and power, and so you can't just learn it straight from the classroom. You have to get out there and do it. In essence too, the key political, to me the building block of any political education is the door knock. It's greeting somebody and trying to persuade them to vote for somebody or to be on your side on something. And that little human interaction is just filled with millions of nuances that you just can't study. You have to go do it and try it.

The youth in the study all talked about starting out participating in one Mikva program and then quickly participating in a range of programs, which ultimately gave them a wide array of experiences. In this sense they were not representative of the larger pool of youth who were touched by Mikva through their involvement with one program or class. However, the perspectives of these youth who were very involved in multiple Mikva programs illuminate why this approach to apprenticing urban youth into the world of politics and governance can be very effective. In particular, using legitimate peripheral participation (Lave & Wenger, 1991) as an analytic lens to understand the youth's experiences in the Mikva programs provides an explanation for why an apprenticeship approach to engaging youth in politics and governance led to a transformative experience in the formation of civic identities.

Lave and Wenger (1991) state: "Legitimate peripheral participation is not itself an educational form, much less a pedagogical strategy or teaching technique. It is an analytical viewpoint on learning, an understanding of learning" (p. 40). They explain that it "crucially involves *participation* as a way of learning—of both absorbing and being absorbed in—the 'culture of practice.' An extended period of legitimate peripherality provides learners with opportunities to make the culture of practice theirs" (p. 95). The youth, staff, and teachers of the Mikva programs all discussed the kinds of skills and knowledge that the youth learned through their participation in the programs. However when they talked about what the youth learned through their involvement with the Mikva programs, no discrete set of skills or knowledge such as those outlined for students to learn in state standards for civic education, emerged. Rather the discussions characterized the learning that took place as more diffuse, individualized, and tied up with identity.

William explained that when he began participating in a Mikva program he did not know how to address community problems. More significantly, he did not think it was his responsibility to do so. He reflected on a time during one of his initial experiences with a Mikva program when the staff posed to him and his peers in a workshop the question "Who addresses community problems?" He said:

> I never knew that it's our job to like tell people that O.K., this is involved in my community. And I thought that was a policeman's job or, you know whoever patrols, or who's ever in charge. Like the alderman, I thought they did it themselves. And you know they [Mikva staff] actually say no, it's like, it's our job that you know, we as the citizens hold all the power about what goes on in our city, in our neighborhood, in our communities, you know. And it's, it's like the activities that they showed us that each, each session was like a different activity with a different focus. Like one, community solving, like problem solving, networking, who to network with.

Despite this initial lack of understanding of or commitment to the political process, William developed a range of political skills that he relished using in the ensuing years. When I asked him what he had learned through his involvement in Mikva, he replied: "The first thing that I, I hold to my heart is how to communicate with the media, because that's a big thing. If you can get the media's attention for, regardless of what the issue is, then you have the attention of whoever you're initially trying to get." He told a specific story of a time that he and a friend in Mikva were attending a State of the City address:

> We kind of walked around in the distance and spoke with all the officials who were there, some of the very important people who were there. . . . Then the cameras showed up. And . . . we immediately darted for the cameras. You know we kind of like hopped in front of the cameras saying . . . we're students and . . . we're here because Mikva gave us the chance to go to the State of the City address. . . . And then we got interviewed. . . . We get some air-time about some of the things that we're going through. You know as students.

William and his friend spoke about the problems with a federal policy related to financial aid for students to attend college. By William's report then, he had learned political skills: He learned to speak directly with "officials . . . very important people" and to use the media to his advantage. These are important lessons of politics. But, more than a set of skills, he learned to make the cultural practices of political engagement his own. He learned to see community issues that he had not even recognized and to develop a range of strategies to address them, and to have the confidence that he could in fact create change in his community. In this sense he had truly absorbed and been absorbed into the culture of political engagement.

Another youth, Kobe, is also an African American man. He went to a parochial high school in Chicago and was attending a prestigious college in the Midwest when he was interviewed. He explained the impact that his involvement in the Mikva programs had on him:

> And then the cool thing about Mikva, it was just like all the Mikva people had faith in the kids, to be able to put them in an environment where . . . teenagers are not normally a part of. It really made me feel a part of the process. Here I was, I couldn't vote, and I came to be a part of the entire election process, yet I was working, and I was campaigning, and I was part of democracy. I liked that a lot . . . the fact that you know, they've made you involved. . .
>
> The most important thing I learned is that you got to participate in the democratic process. Democracy works in two-folds, it's the federal government and the people we elect and their part, you know, the law makers and the law holders, but the part that's missing in America right now is the citizen part. Citizens are supposed to be actively involved in democracy you know. Lobbying and petitioning, and making their voice heard so that the people who make the law and uphold the laws listen. I think Mikva like really ingrained that in me to the point where I felt like I had to be part of the political process.

As Kobe reflects on his experiences with the Mikva programs, it becomes clear that for him, three things are inextricably intertwined: (1) learning skills related to electoral politics—"I was campaigning"; (2) entering a community of practice—"made me feel a part of the process" and "I was part of democracy"; and (3) developing an identity as someone who is politically engaged—"I felt like I had to be part of the political process."

While it is true that the experiential nature of learning in the Mikva programs taught young people things that they could not have learned in books, Kobe's comments suggest something more. They underscore the profound interconnectedness for these youth between learning skills and knowledge about politics and governance, social relations, and identity. Lave and Wenger (1991) argue:

> As an aspect of social practice, learning involves the whole person; it implies not only a relation to specific activities, but a relation to social communities—it implies becoming a full participant, a member, a kind of person. . . . Activities, tasks, functions, and understandings do not exist in isolation; they are part of broader systems of relations in which they have meaning. (p. 53)

Through establishing structured opportunities for these youth to be apprenticed into the real world of politics around them then, the Mikva programs helped these youth, most of whom had been previously disengaged from politics and governance, become absorbed into the culture of political activism. In the process these youth developed their own individual sets of political skills to navigate within the political world as well as strong, positive civic identities.

Moving toward Full Participation: Working with Experts

One of the most unusual aspects of the Mikva programs was the extent to which they put youth into regular, meaningful, face to face contact with people at the core of politics and governance from elected officials to campaign organizers. Robert is a White male who has been teaching for twenty years in a public, neighborhood, Chicago school and has been working with the Mikva programs for about seven years. He compared the Mikva programs to other civics-based programs that he worked with and thought were also excellent. Speaking of the Mikva programs he said:

> There's more experiential learning than perhaps some of the others. And certainly the contacts with people the kids make, and the settings in which they go to are a little unusual. They meet the governor, or they meet the senatorial candidates, or whatever, or presidential candidates. It's something that most of your local organizations don't offer.

Contact happened in a number of ways. Mikva staff invited a wide range of adults in to their private events to meet with the youth. For example, they recruited seven out of eight candidates running for governor for the State of Illinois to meet with and recruit youth to volunteer on their campaigns. The staff took large groups of youth to key events in national politics such as the New Hampshire and the Iowa primaries or to the swing state of Wisconsin in the weeks leading up to the presidential election of 2004 to volunteer on campaigns. Each summer Mikva organized paid internships for youth to work in the offices of public officials. And the youth met with various civic leaders in the city and state to express their opinions and often their own policy ideas on topics of concern to them.

A common theme among participants was that they found it thrilling to meet powerful civic leaders face to face and to do the core work—campaigning, addressing constituents' concerns, lobbying—of politics and governance. Importantly, beyond the rush of that initial experience for each youth, they discussed what they learned from these often extended apprenticeship experiences. Many of them mentioned learning positive things about politics and governance that countered their expectations. For example, a number of youth discussed how their initial distaste for politics and politicians had become tempered, and that their faith in and respect for electoral politics had grown. Elisa is a young Latina woman who graduated from a neighborhood school and was attending college part time in Chicago when I interviewed her. She reflected on her experiences interning in the office of a Latino elected official:

> He was there and you could talk to him. . . . Your title was intern, but they treated you like a staff member, which was pretty cool because some students didn't get the same experience at their offices . . . I've learned a lot from him, like the way he dedicates himself to the community, and how he's always like kind of trying to bring something back . . . That's when I was like, I really want to run for office . . . And little by little doing other programs outside of Mikva, I learned you've got to give back. You grew in this community, but you've got to give back . . . And there's different ways of giving back, and one of the ways he does it is he's a public official, and he brings back resources to his community. The laws he passes you know, that's a really, really good way to effect change.

As this comment indicates, positive experiences campaigning, lobbying, and interning did not occur automatically. The Mikva staff did significant background work with many offices to ensure that the adults with whom the youth worked created meaningful opportunities to participate, rather than trying to pacify them with mindless tasks as some offices did initially. The youth too worked to demonstrate their abilities and to be given meaningful work.

These work experiences in the real world of politics and governance also provided youth with a sense of a future that they had never considered before and thus fueled their motivation to stay involved in Mikva programs. Eleven of the eighteen who had declared their majors in college were majoring in political science, international relations or civic-oriented pre-law in college. Many of the alumni with whom I spoke in interviews, focus groups, or more informally at Mikva events were considering plans to work in electoral politics or government in the future. As they experienced more and more opportunities to interact with civic leaders and to reflect on these experiences through their workshops with Mikva staff members, the youth began to feel that they were more than just members in the world of civically active people. They began to see themselves as leaders and organizers in the world of politics.

Angela is an African American woman who attended a neighborhood high school and was attending college part time in Chicago when I interviewed her. Speaking of her involvement with the Mikva programs she said:

> It opened not only my eyes; it opened my mind and my voice. It allowed me to think outside the box, and say things outside the box . . . And for me just to be able to speak, not only in front of guys, in front of TV audiences, in front of just anyone. In front of politicians, in front of anybody who'll listen.

Angela's comments suggest that at this point, she has come to see herself as someone who can think politically "outside the box," speak her mind "outside the box," and speak to the media or politicians about her concerns. Thus she felt that she had learned to think and act as a leader and with independence in the world of politics. The apprentices became journeymen or, in a few cases, budding masters.

Leadership and independence were evident in different ways. First, all of the youth in the study had become involved in some kind of political and/or community organization outside of and beyond their involvement with the Mikva programs. Whether on college campuses or in community organizations, in traditional party politics or grassroots organizations, the youth that we interviewed were involved collectively in an amazing amount of civically engaged work.

Another way in which the youth demonstrated their leadership and independence was in their nearly unanimous commitment to knowing how a candidate stood on an issue before they would support him or her. While this is a commonly stated ideal of electoral politics in this country, many of these youth spoke of the strong tendency in their communities and among their family members to vote the party line with little critical understanding of how candidates stood on issues that mattered to them. One young African American woman, Keisha, who went to a neighborhood school and attends a branch of the state university, articulated this sentiment most clearly. She said that up until the previous year when she had voted for the first time, outside of Mikva "All I hear was you know, we're Democrat, that's who you vote for." However, she was not satisfied with that approach:

> As far as politics goes, these are the people that are working for us . . . We're putting them in positions of power to keep our messages at heart. Not so that they can come in and ruin our neighborhoods, and like bringing a Wal-Mart in and we get no money. You know what I'm saying? So it was really important for me to be like OK, now . . . since I know how . . . a campaign should be ran, when it's time for somebody to run and I'm looking at their platform and it doesn't seem to add up, or I'm looking at the issues and they are not the most important ones that are affecting us directly, then that's how I know like, OK I shouldn't vote for that person. And then I start to tell other people, because a lot of times, the people that I know have no idea why they're voting for whomever, or what's going on with that. And I mean I'm really a leader in my own right.

Keisha's sense that she had become a leader in her own right was evident in the political and community work that she did after she graduated from high school and her most active involvement with the Mikva programs had ended. This was equally true for the rest of the youth in this study.

Cultural Tensions

For some of the youth, their emerging sense of political confidence, leadership, and independence created more challenges than for others. The youth revealed a passion and excitement about sharing their opinions that met with varied responses from their families. Most of the youth reported that families were proud and supportive of their work with the Mikva programs as well as their growing civic knowledge and involvement. Some reported that their families were not very aware of the specifics of the Mikva programs, but were glad that they were doing something positive with their time. And a few youth reported that their involvement with the Mikva programs had resulted in some conflict with their families. Most of the youth who did report some conflict with family had parents who had immigrated to the United States. Some of these youth had been born in other countries and some had been born within the United States.

Some of the conflict that emerged between youth and their immigrant parents revolved around physical concerns about safety. One of the teachers who taught in a Chicago high school with a predominantly Latino student population talked at length about the challenges of recruiting youth and getting them to stay involved with Mikva programs. She felt strongly that parents, and often the youth themselves, were resistant to physically leaving the neighborhood to attend Mikva events. During one of our focus groups with only alumni from immigrant families, a number of youth echoed this feeling, that their parents had expressed resistance to their traveling around the city to attend such events.

Another point of conflict often arose from parents' strong negative opinions about politics and governance formed in their countries of origin. During one focus group discussion about family reactions to their involvement in Mikva programs, two youths had this exchange:

Akeem: I think some people, not everyone, because like, I've seen stuff where this is all new to them you know, kind of like they have their reservations about this being a new place, all the dangers that are publicized.
Isabel: Yeah, that's what it is I think. My mom fears my involvement with the politics. Sometimes like I know that she doesn't mean this, because she sees Mikva as a positive thing, but sometimes she'll be

like, they're so corrupt, the ideas they're telling you, and this and that. So sometimes it gets in the way of like our relationship and the way I think, because then she'll blame it back to not Mikva, but politics itself. Like oh, it's because you read too much of that stuff. [laughter]

Typically these parental concerns caused some conflict according to the youth, but did not prevent them from participating fully in the Mikva programs. In fact, a few of the youth said that their parents learned to be more trusting of and interested in politics in this country due to their involvement in the Mikva programs.

Some also talked about their emerging sense of confidence in their own political identity escalating authority conflicts with their parents. To disagree, to debate, to back up opinions with evidence and to be independent are all a part of the culture of politics. A number of youth with immigrant parents reported that their parents saw these practices as offensive and thus resisted that culture of practice. One youth, a young Latino man, said in the immigration focus group

My parents, they don't really take such an active role with me, but definitely since I've been in and out of Mikva, or out of high school I think, I'm not sure which it is, but they're like "Oh, you're so different-minded. Why don't you think like you used to?" I'm like, "Hello! Because I noticed the world." [laughter] It's like you know, just because you say something, it so doesn't mean, it's not like it's a black and white issue, it's not one-sided you know. Even in a really good thing you could find some faults, and even in bad things there's something good I guess could happen through it. So it's always, not arguing, but every now and again I'll have to talk to them about it, and it's like you know, it's not just one-sided.

It is important to note that many youth from immigrant families had tremendous support from their families for their involvement in both Mikva and the larger world of politics. And, some families were conflicted, both uneasy about some things and deeply supportive about some things. Again this kind of conflict is often part of the natural developmental process, but it was mentioned somewhat more often by youth from immigrant families than those from non-immigrant families. These findings suggest that further research into family dynamics behind development of civic identity within immigrant families would be fruitful. The fact that these alumni were still involved in Mikva suggests that they and their families found ways to negotiate these conflicts.

Conclusion

This study was exploratory in nature and examined a small number of youth—20 youth more intensively and another 19 youth less intensively—in focus groups and with some participant observation. While this group of youth cannot be seen as truly representative of urban youth in general, the consistency of their experiences suggest that further research examining the ways in which youth become apprenticed into the role of active citizen is worth pursuing. If further research reaches similar conclusions about the processes through which youth, and especially urban youth, develop strong civic identities and patterns of action, the implications for civic education are significant.

These findings of this study suggest that these urban youth experienced their work with a civically and politically oriented community-based organization as deeply social and relational, individual, and inextricably intertwined with a sense of identity. The findings about these youths' experiences run counter to much of the social efficiency logic that under-girds common practices in schools: that teaching and learning can be standardized; that "knowledge, skills, and dispositions" about civic life can be delineated, taught, and tested; that passive or minimally active learning in classrooms will translate into positive dispositions and actions in the civic life of communities; that education myopically focused on economic advancement will produce active and knowledgeable citizens able to sustain the democracy; that the passion and knowledge that individual teachers have about civic life either don't fit within the confines of the overstretched curriculum or can be neatly transformed into learning objectives within the confines of the classroom. Given the clear evidence that youth, and especially urban, low-income, youth of color are feeling alienated by the very politics and governance that infuse all aspects of their lives and indeed every U.S. citizen's life, this apparent disconnect between the current logic of schooling and youth's experiences of learning is sobering.

However, at the same time this study is fundamentally hopeful. It is hopeful because it supports the view that youth, even youth from often

Janet S. Bixby

277

challenging urban and educational environments, are still remarkably open to the influence of positively transformative civic education experiences. It suggests that opportunities carefully orchestrated yet not overly structured that invite them to apprentice into the world of civic and political engagement can have tremendous results. These opportunities, enjoyed by the youth in this study, appear likely to impact the youths' knowledge, skills, and dispositions in enduring ways. They even appear to have impacted the civic engagement of the youths' families and the civic life of their communities in many cases.

This study speaks then to the power and value that community organizations can have in educating youth to become active, informed, and effective citizens. While this work happened most intensively outside of schools for the most part, the role of the schools in this process in this study was significant. It was in the schools, in classrooms, in passing conversations with passionate teachers, in after-school activities that all of the alumni in this study first became involved in Mikva Challenge. The partnership between the community organization and the schools allowed students to take their first tentative steps into the unknown and previously un-enticing world of politics and governance. The partnership also supported teachers with professional respect, financial compensation, opportunities, and curriculum materials that kept them inspired as educators.

The work that Mikva Challenge did in education for democratic citizenship was vital. It had a critical impact on alumni, teachers, families, and communities. By working with youth in ways that recognizes the complex, social, and individual nature of learning, it allowed the youth to transform themselves into civic and political actors, even leaders in their own right. In the process the youth became proof that citizens are made and not born.

Notes

1. All names of people in this chapter are pseudonyms to protect anonymity and confidentiality.
2. The name of the organization is not a pseudonym because it is too large and identifiable to make this feasible.
3. It is important to note here that while there were approximately 450 alumni, a small proportion of those youth had been deeply involved (i.e., over a longer period of time or in more than one Mikva program), and the Mikva Foundation had had very few resources to commit to developing an alumni program. The alumni contact list for example, had only 113 e-mail addresses, the majority of which, it appears, were outdated or rarely used.

4. I would like to thank Judith L. Pace for introducing me to Lave and Wenger's framework and for encouraging me to consider its relevance to this study.
5. Torney-Purta et al. (1999) and Torney-Purta et al. (2001) build upon this conceptual framework in their international study of civic education as well.

References

Baldi, S., Perie, M., Skidmore, A., & Greenberg, E. (2001). *What democracy means to ninth-graders: U.S. results from the International IEA Civic Education Study.* Washington, DC: U.S. Department of Education National Center for Education Statistics.

Cohen, E., & Lotan, R. (Eds.). (1997). *Working for equity in heterogeneous classrooms: Sociological theory in practice.* New York: Teachers College Press.

Conover, P., & Searing, D. (2000). A political socialization perspective. In L. McDonell, Timpane, P., & Benjamin, R. (Eds.) *Rediscovering the democratic purposes of education.* Lawrence: University Press of Kansas.

Flanagan, C. & Van Horn, B. (2003). Youth civic development: A logical next step in community youth development. In F. Villarruel, Perkins, D., Borden, L., & Keith, J. (Eds.) *Community youth development: Programs, policies, and practices* (pp. 273–296). Thousand Oaks, CA.: Sage Publications.

Gibson, C., & Levine, P. (2003). *The civic mission of schools.* New York and Washington, DC: The Carnegie Corporation of New York and the Center for Information and Research on Civic Learning.

Hahn, C. (2002). Education for democratic citizenship: One nation's story. In W. C. Parker (Ed.) *Education for democracy: Contexts, curricula, assessments* (pp. 63–92). Greenwich, CT: Information Age Publishing.

Johanek, M., & Puckett, J. (2005). The state of civic education: Preparing citizens in an era of accountability. In S. Furhman and M. Lazerson (Eds.) *The public schools.* (pp. 130–150). New York: Oxford University Press.

Lave, J., & Wenger, E. (1991). *Situated learning: Legitimate peripheral participation.* Cambridge, England: Cambridge University Press.

Lipman, P. (2004). *High stakes education: Inequality, globalization, and urban school reform.* New York: Routledge Falmer.

McLaughlin, M. W. (2000). *Community counts: How youth organizations matter for youth development.* Washington, DC: Public Education Network.

Newmann, F., & Associates (Eds.). (1996). *Authentic achievement: Restructuring schools for intellectual quality.* San Francisco: Jossey-Bass.

Niemi, R. & Junn, J. (1998). *Civic education: What makes students learn.* New Haven, CT: Yale University Press.

Oakes, J., Wells, A., Jones, M. & Datnow, A. (1997). Detracking: The Social Construction of Ability, Cultural Politics, and Resistance to Reform. *Teachers College Record, 98* (Spring), 482–510.

Putnam, R. D. (2000). *Bowling alone: The collapse and revival of American community.* New York: Simon & Schuster.

Rubin, B. C. (2007). There's still no justice: Youth civic identity development amid distinct school and community contexts. *Teachers College Press, 109*(2), 449–481.

Torney-Purta, J., Lehmann, R., Oswald, H. & Schultz, W. (2001). *Citizenship and education in twenty-eight countries: Civic knowledge and engagement at age fourteen.* Delft:

International Association for the Evaluation of Educational Achievement. More information at: http://www.iea.nl/cived.html

Torney-Purta, J., Schwille, J. & Amadeo, J. (1999). *Civic education across countries: Twenty-four national case studies for the IEA Civic Education Project.* Delft: International Association for the Evaluation of Educational Achievement. More information at: http://www.iea.nl/cived.html

Yates, M. & Youniss, S. (Eds.) (1999). Roots of civic identity: International perspectives on community service and activism in youth. Cambridge, U.K.: Cambridge University Press.

Youniss, J., Bales, S., Christmas-Best, V., Diversi, M., McLaughlin, M. & Sibereisen, R. (2002). Youth civic engagement in the twenty-first century. *Journal of Research on Adolescence, 12*(1), 121–148.

CHAPTER 11

Epilogue: Citizenship Education in Diverse Settings: Findings, Tensions, and Future Research

Judith L. Pace

Educating Citizens in Troubled Times is a unique contribution to our knowledge of citizenship education in the United States with its diverse collection of qualitative studies. Using different methodologies ranging from ethnography to content analysis, the authors describe particular educational efforts in specific locations across the nation, and analyze them by identifying pertinent themes. These themes include the factors that shape teaching for citizenship in the classroom, essential elements of experiential approaches to citizenship education, and the role of sociocultural context in youth's understandings of politics and their relationship to it.

The findings from these studies reflect the diversity that characterizes democracy in the United States. A variety of educational programs exist that provide opportunities for youth who are diverse in their sociocultural identities, experiences with formal schooling, and life circumstances. In addition to providing illustrations and analyses of these programs, this book embodies an argument for further qualitative research on citizenship education. We need to know what specific goals, approaches, topics, structures, and relationships are at play in various settings, and how students interpret them. And we need to know how these features vary across settings, and the factors that influence them.

While this volume captures specificity and variability in citizenship education, at the same time, it addresses a common set of research questions. What do we learn from looking across these chapters about the purposes of citizenship education, understandings of citizenship, and the nature of teaching and learning evident in these programs?

The purposes that drove these educational efforts ranged from transmitting knowledge about the United States government to involving students in direct public action. Even classroom teachers' statements about purposes represent a wide range of ambition. In Pace's chapter, one teacher tentatively said that the goal was "maybe" for students to "start to think a little differently about what government means and what their place can be." Another teacher wanted students to learn "to play their part in democracy . . . that they have to be critical and speak out, be involved." Mr. Sinclair, in Marri's study, tried to empower marginalized students and prepare them to be justice-oriented citizens in a multicultural democracy. And the youth in Nygreen's chapter voluntarily undertook designing and teaching the PARTY class as "part of a larger struggle for collective social change." These young people wanted to empower students, specifically to develop their political voice and speak out against injustice, which they viewed as a form of political action. In contrast, the textbooks studied by Hess, Stoddard, and Murto constrain understandings of 9/11 and terrorism, and foster blind patriotism. Although purposes varied across the different classroom settings described in this volume, in part depending on the conceptions of citizenship education held by teachers, the particular cases described here did not include taking concurrent action outside of the classroom.[1]

However, school programs such as service learning, school governance in Project 540, and those in community-based organizations were deliberately focused on actively engaging youth in the wider community. The service learning programs studied by Root and Billig aimed at developing civic knowledge, skills, and dispositions. But what distinguished their purposes from those of non-service learning classrooms was engagement of students in analyzing and addressing real social problems, so that students understood their complexity and importance, learned to work with others, and developed a commitment to helping others. Likewise, the purpose of Project 540 in Battistoni's chapter was to remedy the problem of youth civic disengagement and to empower high school students through direct participation in school democratic governance. Project 540 aimed to realize the ideal formulated by Dewey almost a century ago—that schools be the "practice grounds" for democracy, by facilitating shared decision-making, student voice, and public problem solving. It may be seen as continuing a legacy of experiments with democratic schooling advanced by the Teachers College, Columbia University Citizenship Education Project of the 1940s and 1950s and Lawrence Kohlberg's Just Community Schools of the 1970s and 1980s.

Outside of the school, the purpose of citizenship education was focused on promoting the public efficacy of young people. In the CBYOs studied by O'Donoghue and Kirshner, this involved learning to interpret public problems, work with others, make decisions, and take action. In Bixby's study the goal was "engaging Chicago youth directly in politics and governance." For the youth themselves it was initially the chance to interact with other youth from across the city, and subsequently, opportunities to work closely with adults in the field of politics, such as elected officials, campaign organizers, and community organizers.

Related to the purposes of educational efforts are the diverse understandings of citizenship manifested in these settings. In Pace's study, according to teachers, citizenship meant the right to freedoms that protect individuals against the government, the political engagement that constitutes a democracy, or the celebration of America's ideals and criticism of its injustices. Mr. Sinclair in Marri's chapter conveyed the more advanced conception that citizenship is a moral endeavor of struggling, both individually and collectively, for justice in a multicultural democracy. Nygreen's students held an even more radical view; for them, citizenship involved subordinated people's expression of power through collective action, which consists of speaking out against injustice. It did not involve standard practices of political involvement, such as voting, organizing, advocating, and protesting.

In the service learning classrooms within three schools, Root and Billig found that teachers supported the notion that for their students, citizenship was a form of leadership that involved responsibility along with the freedom to choose their service-learning project. It also depended on gaining certain kinds of knowledge, skills, and attitudes that empower people to address social problems in the community. Battistoni shows that adults and youth in Project 540 viewed citizenship as being an active member of a community, having a voice and being heard, and engaging with others to make a positive difference. In a similar vein, in O'Donoghue and Kirshner's community-based youth organizations, citizenship was collaborative and experiential. It meant working with others, making decisions, analyzing public problems, and taking action, such as organizing a youth conference on the presence of the U.S. military in their neighborhood. Citizenship also meant seeing oneself as capable of having an impact on the community and voicing one's sense of agency.

Middaugh and Kahne's study addresses conceptions of citizenship held by high school students that bear out previous research findings. Across the focus groups under investigation, students expressed enthusiasm about community service, but little interest in political involvement. However, students articulated different understandings of the political side of citizenship depending on socioeconomic and cultural features of their home communities. Importantly, Bixby's alumni from the Mikva Program understood citizenship as political involvement in government, which seemed to result from their apprenticeships with elected officials and political organizers.

Perhaps the most interesting findings in the book relate to the nature of teaching and learning. The textbooks analyzed by Hess, Stoddard, and Murto communicate that teaching about 9/11 is of paramount importance, yet their explanations of the event are uninformative, unclear, and one-dimensional. Students are asked to blindly accept a constrained version of history and politics and are discouraged from thinking critically. These findings are deeply troubling given prior research on the tremendous influence textbooks have in great numbers of classrooms across the country.

We also see from these studies that institutional settings matter for teaching and learning, which points to the importance of qualitative research that examines the influence of contextual factors on education. In Pace's public school classrooms, the teaching and learning endeavor was knowledge-based; it was academic—meaning text-based and classroom-bound—rather than experiential. Two teachers in one school used more lecture and recitation, while the other two used project and performance-based approaches. In comparison, teaching and learning in Marri's chapter about Mr. Sinclair was inclusive, discussion-based, and critical. Influenced by his knowledge of multicultural and progressive citizenship education, and by his alternative school setting, the teacher engaged students who struggled with school and with life in an exploration of transformational knowledge, for example, the history and psychology of struggles for social justice, rather than mainstream academic knowledge. The PARTY class in Nygreen's chapter, led by youth and also located in an alternative school, also eschewed mainstream academic knowledge and focused on discussion of students' own experiences of oppression and their critiques of the injustices perpetrated by society and the government.

In contrast, teaching and learning outside of the classroom was experiential; students were active with other people in the community. The service learning sites in Root and Billig's chapter involved students in a process of experience, analysis, and reflection. Teachers were deliberate in the design and implementation of their classes, but much of the curricular content depended on the projects students decided to undertake. The same is true in Battistoni's chapter on Project 540. Schools were provided with a design for the process of engaging students in school governance, and adult educators acted as coaches, but the ways in which it played out varied according to what the students did. O'Donoghue and Kirshner's study of CBYOs also found students' choices central to what was learned. However, all of these approaches depended on particular practices that revolved around collaborative learning, decision-making, analysis, and action. Bixby's Mikva Challenge was unique in its employment of apprenticeship. This approach promoted the most intensive and authentic involvement in the workings of politics on community, state, and national levels.

Many of the studies in this book point to tensions related to teaching, learning, and democracy. One tension was over authority, and to what extent adults or youth were in control. Especially when programs purported to empower youth to act as leaders, the role of educators became more ambiguous. Another area of uncertainty was curricular content. When the focus was on social problems in a particular community, then larger issues related to critical contemporary events were neglected, and vice versa. A third tension regarded addressing political conflict in educational settings, specifically issues related to the war on terror. The absence of emphasis on the events of 9/11 in these studies is noteworthy. These tensions suggest questions for future research:

1. In programs that promote civic action, how do educators and youth negotiate authority?
2. How are mainstream texts and alternative materials on 9/11 and the war on terror used by teachers and with what consequences?
3. How do students understand contemporary local, national, and international political conflicts?

It also is vital to acknowledge what is missing from the studies in this volume. As researchers we need to attend much more to educational issues of youth who are not granted U.S. citizenship, and to those whose membership in society is threatened by prejudices against certain groups, most notably Muslims and recent immigrants, during these "troubled times."

These times have pushed us to investigate democratic citizenship education as it is enacted in various settings and through different methods to better understand how we are preparing young people to carry forward a democratic society. We hope these studies will stimulate an increasing number of qualitative investigations into related and new areas of citizenship education, and that deeper understanding will lead to more enlightened and engaged educational practices and policies.

Note

1. In schools that place more emphasis on participatory, action-oriented citizenship, one might see students more civically involved.

Contributors

Richard Battistoni is Professor of Political Science and Public and Community Service Studies at Providence College. His teaching and scholarship intersect the fields of democratic political theory, civic education, and community-based learning.

Shelley H. Billig is Vice President of RMC Research Corporation, Denver, CO. She has served as principal investigator in multiple national studies of civic education, service-learning, and K–12 education reform, particularly for schools and districts serving children from high poverty communities.

Janet S. Bixby is Associate Professor of Education at the Graduate School of Education and Counseling at Lewis & Clark College in Portland, OR. Her research focuses on examining social studies education and the contextual factors that influence the ability of diverse youth populations to develop rich and meaningful understandings of democratic citizenship.

Diana Hess is Associate Professor of Curriculum and Instruction at the University of Wisconsin-Madison. She teaches social studies and democratic education to undergraduate and graduate students, and researches the ideological content of social studies curriculum and how classroom discussions of controversial political issues influence the political and civic engagement of young people.

Joseph Kahne is the Abbie Valley Professor of Education and is Dean of the School of Education at Mills College. Joseph Kahne writes about the democratic purposes of education and on urban school reform. See: www.civicsurvey.org

Ben Kirshner is Assistant Professor in the School of Education at the University of Colorado, Boulder. His current research examines how young people work to overcome educational and socioeconomic inequities through activism, action research, and access to college.

Anand R. Marri is Assistant Professor of social studies and education in the Department of Arts and Humanities at Teachers College, Columbia University. His research focuses on the intersection of civic education and multicultural education, especially in urban schools.

Ellen Middaugh is Research Associate at the Mills College School of Education and doctoral candidate in Human Development and Education at UC Berkeley. Her research interests focus on adolescent social reasoning and social contextual influences on the development of civic identity.

Shannon Murto obtained a master's degree in curriculum and instruction from the University of Wisconsin-Madison under associate professor Diana Hess. Her areas of interest include democratic education and issues surrounding the use of high-stakes, standardized testing.

Kysa Nygreen is Assistant Professor of Education at University of California, Santa Cruz, in the area of Social Context and Policy Studies. Her research and teaching are focused on race, class, culture, and equity in education.

Jennifer L. O'Donoghue received her M.A. in public affairs from the University of Minnesota and her Ph.D. in Educational Administration and Policy Analysis from Stanford University. Her research interests include community-based education and public engagement of traditionally marginalized groups (immigrants and refugees, low-income communities, urban youth), youth participation and development, and citizenship and democracy.

Judith L. Pace is Associate Professor in the Teacher Education Department at the University of San Francisco's School of Education. Her research focuses on classroom relations, curriculum, and pedagogy in history/social studies and English /language arts within the sociocultural and political contexts of schooling.

Walter C. Parker is Professor of social studies education at the University of Washington, Seattle. He studies civic education in its national and global contexts.

Susan Root is Senior Research Associate at RMC Research Corporation, Denver. A former professor of Education at Alma College, her research interests include service-learning impacts on K–12 students and preservice teachers, teacher development, and civic development.

Jeremy D. Stoddard is Assistant Professor in the School of Education at the College of William and Mary. His research applies sociocultural and critical theories to learning contexts, curriculum and pedagogy, and the use of media within social studies education.

Index

Educating Democratic Citizens in Troubled Times

Educating Democratic Citizens in Troubled Times

Qualitative Studies of Current Efforts

Edited by
Janet S. Bixby
and
Judith L. Pace

Published by
State University of New York Press, Albany

© 2008 State University of New York

All rights reserved

Published in the United States of America

For information, contact State University of New York Press, Albany, NY
www. sunypress. edu

Production by Kelli LeRoux
Marketing by Michael Campochiaro

Library of Congress Cataloging-in-Publication Data
Educating democratic citizens in troubled times : qualitative studies of current
efforts / edited by Judith L. Pace and Janet S. Bixby ; foreword by Walter C. Parker.
    p.   cm.
Includes bibliographical references and index.
ISBN 978-0-7914-7639-0 (hardcover : alk. paper) — ISBN 978-0-7914-7640-6
(pbk. : alk. paper)
    1. Citizenship—Study and teaching—United States. 2. Democracy—United States.
I. Pace, Judith L. II. Bixby, Janet S.
LC1091.E3835 2009
370.11'5—dc22   2008003125

10 9 8 7 6 5 4 3 2 1

Contents

In the Community